THE PELICAN SHAKESPEARE
GENERAL EDITORS

STEPHEN ORGEL
A. R. BRAUNMULLER

King Lear
The 1608 Quarto and 1623 Folio Texts

D0169528

Ellen Terry as Cordelia, 1892

William Shakespeare

King Lear

The 1608 Quarto and 1623 Folio Texts

EDITED BY STEPHEN ORGEL

PENGUIN BOOKS

PENGUIN BOOKS

Published by the Penguin Group

Penguin Putnam Inc., 375 Hudson Street,
New York, New York 10014, U.S.A.
Penguin Books Ltd, 27 Wrights Lane,
London W8 5TZ, England
Penguin Books Australia Ltd, Ringwood,
Victoria, Australia
Penguin Books Canada Ltd, 10 Alcorn Avenue,
Toronto, Ontario, Canada M4V 3B2
Penguin Books (N.Z.) Ltd, 182–190 Wairau Road,
Auckland 10, New Zealand

Penguin Books Ltd, Registered Offices:
Harmondsworth, Middlesex, England

This edition published in Penguin Books 2000

1 3 5 7 9 10 8 6 4 2

Copyright © Penguin Putnam Inc., 2000
All rights reserved

ISBN 0-14-07.1490-1

Printed in the United States of America
Set in Garamond
Designed by Virginia Norey

Except in the United States of America, this
book is sold subject to the condition that it
shall not, by way of trade or otherwise, be lent,
re-sold, hired out, or otherwise circulated
without the publisher's prior consent in any form
of binding or cover other than that in which it
is published and without a similar condition including this
condition being imposed on the subsequent purchaser.

Contents

Publisher's Note

IT IS ALMOST half a century since the first volumes of the Pelican Shakespeare appeared under the general editorship of Alfred Harbage. The fact that a new edition, rather than simply a revision, has been undertaken reflects the profound changes textual and critical studies of Shakespeare have undergone in the past twenty years. For the new Pelican series, the texts of the plays and poems have been thoroughly revised in accordance with recent scholarship, and in some cases have been entirely reedited. New introductions and notes have been provided in all the volumes. But the new Shakespeare is also designed as a successor to the original series; the previous editions have been taken into account, and the advice of the previous editors has been solicited where it was feasible to do so.

Certain textual features of the new Pelican Shakespeare should be particularly noted. All lines are numbered that contain a word, phrase, or allusion explained in the glossarial notes. In addition, for convenience, every tenth line is also numbered, in italics when no annotation is indicated. The intrusive and often inaccurate place headings inserted by early editors are omitted (as is becoming standard practice), but for the convenience of those who miss them, an indication of locale now appears as the first item in the annotation of each scene.

In the interest of both elegance and utility, each speech prefix is set in a separate line when the speaker's lines are in verse, except when those words form the second half of a verse line. Thus the verse form of the speech is kept visually intact. What is printed as verse and what is printed as prose has, in general, the authority of the original texts. Departures from the original texts in this regard have only the authority of editorial tradition and the judgment of the Pelican editors; and, in a few instances, are admittedly arbitrary.

The Theatrical World

Economic realities determined the theatrical world in which Shakespeare's plays were written, performed, and received. For centuries in England, the primary theatrical tradition was nonprofessional. Craft guilds (or "mysteries") provided religious drama – mystery plays – as part of the celebration of religious and civic festivals, and schools and universities staged classical and neoclassical drama in both Latin and English as part of their curricula. In these forms, drama was established and socially acceptable. Professional theater, in contrast, existed on the margins of society. The acting companies were itinerant; playhouses could be any available space – the great halls of the aristocracy, town squares, civic halls, inn yards, fair booths, or open fields – and income was sporadic, dependent on the passing of the hat or on the bounty of local patrons. The actors, moreover, were considered little better than vagabonds, constantly in danger of arrest or expulsion.

In the late 1560s and 1570s, however, English professional theater began to gain respectability. Wealthy aristocrats fond of drama – the Lord Admiral, for example, or the Lord Chamberlain – took acting companies under their protection so that the players technically became members of their households and were no longer subject to arrest as homeless or masterless men. Permanent theaters were first built at this time as well, allowing the companies to control and charge for entry to their performances.

Shakespeare's livelihood, and the stunning artistic explosion in which he participated, depended on pragmatic and architectural effort. Professional theater requires ways to restrict access to its offerings; if it does not, and admission fees cannot be charged, the actors do not get paid, the costumes go to a pawnbroker, and there is no such thing as a professional, ongoing theatrical tradition. The answer to that economic need arrived in the late 1560s and 1570s with the creation of the so-called public or amphitheater playhouse. Recent discoveries indicate that the precursor of the Globe playhouse in London (where Shakespeare's mature plays were presented) and the Rose theater (which presented Christopher Marlowe's plays and some of Shakespeare's earliest ones) was the Red Lion theater of 1567. Archaeological studies of the foundations of the Rose and Globe theaters have revealed that the open-air theater of the 1590s and later was probably a polygonal building with fourteen to twenty or twenty-four sides, multistoried, from 75 to 100 feet in diameter, with a raised, partly covered "thrust" stage that projected into a group of standing patrons, or "groundlings," and a covered gallery, seating up to 2,500 or more (very crowded) spectators.

These theaters might have been about half full on any given day, though the audiences were larger on holidays or when a play was advertised, as old and new were, through printed playbills posted around London. The metropolitan area's late-Tudor, early-Stuart population (circa 1590-1620) has been estimated at about 150,000 to 250,000. It has been supposed that in the mid-1590s there were about 15,000 spectators per week at the public theaters; thus, as many as 10 percent of the local population went to the theater regularly. Consequently, the theaters' repertories – the plays available for this experienced and frequent audience – had to change often: in the month between September 15 and October 15, 1595, for instance, the Lord Admiral's Men performed twenty-eight times in eighteen different plays.

Since natural light illuminated the amphitheaters' stages, performances began between noon and two o'clock and ran without a break for two or three hours. They often concluded with a jig, a fencing display, or some other nondramatic exhibition. Weather conditions determined the season for the amphitheaters: plays were performed every day (including Sundays, sometimes, to clerical dismay) except during Lent – the forty days before Easter – or periods of plague, or sometimes during the summer months when law courts were not in session and the most affluent members of the audience were not in London.

To a modern theatergoer, an amphitheater stage like that of the Rose or Globe would appear an unfamiliar mixture of plainness and elaborate decoration. Much of the structure was carved or painted, sometimes to imitate marble; elsewhere, as under the canopy projecting over the stage, to represent the stars and the zodiac. Appropriate painted canvas pictures (of Jerusalem, for example, if the play was set in that city) were apparently hung on the wall behind the acting area, and tragedies were accompanied by black hangings, presumably something like crepe festoons or bunting. Although these theaters did not employ what we would call scenery, early modern spectators saw numerous large props, such as the "bar" at which a prisoner stood during a trial, the "mossy bank" where lovers reclined, an arbor for amorous conversation, a chariot, gallows, tables, trees, beds, thrones, writing desks, and so forth. Audiences might learn a scene's location from a sign (reading "Athens," for example) carried across the stage (as in Bertolt Brecht's twentieth-century productions). Equally captivating (and equally irritating to the theater's enemies) were the rich costumes and personal props the actors used: the most valuable items in the surviving theatrical inventories are the swords, gowns, robes, crowns, and other items worn or carried by the performers.

Magic appealed to Shakespeare's audiences as much as it does to us today, and the theater exploited many deceptive and spectacular devices. A winch in the loft above the stage, called "the heavens," could lower and raise actors playing gods, goddesses, and other supernatural figures to and from the main acting area, just as one or more trapdoors permitted entrances and exits to and from the area, called "hell," beneath the stage. Actors wore elementary makeup such as wigs, false beards, and face paint, and they employed pig's bladders filled with animal blood to make wounds seem more real. They had rudimentary but effective ways of pretending to behead or hang a person. Supernumeraries (stagehands or actors not needed in a particular scene) could make thunder sounds (by shaking a metal sheet or rolling an iron ball down a chute) and show lightning (by blowing inflammable resin through tubes into a flame). Elaborate fireworks enhanced the effects of dragons flying through the air or imitated such celestial phenomena as comets, shooting stars, and multiple suns. Horses' hoofbeats, bells (located perhaps in the tower above the stage), trumpets and drums, clocks, cannon shots and gunshots, and the like were common sound effects. And the music of viols, cornets, oboes, and recorders was a regular feature of theatrical performances.

For two relatively brief spans, from the late 1570s to 1590 and from 1599 to 1614, the amphitheaters competed with the so-called private, or indoor, theaters, which originated as, or later represented themselves as, educational institutions training boys as singers for church services and court performances. These indoor theaters had two features that were distinct from the amphitheaters': their personnel and their playing spaces. The amphitheaters' adult companies included both adult men, who played the male roles, and boys, who played the female roles; the private, or indoor, theater companies, on the other hand, were entirely composed of boys aged about 8 to 16, who were, or could pretend to be, candidates for singers in a church or a royal boys' choir. (Until 1660, professional theatrical companies included no women.) The playing space would appear much more familiar to modern audiences than the long-vanished amphitheaters; the later indoor theaters were, in fact, the ancestors of the typical modern theater. They were enclosed spaces, usually rectangular, with the stage filling one end of the rectangle and the audience arrayed in seats or benches across (and sometimes lining) the building's longer axis. These spaces staged plays less frequently than the public theaters (perhaps only once a week) and held far fewer spectators than the amphitheaters: about 200 to 600, as opposed to 2,500 or more. Fewer patrons mean a smaller gross income, unless each pays more. Not surprisingly, then, private theaters charged higher prices than the amphitheaters, probably sixpence, as opposed to a penny for the cheapest entry.

Protected from the weather, the indoor theaters presented plays later in the day than the amphitheaters, and used artificial illumination – candles in sconces or candelabra. But candles melt, and need replacing, snuffing, and trimming, and these practical requirements may have been part of the reason the indoor theaters introduced breaks in the performance, the intermission so dear to the heart of theatergoers and to the pocketbooks of theater concessionaires ever since. Whether motivated by the need to tend to the candles or by the entrepreneurs' wishing to sell oranges and liquor, or both, the indoor theaters eventually established the modern convention of the non-continuous performance. In the early modern "private" theater, musical performances apparently filled the intermissions, which in Stuart theater jargon seem to have been called "acts."

At the end of the first decade of the seventeenth century, the distinction between public amphitheaters and private indoor companies ceased. For various cultural, political, and economic reasons, individual companies gained control of both the public, open-air theaters and the indoor ones, and companies mixing adult men and boys took over the formerly "private" theaters. Despite the death of the boys' companies and of their highly innovative theaters (for which such luminous playwrights as Ben Jonson, George Chapman, and John Marston wrote), their playing spaces and conventions had an immense impact on subsequent plays: not merely for the intervals (which stressed the artistic and architectonic importance of "acts"), but also because they introduced political and social satire as a popular dramatic ingredient, even in tragedy, and a wider range of actorly effects, encouraged by their more intimate playing spaces.

Even the briefest sketch of the Shakespearean theatrical world would be incomplete without some comment on the social and cultural dimensions of theaters and playing in the period. In an intensely hierarchical and status-conscious society, professional actors and their ventures had hardly any respectability; as we have indicated, to protect themselves against laws designed to curb vagabondage and the increase of masterless men, actors resorted to the near-fiction that they were the servants of noble masters, and wore their distinctive livery. Hence the company for which Shakespeare wrote in the 1590s called itself the Lord Chamberlain's Men and pretended that the public, money-getting performances were in fact rehearsals for private performances before that high court official. From 1598, the Privy Council had licensed theatrical companies, and after 1603, with the accession of King James I, the companies gained explicit royal protection, just as the Queen's Men had for a time under Queen Elizabeth. The Chamberlain's Men became the King's Men, and the other companies were patronized by the other members of the royal family.

These designations were legal fictions that half-concealed an important economic and social development, the evolution away from the theater's organization on the model of the guild, a self-regulating confraternity of individual artisans, into a proto-capitalist organization. Shakespeare's company became a joint-stock company, where persons who supplied capital and, in some cases, such as Shakespeare's, capital and talent, employed themselves and others in earning a return on that capital. This development meant that actors and theater companies were outside both the traditional guild structures, which required some form of civic or royal charter, and the feudal household organization of master-and-servant. This anomalous, maverick social and economic condition made theater companies practically unruly and potentially even dangerous; consequently, numerous official bodies – including the London metropolitan and ecclesiastical authorities as well as, occasionally, the royal court itself – tried, without much success, to control and even to disband them.

Public officials had good reason to want to close the theaters: they were attractive nuisances – they drew often riotous crowds, they were always noisy, and they could be politically offensive and socially insubordinate. Until the Civil War, however, anti-theatrical forces failed to shut down professional theater, for many reasons – limited surveillance and few police powers, tensions or outright hostilities among the agencies that sought to check or channel theatrical activity, and lack of clear policies for control. Another reason must have been the theaters' undeniable popularity. Curtailing any activity enjoyed by such a substantial percentage of the population was difficult, as various Roman emperors attempting to limit circuses had learned, and the Tudor-Stuart audience was not merely large, it was socially diverse and included women. The prevalence of public entertainment in this period has been underestimated. In fact, fairs, holidays, games, sporting events, the equivalent of modern parades, freak shows, and street exhibitions all abounded, but the theater was the most widely and frequently available entertainment to which people of every class had access. That fact helps account both for its quantity and for the fear and anger it aroused.

WILLIAM SHAKESPEARE OF
STRATFORD-UPON-AVON, GENTLEMAN

Many people have said that we know very little about William Shakespeare's life – pinheads and postcards are often mentioned as appropriately tiny surfaces on which to record the available information. More imaginatively and perhaps more correctly, Ralph Waldo Emerson wrote, "Shakespeare is the only biographer of Shakespeare. . . . So far from Shakespeare's being the least known, he is the one person in all modern history fully known to us."

In fact, we know more about Shakespeare's life than we do about almost any other English writer's of his era. His last will and testament (dated March 25, 1616) survives, as do numerous legal contracts and court documents involving Shakespeare as principal or witness, and parish records in Stratford and London. Shakespeare appears quite often in official records of King James's royal court, and of course Shakespeare's name appears on numerous title pages and in the written and recorded words of his literary contemporaries Robert Greene, Henry Chettle, Francis Meres, John Davies of Hereford, Ben Jonson, and many others. Indeed, if we make due allowance for the bloating of modern, run-of-the-mill bureaucratic records, more information has survived over the past four hundred years about William Shakespeare of Stratford-upon-Avon, Warwickshire, than is likely to survive in the next four hundred years about any reader of these words.

What we do not have are entire categories of information – Shakespeare's private letters or diaries, drafts and revisions of poems and plays, critical prefaces or essays, commendatory verse for other writers' works, or instructions guiding his fellow actors in their performances, for instance – that we imagine would help us understand and appreciate his surviving writings. For all we know, many such data never existed as written records. Many literary and theatrical critics, not knowing what might once have existed, more or less cheerfully accept the situation; some even make a theoretical virtue of it by claiming that such data are irrelevant to understanding and interpreting the plays and poems.

So, what do we know about William Shakespeare, the man responsible for thirty-seven or perhaps more plays, more than 150 sonnets, two lengthy narrative poems, and some shorter poems?

While many families by the name of Shakespeare (or some variant spelling) can be identified in the English Midlands as far back as the twelfth century, it seems likely that the dramatist's grandfather, Richard, moved to Snitterfield, a town not far from Stratford-upon-Avon, sometime before 1529. In Snitterfield, Richard Shakespeare leased farmland from the very wealthy Robert Arden. By 1552, Richard's son John had moved to a large house on Henley Street in Stratford-upon-Avon, the house that stands today as "The Birthplace." In Stratford, John Shakespeare traded as a glover, dealt in wool, and lent money at interest; he also served in a variety of civic posts, including "High Bailiff," the municipality's equivalent of mayor. In 1557, he married Robert Arden's youngest daughter, Mary. Mary and John had four sons – William was the oldest – and four daughters, of whom only Joan outlived her most celebrated sibling. William was baptized (an event entered in the Stratford parish church records) on April 26, 1564, and it has become customary, without any good factual support, to suppose he was born on April 23, which happens to be the feast day of Saint George, patron saint of England, and is also the date on which he died, in 1616. Shakespeare married Anne Hathaway in 1582, when he was eighteen and she was twenty-six; their first child was born five months later. It has been generally assumed that the marriage was enforced and subsequently unhappy, but these are only assumptions; it has been estimated, for instance, that up to one third of Elizabethan brides were pregnant when they married. Anne and William Shakespeare had three children: Susanna, who married a prominent local physician, John Hall; and the twins Hamnet, who died young in 1596, and Judith, who married Thomas Quiney – apparently a rather shady individual. The name Hamnet was unusual but not unique: he and his twin sister were named for their godparents, Shakespeare's neighbors Hamnet and Judith Sadler. Shakespeare's father died in 1601 (the year of *Hamlet*), and Mary Arden Shakespeare died in 1608 (the year of *Coriolanus*). William Shakespeare's last surviving direct descendant was his granddaughter Elizabeth Hall, who died in 1670.

Between the birth of the twins in 1585 and a clear reference to Shakespeare as a practicing London dramatist in Robert Greene's sensationalizing, satiric pamphlet, *Greene's Groatsworth of Wit* (1592), there is no record of where William Shakespeare was or what he was doing. These seven so-called lost years have been imaginatively filled by scholars and other students of Shakespeare: some think he traveled to Italy, or fought in the Low Countries, or studied law or medicine, or worked as an apprentice actor/writer, and so on to even more fanciful possibilities. Whatever the biographical facts for those "lost" years, Greene's nasty remarks in 1592 testify to professional envy and to the fact that Shakespeare already had a successful career in London. Speaking to his fellow playwrights, Greene warns both generally and specifically:

... trust them [actors] not: for there is an upstart crow, beautified with our feathers, that with his tiger's heart wrapped in a player's hide supposes he is as well able to bombast out a blank verse as the best of you; and being an absolute Johannes Factotum, is in his own conceit the only Shake-scene in a country.

The passage mimics a line from *3 Henry VI* (hence the play must have been performed before Greene wrote) and seems to say that "Shake-scene" is both actor and play-wright, a jack-of-all-trades. That same year, Henry Chettle protested Greene's remarks in *Kind-Heart's Dream*, and each of the next two years saw the publication of poems – *Venus and Adonis* and *The Rape of Lucrece*, respectively – publicly ascribed to (and dedicated by) Shakespeare. Early in 1595 he was named one of the senior members of a prominent acting company, the Lord Chamberlain's Men, when they received payment for court performances dur-ing the 1594 Christmas season.

Clearly, Shakespeare had achieved both success and reputation in London. In 1596, upon Shakespeare's appli-cation, the College of Arms granted his father the now-familiar coat of arms he had taken the first steps to obtain almost twenty years before, and in 1598, John's son – now permitted to call himself "gentleman" – took a 10 percent share in the new Globe playhouse. In 1597, he bought a substantial bourgeois house, called New Place, in Stratford – the garden remains, but Shakespeare's house, several times rebuilt, was torn down in 1759 – and over the next few years Shakespeare spent large sums buying land and making other investments in the town and its environs. Though he worked in London, his family re-mained in Stratford, and he seems always to have consid-ered Stratford the home he would eventually return to. Something approaching a disinterested appreciation of Shakespeare's popular and professional status appears in Francis Meres's *Palladis Tamia* (1598), a not especially imaginative and perhaps therefore persuasive record of lit-erary reputations. Reviewing contemporary English writ-ers, Meres lists the titles of many of Shakespeare's plays, including one not now known, *Love's Labor's Won*, and praises his "mellifluous & hony-tongued" "sugred Son-nets," which were then circulating in manuscript (they were first collected in 1609). Meres describes Shakespeare as "one of the best" English playwrights of both comedy and tragedy. In *Remains . . . Concerning Britain* (1605),

William Camden – a more authoritative source than the imitative Meres – calls Shakespeare one of the "most pregnant witts of these our times" and joins him with such writers as Chapman, Daniel, Jonson, Marston, and Spenser. During the first decades of the seventeenth century, publishers began to attribute numerous play quartos, including some non-Shakespearean ones, to Shakespeare, either by name or initials, and we may assume that they deemed Shakespeare's name and supposed authorship, true or false, commercially attractive.

For the next ten years or so, various records show Shakespeare's dual career as playwright and man of the theater in London, and as an important local figure in Stratford. In 1608-9 his acting company – designated the "King's Men" soon after King James had succeeded Queen Elizabeth in 1603 – rented, refurbished, and opened a small interior playing space, the Blackfriars theater, in London, and Shakespeare was once again listed as a substantial sharer in the group of proprietors of the playhouse. By May 11, 1612, however, he describes himself as a Stratford resident in a London lawsuit – an indication that he had withdrawn from day-to-day professional activity and returned to the town where he had always had his main financial interests. When Shakespeare bought a substantial residential building in London, the Blackfriars Gatehouse, close to the theater of the same name, on March 10, 1613, he is recorded as William Shakespeare "of Stratford upon Avon in the county of Warwick, gentleman," and he named several London residents as the building's trustees. Still, he continued to participate in theatrical activity: when the new Earl of Rutland needed an allegorical design to bear as a shield, or *impresa,* at the celebration of King James's Accession Day, March 24, 1613, the earl's accountant recorded a payment of 44 shillings to Shakespeare for the device with its motto.

For the last few years of his life, Shakespeare evidently

concentrated his activities in the town of his birth. Most of the final records concern business transactions in Stratford, ending with the notation of his death on April 23, 1616, and burial in Holy Trinity Church, Stratford-upon-Avon.

THE QUESTION OF AUTHORSHIP

The history of ascribing Shakespeare's plays (the poems do not come up so often) to someone else began, as it continues, peculiarly. The earliest published claim that someone else wrote Shakespeare's plays appeared in an 1856 article by Delia Bacon in the American journal *Putnam's Monthly* – although an Englishman, Thomas Wilmot, had shared his doubts in private (even secretive) conversations with friends near the end of the eighteenth century. Bacon's was a sad personal history that ended in madness and poverty, but the year after her article, she published, with great difficulty and the bemused assistance of Nathaniel Hawthorne (then United States Consul in Liverpool, England), her *Philosophy of the Plays of Shakspere Unfolded.* This huge, ornately written, confusing farrago is almost unreadable; sometimes its intents, to say nothing of its arguments, disappear entirely beneath near-raving, ecstatic writing. Tumbled in with much supposed "philosophy" appear the claims that Francis Bacon (from whom Delia Bacon eventually claimed descent), Walter Ralegh, and several other contemporaries of Shakespeare's had written the plays. The book had little impact except as a ridiculed curiosity.

Once proposed, however, the issue gained momentum among people whose conviction was the greater in proportion to their ignorance of sixteenth- and seventeenth-century English literature, history, and society. Another American amateur, Catherine P. Ashmead Windle, made the next influential contribution to the cause when she published *Report to the British Museum* (1882), wherein she promised to open "the Cipher of Francis Bacon," though what she mostly offers, in the words of S. Schoenbaum, is "demented allegorizing." An entire new cottage industry grew from Windle's suggestion that the texts contain hidden, cryptographically discoverable ciphers – "clues" – to their authorship; and today there are not only books devoted to the putative ciphers, but also pamphlets, journals, and newsletters.

Although Baconians have led the pack of those seeking a substitute Shakespeare, in *"Shakespeare" Identified* (1920), J. Thomas Looney became the first published "Oxfordian" when he proposed Edward de Vere, seventeenth earl of Oxford, as the secret author of Shakespeare's plays. Also for Oxford and his "authorship" there are today dedicated societies, articles, journals, and books. Less popular candidates – Queen Elizabeth and Christopher Marlowe among them – have had adherents, but the movement seems to have divided into two main contending factions, Baconian and Oxfordian. (For further details on all the candidates for "Shakespeare," see S. Schoenbaum, *Shakespeare's Lives,* 2nd ed., 1991.)

The Baconians, the Oxfordians, and supporters of other candidates have one trait in common – they are snobs. Every pro-Bacon or pro-Oxford tract sooner or later claims that the historical William Shakespeare of Stratford-upon-Avon could not have written the plays because he could not have had the training, the university education, the experience, and indeed the imagination or background their author supposedly possessed. Only a learned genius like Bacon or an aristocrat like Oxford could have written such fine plays. (As it happens, lucky male children of the middle class had access to better education than most aristocrats in Elizabethan England – and Oxford was not particularly well educated.) Shakespeare received in the Stratford grammar school a formal education that would daunt many college graduates today; and popular rival playwrights such as the very learned Ben Jonson and George Chapman, both of whom also lacked university training, achieved great artistic success, without being taken as Bacon or Oxford.

Besides snobbery, one other quality characterizes the authorship controversy: lack of evidence. A great deal of testimony from Shakespeare's time shows that Shakespeare wrote Shakespeare's plays and that his contemporaries recognized them as distinctive and distinctly superior. (Some of that contemporary evidence is collected in E. K. Chambers, *William Shakespeare: A Study of Facts and Problems,* 2 vols., 1930.) Since that testimony comes from Shakespeare's enemies and theatrical competitors as well as from his co-workers and from the Elizabethan equivalent of literary journalists, it seems unlikely that, if any one of these sources had known he was a fraud, they would have failed to record that fact.

Books About Shakespeare's Theater

Useful scholarly studies of theatrical life in Shakespeare's day include: G. E. Bentley, *The Jacobean and Caroline Stage,* 7 vols. (1941-68), and the same author's *The Professions of Dramatist and Player in Shakespeare's Time, 1590-1642* (1986); E. K. Chambers, *The Elizabethan Stage,* 4 vols. (1923); R. A. Foakes, *Illustrations of the English Stage, 1580-1642* (1985); Andrew Gurr, *The Shakespearean Stage,* 3rd ed. (1992), and the same author's *Play-going in Shakespeare's London,* 2nd ed. (1996); Edwin Nungezer, *A Dictionary of Actors* (1929); Carol Chillington Rutter, ed., *Documents of the Rose Playhouse* (1984).

Books About Shakespeare's Life

The following books provide scholarly, documented accounts of Shakespeare's life: G. E. Bentley, *Shakespeare: A Biographical Handbook* (1961); E. K. Chambers, *William Shakespeare: A Study of Facts and Problems,* 2 vols. (1930); S. Schoenbaum, *William Shakespeare: A Compact*

Documentary Life (1977); and *Shakespeare's Lives,* 2nd ed. (1991), by the same author. Many scholarly editions of Shakespeare's complete works print brief compilations of essential dates and events. References to Shakespeare's works up to 1700 are collected in C. M. Ingleby et al., *The Shakespeare Allusion-Book,* rev. ed., 2 vols. (1932).

The Texts of Shakespeare

As far as we know, only one manuscript conceivably in Shakespeare's own hand may (and even this is much disputed) exist: a few pages of a play called *Sir Thomas More*, which apparently was never performed. What we do have, as later readers, performers, scholars, students, are printed texts. The earliest of these survive in two forms: quartos and folios. Quartos (from the Latin for "four") are small books, printed on sheets of paper that were then folded in fours, to make eight double-sided pages. When these were bound together, the result was a squarish, eminently portable volume that sold for the relatively small sum of sixpence (translating in modern terms to about $5.00). In folios, on the other hand, the sheets are folded only once, in half, producing large, impressive volumes taller than they are wide. This was the format for important works of philosophy, science, theology, and literature (the major precedent for a folio Shakespeare was Ben Jonson's *Works*, 1616). The decision to print the works of a popular playwright in folio is an indication of how far up on the social scale the theatrical profession had come during Shakespeare's lifetime. The Shakespeare folio was an expensive book, selling for between fifteen and eighteen shillings, depending on the binding (in modern terms, from about $150 to $180). Twenty Shakespeare plays of the thirty-seven that survive first appeared in quarto, seventeen of which appeared during Shakespeare's lifetime; the rest of the plays are found only in folio.

The First Folio was published in 1623, seven years after Shakespeare's death, and was authorized by his fellow actors, the co-owners of the King's Men. This publication was certainly a mark of the company's enormous respect for Shakespeare; but it was also a way of turning the old plays, most of which were no longer current in the playhouse, into ready money (the folio includes only Shakespeare's plays, not his sonnets or other nondramatic verse). Whatever the motives behind the publication of the folio, the texts it preserves constitute the basis for almost all later editions of the playwright's works. The texts, however, differ from those of the earlier quartos, sometimes in minor respects but often significantly – most strikingly in the two texts of *King Lear,* but also in important ways in *Hamlet, Othello,* and *Troilus and Cressida.* (The variants are recorded in the textual notes to each play in the new Pelican series.) The differences in these texts represent, in a sense, the essence of theater: the texts of plays were initially not intended for publication. They were scripts, designed for the actors to perform – the principal life of the play at this period was in performance. And it follows that in Shakespeare's theater the playwright typically had no say either in how his play was performed or in the disposition of his text – he was an employee of the company. The authoritative figures in the theatrical enterprise were the shareholders in the company, who were for the most part the major actors. They decided what plays were to be done; they hired the playwright and often gave him an outline of the play they wanted him to write. Often, too, the play was a collaboration: the company would retain a group of writers, and parcel out the scenes among them. The resulting script was then the property of the company, and the actors would revise it as they saw fit during the course of putting it on stage. The resulting text belonged to the company. The playwright had no rights in it once he had been paid. (This system survives largely intact in the movie industry, and most of the playwrights of Shakespeare's time were as anonymous as most screenwriters are today.) The script could also, of course, continue to

change as the tastes of audiences and the requirements of
the actors changed. Many – perhaps most – plays were revised when they were reintroduced after any substantial
absence from the repertory, or when they were performed
by a company different from the one that originally com-
missioned the play.

Shakespeare was an exceptional figure in this world
because he was not only a shareholder and actor in his
company, but also its leading playwright – he was literally
his own boss. He had, moreover, little interest in the
publication of his plays, and even those that appeared
during his lifetime with the authorization of the company
show no signs of any editorial concern on the part of
the author. Theater was, for Shakespeare, a fluid and
supremely responsive medium – the very opposite of the
great classic canonical text that has embodied his works
since 1623.

The very fluidity of the original texts, however,
has meant that Shakespeare has always had to be edited.
Here is an example of how problematic the editorial pro-
ject inevitably is, a passage from the most famous speech
in *Romeo and Juliet,* Juliet's balcony soliloquy beginning
"O Romeo, Romeo, wherefore art thou Romeo?" Since
the eighteenth century, the standard modern text has
read,

> What's Montague? It is nor hand, nor foot,
> Nor arm, nor face, nor any other part
> Belonging to a man. O be some other name!
> What's in a name? That which we call a rose
> By any other name would smell as sweet.
> (II.2.40-44)

Editors have three early texts of this play to work from,
two quarto texts and the folio. Here is how the First
Quarto (1597) reads:

> Whats *Mountague?* It is nor hand nor foote,
> Nor arme,nor face, nor any other part.
> Whats in a name? That which we call a Rofe,
> By any other name would fmell as fweet:

Here is the Second Quarto (1599):

> Whats *Mountague?* it is nor hand nor foote,
> Nor arme nor face, ô be fome other name
> Belonging to a man.
> Whats in a name that which we call a rofe,
> By any other word would fmell as fweete,

And here is the First Folio (1623):

> What's *Mountague?* it is nor hand nor foote,
> Nor arme,nor face,O be fome other name
> Belonging to a man.
> What? in a names that which we call a Rofe,
> By any other word would fmell as fweete,

There is in fact no early text that reads as our modern text does – and this is the most famous speech in the play. Instead, we have three quite different texts, all of which are clearly some version of the same speech, but none of which seems to us a final or satisfactory version. The transcendently beautiful passage in modern editions is an editorial invention: editors have succeeded in conflating and revising the three versions into something we recognize as great poetry. Is this what Shakespeare "really" wrote? Who can say? What we can say is that Shakespeare always had performance, not a book, in mind.

Books About the Shakespeare Texts

The standard study of the printing history of the First Folio is W. W. Greg, *The Shakespeare First Folio* (1955). J. K. Walton, *The Quarto Copy for the First Folio of Shakespeare* (1971), is a useful survey of the relation of the quartos to the folio. The second edition of Charlton Hinman's *Norton Facsimile* of the First Folio (1996), with a new introduction by Peter Blayney, is indispensable. Stanley Wells and Gary Taylor, *William Shakespeare: A Textual Companion,* keyed to the Oxford text, gives a comprehensive survey of the editorial situation for all the plays and poems.

THE GENERAL EDITORS

Introduction

*K*ING *LEAR* HAS COME DOWN to us in two significantly different versions, a quarto published in 1608 and the text printed in the First Folio of 1623. Each of these includes material missing from the other: the folio has 115 lines not in the quarto, while the quarto has 285 lines (including a whole scene, and a large part of another) not in the folio. There are many smaller variations as well, in individual words, speech designations, lineation. It is generally, though not universally, agreed now that the quarto represents a version of the heavily corrected and revised manuscript that came from Shakespeare's hand, and that the folio represents a later performing version of the play. The implication is that the quarto represents the play *before* it was performed, the play as it went to the acting company to be transcribed and turned into a performing text, and that the folio version represents the performing text, though not necessarily the only version the company had performed in the years between 1605 and 1623.

Since Lewis Theobald's edition of Shakespeare's plays published in 1733, the standard text of *King Lear* has been a conflation of the quarto and folio texts, with the presumption being that both are cut versions of a longer original. Because the two texts disagree on many matters, however, it is not possible simply to combine them, and a good deal of editorial judgment has always been required to produce a final version. Even editors who do not believe that behind the two texts lies a single Shakespearean original have nevertheless, until recently, preferred a conflated text simply because it gives us more Shakespeare – the quarto, indeed, is our only source for one of the most famous moments in the play, Lear's mock-trial of his daughters in III.6, and even if we believe Shakespeare edited this out of the final script, it is a scene later actors, directors, and editors have been loath to lose.

This volume presents modernizations of the two texts. They have been printed separately, not *en face*, so that the reader may consider them as two discrete stages of the play, not merely as the play in the process of revision, which would privilege the folio text. (It should be emphasized that the two *Lears* do not necessarily represent the only two versions of the play in Shakespeare's time, but merely the only two versions that were preserved in print.) To facilitate comparison of the two, however, act and scene numbers have been supplied for the quarto to enable cross references (see below). A summary of the major differences between the two versions follows the general introduction.

Shakespeare's overwhelming study of the tragedy of old age and the politics of the family has held the stage continuously since its first performance in 1606. In recent years it has rivaled *Hamlet* and *Romeo and Juliet* as the most frequently produced and intensely studied of Shakespeare's tragedies; its analysis of the disintegration of the closest family ties, the resentment and violence underlying the most intimate relationships, has seemed to speak to peculiarly modern concerns. In Shakespeare's own time it spoke as well to much larger political issues: the responsibilities of kingship, the continuity of rule, the unity of the commonwealth, and perhaps most troubling of all, the profound tenuousness of a patriarchal social order – of the assumption that the model for the commonwealth was the family, and that on all levels of society, father was king. Indeed, even overtly political tragedy, for Shakespeare, invariably starts in the family. It is Richard II's behavior toward his uncles and cousins that prompts the rebellion that deposes him; the tragedy of Hamlet begins with fratricide and incest, and takes shape around the complex relations of parents and children; Macbeth, assassinating Duncan at the urging of his wife, is murdering his first cousin; Lear's tragedy is from beginning to end a family matter. It is to the point that when James I came to the English throne in 1603, there was a fully constituted royal family at the center of English society for the first time since the death of Henry VIII. The first recorded performance of *King Lear*, on December 26, 1606, was at Whitehall Palace before King James – though the play seems to have been written in the previous year, the court performance may well have been the first, since plague had closed the public theaters for the season. If this is the case, Shakespeare's play began its life with Britain's royal patriarch at the center of its audience.

But the opening scene hardly mirrors the Jacobean court. Though the story of Lear comes from the chronicles of ancient Britain, the action belongs more to the world of legend than history. Lear's court initially seems like a fairy tale world, where momentous decisions are determined by trifles. The opening moments of the play invite us not to take the action seriously. The declarations of love Lear demands from his three daughters are to be performances, set pieces. Nothing apparently depends on them, since the division of the kingdom has already been decided upon – Lear arrives with a map already prepared. His daughters understand perfectly what is required of them; they have only to play their parts. Cordelia, refusing to produce her accolade, is disrupting both a courtly ceremonial and a family game, and it comes as a profound surprise to everyone present. In insisting on her right to silence, she is not only refusing to play, but is changing the rules.

How are we to take this scene? We could say that it is a debate between style and meaning, with Goneril and Regan showing their rhetorical art, and Cordelia, distrusting language, refusing to say what she does not believe.

The older sisters' performances purport to be deeds, acts of homage to the king their father; but Cordelia objects that words are not deeds. From Goneril and Regan's perspective, these performances are noble ceremonies, hyperbolic and therefore appropriate responses to their royal father; from Cordelia's, they are merely specious shows, cheapening the king because they are inherently dishonest. If we look at the scene this way, it constitutes a debate between rhetoricians and plain-speakers, and it includes a good deal of the Elizabethan distrust of the theater as well – the fear that its representations will be taken for, and will thereby undermine or subvert, reality. Significantly here, it is the villains who are the performers.

We could look at the scene another way and say that the three sisters are being asked to sign a loyalty oath. Goneril and Regan agree to it because they are aware that the oath is really meaningless, and Cordelia refuses for exactly the same reason: because she too is aware that the oath is meaningless – the same perceptions can produce opposite actions, and motives for action are incalculable. The moral implications of the scene are immensely complicated because the issues are so trifling. Is Lear at fault for demanding the performance, for requiring the oath? As it turns out, he is, but we can imagine a different outcome, in which the willing adherence to the honorable forms of ceremonial behavior is seen as the essence of civilized society. These are precisely the values that Hamlet is nostalgic for, the old chivalric world, the world Macbeth destroys with his murder of Duncan. Whether Lear is at fault or not is almost beside the point: the point, as the scene proceeds, is much more schematic, and reminds us of Macbeth's world of paradoxes. The good daughter cannot express her love while the bad daughters are believed; speech is lying and silence is truth; the richest reality is nothing – what Cordelia says, what her dowry is.

These issues relate to the larger question of the nature of power. In this scene about royalty and its dependencies, what constitutes power? In the case of the sisters, it is the ability to speak and please the king. The king's power is, to begin with, the power to bestow the monarchy. But Lear thinks of it in much less practical and more metaphysical ways, as the power of his senses –

Hence, and avoid my sight! (123)*

– and even more significantly, as the power of his language. Kent, urging Lear to rescind his decree, has sought "To come between our sentence and our power": a *sentence*, the crucial unit of structured language, is also the exercise of judicial authority. In our legal system, the full power of the law is still imposed by that word "sentence." To punish criminals, we sentence them.

What Lear does *not* conceive his power to be is his position, the mere fact that he is king. But this, of course, is the sole source of his power, and he makes clear the way the drama is to move by resigning his office but nevertheless undertaking to retain "the name, and all th'addition to a king" (135). A question the play examines most intensely is what the name of king is – is it another nothing? What "addition" can a nothing have – what more than nothing is a nothing entitled to? And what is authority, which Kent sees in the face of the mad Lear? Can there be authority without power? What are the bases of judgment, essential for effective government? This question is central to *Macbeth*, too, as King Duncan observes of the thane who has betrayed him: "There's no art / To find the mind's construction in the face" (I.4.11–12).

Clearly the basis of judgment is not loyalty oaths. Even the victorious sisters realize how foolish Lear has been, observing, "with what poor judgment he hath now cast [Cordelia] off appears too grossly" (291–92). More important is their observation that "he hath ever but slen-

---

*Citations are to the folio text.

derly known himself" (293-94); it implies that Lear's behavior is not simply a function of old age, but is both characteristic and at the heart of the play's disruptions. A king without self-knowledge is notoriously a danger to the commonwealth. But is Lear really responsible for the ensuing tragedy? How far could even the best of kings contain the villainy of Goneril, Regan, Cornwall, Edmund? Could Cordelia do so?

Moreover, though it is Kent who initially objects to Lear's bad judgment, only the villains assume that it renders him unfit to rule. In fact, elsewhere in the play Lear is referred to not as blind, foolish, irascible, self-centered, tyrannical, but as *kind* – Kent deplores "the hard rein which both of them hath borne / Against the old kind king . . ." (III.1.19-20). Lear on himself, "So kind a father!" (I.5.32), is presumably to be taken ironically, but his later characterization of himself, "Your old kind father, whose frank heart gave all" (III.4.20), is, objectively, true, though of course not the whole truth. When Richard Burbage, the leading tragedian of Shakespeare's company, died in 1618, his elegy listed the roles that made him famous:

No more young Hamlet, old Hieronymo,
Kind Lear, the grievèd Moor . . . *

The point here is not only that Lear is entitled to respect and pity, but even more significantly, that in a monarchy based on a philosophy of Divine Right, a bad king is still the king. This is no doubt why King James liked this play about the extreme precariousness of kingship enough to have it performed at court. The play was, in this respect, for its original audiences, both politically conservative and basically sentimental. Modern audiences and critics

---

The Shakespeare Allusion Book, ed. John Munro (London: Oxford University Press, 1932); 1:272.

who focus on Lear's irrationality and incompetence have adopted the point of view of the villains.

As Lear's plot derives from both ancient history and Jacobean politics, the parallel plot of Gloucester and his good and bad sons derives from contemporary romance. Shakespeare took the story from Sir Philip Sidney's immensely popular novel *Arcadia*, written in the 1580s, and an instant classic – by 1605 it had already gone through four editions. Gloucester's tragedy provides a running commentary on that of Lear and his daughters, but it also has its own momentum. Modern audiences find the casualness of Gloucester's attitude to Edmund's bastardy in the opening exchange with Kent at least disconcerting, if not reprehensible; but illegitimacy was a commonplace fact of Shakespeare's England, as it must be of any society without reliable methods of birth control, and though illegitimate children were barred from the line of succession and the inheritance of landed estates, no stigma was attached to the fact of bastardy itself. Noblemen freely acknowledged their illegitimate children, and often provided handsomely for them, and illegitimacy was no bar to social and political success: Elizabeth's powerful minister the Earl of Leicester was illegitimate, as were, technically, both Elizabeth herself and her predecessor on the throne Queen Mary I. Edmund complains of his bastardy, etymologizing it (incorrectly) from "base," but it is important to emphasize that he loses nothing on account of it. He is younger than the legitimate son Edgar, not older, and therefore even if he were not illegitimate, he would be entitled only to whatever his father chooses to give him: under the English law of primogeniture, the eldest son inherits the title, and the bulk of the estate. In fact, Edmund is contemptuous of his father precisely because he makes no distinction between his two sons, but loves and trusts them equally – contemptuous not because Gloucester is blind to the fact that Edmund is a bastard, but because he is blind to the fact that he is a villain.

But Edmund is more than a villain. He is in his way the great realist of the play. Invoking Nature as his goddess in a powerful soliloquy at the opening of Act I, scene 2, he defies conventional morality in favor of an ethic of pure self-interest. Shakespeare's contemporaries would have seen him as a Machiavellian figure, and to that extent a conventional stage villain; but what is probably most striking about him for us is the way he analyzes and overturns the idea of nature so central to the largest ethical claims of the play, the idea of nature as a benign and humane force. From Lear's and Cordelia's perspective, Goneril and Regan are behaving unnaturally; from Edmund's, they are fulfilling nature's law, what we would call the law of the jungle. It is Goneril and Regan who are the play's conventional villains; Edmund is a genuinely subversive figure. He loses in the end, certainly, but so do Lear and Cordelia; and what he introduces into the play is a serious question about the basis of ethical behavior.

The Nature Edmund invokes is anarchic, full of competing claims, not ordered and hierarchical. To acknowledge such a Nature is to acknowledge the reality, force, and validity of the individual will – to acknowledge that all of us have claims that conflict with claims about the deference due to fathers and kings, about the hierarchy of society and what is natural within the family. This is the recognition that Edmund brings into *King Lear* when he invokes Nature as his goddess. It is a Nature that is not the image of divine order, but one in which the strongest and craftiest survive – and when they survive, they then go on to devise claims about Nature that justify their success, claims about hierarchies, natural law and order, the divine right of kings, the sanctity of the father. Edmund is a villain, but if he were ultimately successful he would be indistinguishable from the Lears and Cordelias (and James I's) of Shakespeare's world.

Such concerns may seem to us anachronistic: we tend to believe that for Shakespeare's society the order of nature was a norm, the sanctity of patriarchy unquestionable. But ambivalence about what is natural within the family was built into the very language of Elizabethan England: the alternative term for an illegitimate child was a natural child – it is the legitimate, here, that is unnatural. Edmund raises all the issues that Machiavelli had introduced into Renaissance political discourse, and the fear generated by the figure of the Machiavel in Renaissance England is a measure of how genuinely subversive those issues were. The fact that Edmund must live by his wits, that he is entitled only to what he can gain by his own efforts, actually makes him representative of a large segment of Shakespeare's audience: his situation is not only that of bastards, but of every younger son in a culture that practices primogeniture. Edmund stands, disturbingly, at the center of the society's doubts about itself.

The ease with which Edmund's elder brother Edgar, Gloucester's legitimate heir, is displaced, is a measure of how forcefully those doubts were felt. Gloucester's whole sense of the beloved Edgar is overturned in an instant by Edmund's deception, as Lear's sense of Cordelia is overturned by a single act of obduracy. At the heart of the play, in both Lear's and Gloucester's families, is a conviction that human nature, even the nature of those closest to us, is essentially unknowable. Doubtless both Gloucester's and Edgar's gullibility are strongly contributing factors in the success of Edmund's schemes, but that gullibility stems precisely from their faith in the essential goodness and honesty of human nature. Would skepticism be sufficient protection against Edmund's villainy?

Once the enabling actions of the opening two scenes have occurred, the tragedy takes shape with extraordinary swiftness. Lear's reduction from monarch to "a poor old man, / As full of grief as age, wretched in both" (II.4.265-66) is complete by the end of Act II, the blinding of Gloucester by the end of Act III. The whole action of the play covers no more than a few weeks. It is not only the

speed of this that is notable, but its violence, the abject-
ness of Lear's misery and madness, the savagery of
Gloucester's treatment at the hands of Cornwall, Regan,
and Goneril. The savagery is visited, moreover, not only
on the characters, but on the audience as well: deaths,
even murders, take place on Shakespeare's stage in every
tragedy, but the blinding of Gloucester is all but unique –
the closest parallel, the mutilation of Lavinia in *Titus An-
dronicus*, takes place offstage.

Along with the violence, the play has a strong erotic element, though it has little to do with the issues of marriage that fill the opening scene –"tell me how much you
love me" is what fathers say to children in this play, not
what lovers say to each other. The most powerful erotic
forces of the play are those of the villains, the adulterous
passion of Goneril and Regan for Edmund. It is this that
turns the sisters from natural allies to natural enemies.
Even so, the play includes no love scenes.

What, then, are the erotics of the opening scene? Burgundy and France have, after all, come to woo Cordelia,
but for both, the issue of inheritance is the primary one.
There is nothing culturally inappropriate about this: the
reason women in Early Modern cultures are provided
with dowries is that men will not marry them otherwise.
In patriarchal societies, women are property, and no matter how intelligent, accomplished, charming, or beautiful
they may be, the property is essential, and the more property they represent the more desirable they are. Love is not
irrelevant to marriage, but neither is it the sole nor even
the primary consideration, and it is often represented as
what follows from a prosperous marriage, not what brings
it about. Lear dividing the kingdom among his three
daughters, moreover, is following the dictates of English
law: primogeniture applied exclusively to male heirs. If
there were only daughters, they inherited equally – Lear's
willfulness in the matter is manifested merely in his deter-

mination to give Cordelia a better portion than her sisters.

Why then does Cordelia become more attractive to the king of France when she is dowryless, and out of favor with her father? This, in fact, is the romance element in the plot: the love interest is represented as both chivalric and quixotic. Of course, France's romantic passion can also be seen cynically (or realistically), as representing basically an investment. The French king supporting, indeed, urging, an invasion of England by an army led by his wife on behalf of his father-in-law is hardly disinterested. France is not concerned solely to get Lear in out of the rain; to rescue Lear means repossessing at least Cordelia's original third of the kingdom, and perhaps all of it. Cordelia is a gamble, but in all the sources the gamble pays off handsomely: in Holinshed's *Chronicles*, from which Shakespeare took his history, Cordelia's army wins, Lear retrieves his throne, and Cordelia succeeds him. The surprise for a Jacobean audience would have been that in Shakespeare the gamble fails.

The parallel between Lear and Gloucester plays itself out as a double tragedy with two quite different morals. Both men are attended by the figures they have decisively rejected, either in disguise, like Kent and Edgar, or in the plain-speaking Fool, a surrogate Cordelia. Edgar leads his blind father out of despair through a little staged miracle, the extraordinary imagined fall from Dover Cliff in IV.5. But the resulting patience and acceptance lead to nothing but death, without even the recognition and reconciliation scene we have surely been primed to expect – and which is an essential element of the story in Shakespeare's source for the Gloucester plot, the episode of the Paphlagonian king in Sidney's *Arcadia* (Book 2, Chapter 10). In Sidney, the reconciliation has taken place even before the story is recounted, and is, in a sense, a determining condition of the story. Shakespeare's Edgar, almost at the play's end, merely reports that at the moment of Gloucester's death he did finally reveal his identity – the shock of recognition, in fact, is what killed Gloucester. But the announcement comes almost as an afterthought, the tying up of a loose end.

Gloucester is effectively abandoned by the play. His tragedy is framed, moreover, with a simplistic moral. Edgar, confronting Edmund at the end, says

> The gods are just, and of our pleasant vices [Q: virtues]
> Make instruments to plague us.
> The dark and vicious place where thee he got
> Cost him his eyes.
>
> (V.3.163-65)

Edmund agrees: "Thou'st spoken right; 'tis true / The wheel is come full circle." But as a summation of Gloucester's tragedy, the lines seem singularly obtuse: Gloucester dies blaming his gullibility and imperceptiveness; he never gives any sign of regret for his youthful adultery. We will be especially unpersuaded by Edgar's conviction of the economy of divine justice if we think of Cordelia's fate, and even of Lear's, which seem more appropriately summed up with Gloucester's own cosmic epigram,

> As flies to wanton boys are we to th' gods;
> They kill us for their sport.
>
> (IV.1.36-67)

Tragedy may be a moralizing form, but it is not an equitable one: the innocent invariably suffer with the guilty, and often more than the guilty. If tragedy has a moral, it is surely that we *do not* get what we deserve. We might contrast the sense Edgar makes of his tragedy with the sense Cordelia, stoical in defeat, makes of hers: "We are not the first / Who with best meaning have incurred the worst" (V.3.3-4).

In the tragedy of Lear and Cordelia, the moral is obscure but the suffering and awareness are the measures of value. Renaissance philosophy and theology almost without exception took the position of Lear and Cordelia. Edgar's notion of cosmic justice would have been considered to be like a belief in horoscopes, naive and simplistic. Providence works on far too vast a scale for individual suffering to be included in it – the heavens do not provide comfort: that one must make for oneself. Virtue, proverbial wisdom tells us, is its own reward: the virtuous gain nothing but the thing itself, the knowledge that they are virtuous. This is not a philosophy designed to produce happy endings.

Renaissance Christianity was not a cozy or friendly faith; whether Protestant or Catholic, the church was fierce and uncompromising, not the welcoming mother one could always return to, but an omnipotent and largely disapproving father. The notion of a comforting Christianity, gentle Jesus meek and mild, is a relatively modern development; for Milton, God's ways have to be *justified* to man, and the task is not an easy one.

In the final scene we find Lear creating a play world, the reconciliation with Cordelia allowing nothing more than a childish fantasy:

> Come, let's away to prison.
> We two alone will sing like birds i' th' cage.
>   (V.3.8–9)

The point about birds in a cage is that they are happier than we are. Lear conceives of themselves getting clear out of the world of action and passion, spies for a God who has left the world unattended (why else would God need spies?), and thus creating the only permanence in a world of change. Of course this is a fantasy, not merely because of the real pathos of Lear's condition, but because it leaves out of account all the other realities of his world – the villainy of Edmund, who has ordered them killed; but also the realities of what even the men of good will in this play are like. Albany has to be *reminded* by Kent of the king and Cordelia, and he replies, "Great thing of us forgot" (212). Forgetting a great thing makes it a nothing. Cordelia and Lear are killed as much by passive forgetfulness as by active villainy. Even in the play's last moments, lack of awareness is the destructive element.

Albany's pious prayer, "The gods defend her" (232), is immediately followed by Lear carrying Cordelia's corpse, howling like a beast; and it seems to Kent and Edgar the Day of Judgment –"Is this the promised end?" "Or image of that horror?" (239-40) – though characteristically it seems real to Kent, an image to Edgar. For Lear now, the only possible redemption is that Cordelia might not be dead. For a moment he thinks that she is alive, cruelly deceived; and then, when it is clear that she is not, raging again, he accuses the best and most faithful of friends, Kent and Edgar, of having murdered her. Good will counts for nothing, nothing redeems sorrows; Kent says it: "All's cheerless, dark, and deadly" (266). The final realization, the final truth of plain-speaking, is five *nevers*:

> Thou'lt come no more.
> Never, never, never, never, never.
>
> (284)

Lear heartbreakingly extends Cordelia's *nothing* into the scheme of time. He returns momentarily to the fantasy that she lives –"Look on her! Look, her lips"– and with that false hope he dies.

It is important to emphasize that the exceptional bleakness of this conclusion is all Shakespeare's. In the story as he found it in every one of the sources, Cordelia's army is victorious, and Lear reascends his throne. Kent's simple eulogy does no more than accept the facts, and proposes no moral:

He hates him
That would upon the rack of this tough world
Stretch him out longer.

The world is an instrument of torture, and the only comfort is in the nothing, the never, of death. The heroic vision is of suffering, unredeemed and unmitigated. Kent says, "The wonder is, he hath endured so long."

STEPHEN ORGEL
Stanford University

Note on the Texts

The Quarto and the Folio

To BEGIN AT THE beginning, the title page of the quarto describes the play as follows:

> Master William Shakespeare: his chronicle history of the life and death of King Lear and his three daughters. With the unfortunate life of Edgar, son and heir to the Earl of Gloucester, and his sullen and assumed humor of Tom of Bedlam.

The attractions here for the book buyer include Shakespeare's name (which by 1608 in itself guaranteed a good sale), a tragic subject from British history, and a subsidiary tragedy about aristocrats, enlivened by mad scenes. (A Second Quarto, published in 1619 with a false date of 1608, is essentially a slightly edited version of the First Quarto.) The play in the folio is simply *The Tragedy of King Lear*. The change from chronicle history to tragedy suggests a change of focus, but in fact it probably signals only the folio editors' desire for neat categories: history was reserved for English history after the Norman Conquest – so the play called in quarto *The Tragedy of King Richard the Second* becomes in the folio *The Life and Death of Richard the Second*, and appears in the section of Histories, not of Tragedies; these categories, obviously, were not mutually exclusive. Certainly the quarto's history of Lear is no less tragic than the folio's tragedy of Lear, and the folio makes as much of Gloucester's and Edgar's story as the quarto does.

The two versions differ significantly, however, in their presentation. The action of the quarto *King Lear* is uninterrupted, with no act and scene divisions – indeed, the book does not even have page numbers. None of this is unusual in play quartos of the period. Acts and scenes in Shakespeare are for the most part a feature of the plays as edited for the folio, to give these modern classics the look, in print, of classical drama. In the present edition, the quarto has been supplied with act and scene numbers based on those of the folio to facilitate reference and comparison.

Here is a summary of the major differences between the two texts – there are many less significant ones not noted here:

F I.1.41–45 A direct address to the sons-in-law has been added. They also have a joint line, interposing in the fight between Lear and Kent, "Dear sir, forbear" (161), not in Q.

F III.2.82–97 Only F has the fool's prophecy.

Q III.6.16–51 Only Q has the mock-trial.

Q III.6.91–109 Only Q has Kent's speech and Edgar's soliloquy.

Q III.7.103–11 Only Q has the servants aid Gloucester.

Q IV.2.30–49 Only Q has the argument between Albany and Goneril.

Q IV.3a Only Q has the scene of Kent and the gentleman discussing the political situation, the account of Cordelia, and the account of Lear's unwillingness to meet her (this contradicts IV.6, in which Lear is unaware that Cordelia is no longer in France).

Q V.3.185–95 Only Q has Edgar's account of meeting Kent.

The final speech is spoken by Albany in Q, by Edgar in F. (Either makes good sense: Albany is the highest-ranking person left alive, but Edgar is the successor to Lear's throne.)

The following is a list of departures from the copy texts of this edition.

The History of King Lear

I.1   134 mad] F; man Q   215 may know] Q; make known F. All editors emend this, since to keep it involves Cordelia in a change of address from Lear to France in the middle of the speech. But onstage this would pose no problem, and though Shakespeare apparently later thought better of it, that is no reason to change it.   230 a dower] and dowre Q; a dowrie F

I.2   15 Well then,] F; well the Q   110 honesty] F; honest Q   117 spherical] F; spiritual Q

I.4   101 my] F; any Q   108 the brach] Steevens; oth'e brach Q; the Lady Brach F   223 notion weakens] F; notion, weaknes Q   224 lethargied] F; lethargie Q   254 my] F; any Q   258 are] F; and Q   279 cadent] F; accent Q

II.2   71 too entrenched] to intrench Q; t'intrince F   73 fire] F; stir Q   76 dogs] F; dayes Q   162 miracles] F; my wracke Q

II.4   1 home] F; hence Q   7 heads] F; heeles Q

III.3   3 took] F; tooke me Q

III.4   7 contentious] F; crulentious Q; tempestious Q corr.

III.5   11 were not] F; were Q

III.6   21 burn] Capell; broome Q

III.7   62 bowed] Greg; lou'd Q; lowd Q corr.; bare F   63 buoyed] Q (bod); F

IV.1   4 esperance] F; experience Q   35 kill] F; bitt Q

IV.2   10 dislike] F; desire Q   28 A . . . bed] Q corr.; My foote vsurps my body Q; My Foole vsurps my body F

IV.3a   32 moistened] Capell; moistened her Q

IV.3b   2 vexed] F; vent Q

V.1   54 Here] F; Hard Q

V.3   24 good years] F (good yeares); good Q   131 Conspirant] F; conspicuate Q   256 you] Q2, F; your Q   286 first] F; life Q   289 fordone] F; foredoome Q; fore-doom'd Q2

The Tragedy of King Lear

I.1   281 pleated] Q, F (plighted)

I.4   160 fools] Q; foole F   181 nor crumb] not crumb F

II.1   78 why] Q; wher F   86 strange news] Q; strangenesse F

II.2   74 too intrince] t'intrince F; too entrenched Q   107 flick'ring] flicking F; flitkering Q   122 dread] Q; dead F

II.4   2 messenger] Q; messengers F   178 sickly] F3; fickly F; fickle Q

III.2   57 Hast] Q; ha's F

III.4 53 ford] Q (foorde); Sword F   115 till the] Q; at F   134 had] Q;
not in F
III.6 29 tyke] Q (tike); tight F
IV.2 43 thereat enraged] Q (inraged); threat-enrag'd F
IV.3 18 distress] Q; desires F
IV.6 25 not] Q; not in F
V.1 13 me] Q; not in F   36 love] Q; loues F

The History of King Lear

1608 Quarto Text

[Names of the Actors

LEAR, *King of Britain*
KING OF FRANCE
GONERIL, *Lear's eldest daughter*
DUKE OF ALBANY, *Goneril's husband*
REGAN, *Lear's second daughter*
DUKE OF CORNWALL, *Regan's husband*
CORDELIA, *Lear's youngest daughter*
DUKE OF BURGUNDY
EARL OF KENT
EARL OF GLOUCESTER
EDGAR, *Gloucester's elder son, later disguised as*
   Tom o' Bedlam
EDMUND, *Gloucester's younger, bastard son*
OSWALD, *Goneril's steward*
OLD MAN, *Gloucester's tenant*
CURAN, *Gloucester's servant*
FOOL, *attending on Lear*
DOCTOR
SERVANTS, CAPTAINS, HERALD, KNIGHT,
   MESSENGER, GENTLEMEN, SOLDIERS, *etc.*

SCENE: *Britain*]
*

The History of King Lear

∾ I.1 *Enter Kent, Gloucester, and Bastard [Edmund].*

KENT I thought the king had more affected the Duke of   1
Albany than Cornwall.   2
GLOUCESTER It did always seem so to us, but now in the
division of the kingdoms, it appears not which of the
dukes he values most, for equalities are so weighed that   5
curiosity in neither can make choice of either's moiety.   6
KENT Is not this your son, my lord?
GLOUCESTER His breeding, sir, hath been at my charge.
I have so often blushed to acknowledge him that now I
am brazed to it.   10
KENT I cannot conceive you.   11
GLOUCESTER Sir, this young fellow's mother could,
whereupon she grew round-wombed and had indeed,
sir, a son for her cradle ere she had a husband for her
bed. Do you smell a fault?
KENT I cannot wish the fault undone, the issue of it
being so proper.   17
GLOUCESTER But I have, sir, a son by order of law, some   18
year elder than this, who yet is no dearer in my ac-   19
count. Though this knave came something saucily into   20
the world before he was sent for, yet was his mother

I.1 Lear's palace **s.d.** *Gloucester* (pronounced "Gloster") **1–2** *more af-*
fected . . . than preferred . . . to **2** *Albany* i.e., Scotland **5** *equalities . . .*
weighed their qualities are so equal **6** *curiosity . . . moiety* thorough examina-
tion cannot find either's share preferable **10** *brazed* brazened **11** *conceive*
understand **17** *proper* handsome **18** *by . . . law* legitimate **19–20** *account*
esteem **20** *something saucily* somewhat impertinently

fair; there was good sport at his making, and the
23   whoreson must be acknowledged. Do you know this
noble gentleman, Edmund?
EDMUND   No, my lord.
GLOUCESTER   My lord of Kent. Remember him hereafter
as my honorable friend.
EDMUND   My services to your lordship.
29   KENT   I must love you, and sue to know you better.
30   EDMUND   Sir, I shall study deserving.
31   GLOUCESTER   He hath been out nine years, and away he
32   shall again. The king is coming.
> *Sound a sennet. Enter one bearing a coronet, then*
> *Lear, then the Dukes of Albany and Cornwall; next*
> *Goneril, Regan, Cordelia, with Followers.*

LEAR
Attend my lords of France and Burgundy, Gloucester.
GLOUCESTER   I shall, my liege.   *Exit.*
LEAR
35   Meantime we will express our darker purposes.
The map there. Know we have divided
In three our kingdom, and 'tis our first intent
To shake all cares and business of our state,
Confirming them on younger years.
40   The two great princes, France and Burgundy,
Great rivals in our youngest daughter's love,
Long in our court have made their amorous sojourn,
And here are to be answered. Tell me, my daughters,
Which of you shall we say doth love us most,
That we our largest bounty may extend
Where merit doth most challenge it?
Goneril, our eldest born, speak first.

---

23 *whoreson* (literally "bastard," but the word was also an affectionate term,
like "scamp")   29 *sue* seek   30 *study deserving* undertake to deserve it   31
out away   32 s.d. *sennet* trumpet fanfare   35 *darker purposes* secret plan

GONERIL
    Sir, I do love you more than words can wield the matter, 48
    Dearer than eyesight, space, or liberty, 49
    Beyond what can be valued rich or rare, 50
    No less than life, with grace, health, beauty, honor;
    As much as child e'er loved, or father, friend;
    A love that makes breath poor and speech unable. 53
    Beyond all manner of so much I love you.
CORDELIA   *[Aside]*
    What shall Cordelia do? Love and be silent.
LEAR
    Of all these bounds, even from this line to this,
    With shady forests and wide-skirted meads, 57
    We make thee lady. To thine and Albany's issue 58
    Be this perpetual. What says our second daughter,
    Our dearest Regan, wife to Cornwall? Speak. 60
REGAN
    Sir, I am made
    Of the selfsame mettle that my sister is,
    And prize me at her worth in my true heart. 63
    I find she names my very deed of love;
    Only she came short, that I profess 65
    Myself an enemy to all other joys
    Which the most precious square of sense possesses, 67
    And find I am alone felicitate 68
    In your dear highness' love.
CORDELIA   *[Aside]*   Then poor Cordelia!
    And yet not so, since I am sure my love's 70
    More richer than my tongue.
LEAR
    To thee and thine hereditary ever

---

48 *wield the matter* express the subject   **49** *space* scope (to enjoy "liberty")
53 *breath* voice   **57** *wide-skirted meads* spreading meadows   **58** *issue* heirs
63 *prize me* value myself   **65** *that* in that   **67** *most . . . possesses* measure of
perception holds to be most precious (?)   **68** *felicitate* made happy

Remain this ample third of our fair kingdom,
74 No less in space, validity, and pleasure
Than that confirmed on Goneril. But now, our joy,
Although the last, not least in our dear love,
What can you say to win a third more opulent
Than your sisters?

CORDELIA   Nothing, my lord.

LEAR   How!
79 Nothing can come of nothing; speak again.

CORDELIA
80 Unhappy that I am, I cannot heave
My heart into my mouth. I love your majesty
82 According to my bond, nor more nor less.

LEAR
Go to, go to, mend your speech a little
Lest it may mar your fortunes.

CORDELIA   Good my lord,
You have begot me, bred me, loved me.
86 I return those duties back as are right fit,
Obey you, love you, and most honor you.
Why have my sisters husbands, if they say
They love you all? Happily when I shall wed
90 That lord whose hand must take my plight shall carry
Half my love with him, half my care and duty.
Sure I shall never marry like my sisters,
To love my father all.

LEAR
But goes this with thy heart?

CORDELIA   Ay, good my lord.

LEAR
So young and so untender?

CORDELIA
96 So young, my lord, and true.

---

74 *validity* value 79 *Nothing ... nothing* (quoting a famous scholastic
maxim derived from Aristotle, *nihil ex nihilo fit*) 82 *bond* duty 86 *I ... fit*
I am properly dutiful in return 90 *plight* marriage vow 96 *true* honest

LEAR
 Well, let it be so. Thy truth then be thy dower,
 For by the sacred radiance of the sun,
 The mysteries of Hecate and the night,   99
 By all the operation of the orbs,   100
 From whom we do exist and cease to be,
 Here I disclaim all my paternal care,
 Propinquity, and property of blood,   103
 And as a stranger to my heart and me
 Hold thee from this forever. The barbarous Scythian, 105
 Or he that makes his generation   106
 Messes to gorge his appetite, shall be
 As well neighbored, pitied, and relieved
 As thou my sometime daughter.
KENT   Good my liege –
LEAR
 Peace, Kent! Come not between the dragon and his *110*
 wrath.
 I loved her most, and thought to set my rest
 On her kind nursery. *[To Cordelia]* Hence, and avoid my 112
 sight!
 So be my grave my peace as here I give   113
 Her father's heart from her. Call France – who stirs?
 Call Burgundy. Cornwall and Albany,
 With my two daughters' dowers digest this third.
 Let pride, which she calls plainness, marry her.
 I do invest you jointly in my power,
 Preeminence, and all the large effects   119
 That troop with majesty. Ourself by monthly course, 120
 With reservation of an hundred knights,   121
 By you to be sustained, shall our abode

---

99 *Hecate* goddess of the underworld, patron of witchcraft **100** *opera-tion . . . orbs* astrological influences **103** *Propinquity . . . blood* blood rela-tionship **105** *this* this time; *Scythian* Crimean tribesman, notorious for cruelty **106–7** *makes . . . Messes* devours his children **112** *nursery* care **113** *So . . . peace* let my peace be in my grave **119** *large effects* rich trappings **120** *troop with* accompany **121** *With reservation of* legally retaining

Make with you by due turns. Only we still retain
124 The name and all the additions to a king.
125 The sway, revenue, execution of the rest,
Belovèd sons, be yours; which to confirm,
127 This coronet part betwixt you.
KENT   Royal Lear,
Whom I have ever honored as my king,
Loved as my father, as my master followed,
130 As my great patron thought on in my prayers –
LEAR
131 The bow is bent and drawn; make from the shaft.
KENT
132 Let it fall rather, though the fork invade
The region of my heart. Be Kent unmannerly
When Lear is mad. What wilt thou do, old man?
Think'st thou that duty shall have dread to speak
136 When power to flattery bows? To plainness honor's
bound
137 When majesty stoops to folly. Reverse thy doom,
And in thy best consideration check
139 This hideous rashness. Answer my life my judgment:
140 Thy youngest daughter does not love thee least,
Nor are those empty-hearted whose low sound
142 Reverbs no hollowness.
LEAR   Kent, on thy life, no more.
KENT
144 My life I never held but as a pawn
145 To wage against thy enemies, nor fear to lose it,
146 Thy safety being the motive.

---

124 *all the additions* i.e., the honors and prerogatives 125 *sway* authority
127 *coronet* (which would have crowned Cordelia)   131 *make from* get out
of the way of   132 *fall* strike; *fork* (two-pronged) arrowhead   136 *plainness*
straight talk   137 *doom* decision   139 *Answer my life* I stake my life on
142 *Reverbs no hollowness* does not resonate hollowly   144 *pawn* (1) stake,
(2) the least valuable chess piece   145 *wage* wager, risk   146 *motive* motivation

LEAR   Out of my sight!
KENT
  See better, Lear, and let me still remain   147
  The true blank of thine eye.   148
LEAR   Now by Apollo —
KENT
  Now by Apollo, king, thou swearest thy gods in vain.   149
LEAR Vassal, recreant!   150
KENT
  Do, kill thy physician,
  And the fee bestow upon the foul disease.
  Revoke thy doom, or whilst I can vent clamor
  From my throat, I'll tell thee thou dost evil.
LEAR
  Hear me, on thy allegiance hear me!
  Since thou hast sought to make us break our vow,
  Which we durst never yet and with strayed pride   157
  To come between our sentence and our power,   158
  Which nor our nature nor our place can bear,   159
  Our potency made good, take thy reward: 160
  Four days we do allot thee for provision
  To shield thee from diseases of the world,
  And on the fifth to turn thy hated back
  Upon our kingdom. If on the tenth day following
  Thy banished trunk be found in our dominions,   165
  The moment is thy death. Away! By Jupiter,
  This shall not be revoked.
KENT
  Why, fare thee well, king; since thus thou wilt appear,
  Friendship lives hence, and banishment is here.
    [To Cordelia]

---

147 *still* always 148 *true blank* exact bull's-eye 149 *Apollo* the sun god
150 *recreant* (1) traitor, (2) infidel 157 *strayed* undutiful 158 *our power*
the power to execute them 159 *place* royal office 160 *Our . . . good* hereby
demonstrating my power 165 *trunk* body

170   The gods to their protection take thee, maid,
       That rightly thinks, and hast most justly said.
       [To Goneril and Regan]
172   And your large speeches may your deeds approve,
       That good effects may spring from words of love.
       Thus Kent, O princes, bids you all adieu;
       He'll shape his old course in a country new.   *[Exit.]*
       Enter [the King of] France and [the Duke of]
       Burgundy, with Gloucester.
       GLOUCESTER
       Here's France and Burgundy, my noble lord.
       LEAR
       My lord of Burgundy,
       We first address towards you, who with a king
       Hath rivaled for our daughter. What in the least
180   Will you require in present dower with her,
       Or cease your quest of love?
       BURGUNDY   Royal majesty,
       I crave no more than what your highness offered,
183   Nor will you tender less.
       LEAR   Right noble Burgundy,
       When she was dear to us we did hold her so;
       But now her price is fallen. Sir, there she stands.
186   If aught within that little seeming substance,
187   Or all of it, with our displeasure pieced
188   And nothing else, may fitly like your grace,
       She's there, and she is yours.
       BURGUNDY   I know no answer.
       LEAR
190   Sir, will you with those infirmities she owes,
       Unfriended, new-adopted to our hate,

---

172 *your . . . approve* i.e., may your actions justify your words   183 *tender*
offer   186 *aught* anything; *little . . . substance* (1) mere shell of a person, (2)
person with few pretensions   187 *pieced* joined   188 *like* please   190 *owes*
owns

Covered with our curse, and strangered with our oath,   192
Take her or leave her?
BURGUNDY   Pardon me, royal sir;
Election makes not up on such conditions.   194
LEAR
Then leave her, sir; for, by the power that made me,
I tell you all her wealth. *[To France]* For you, great king,
I would not from your love make such a stray   197
To match you where I hate; therefore beseech you
To avert your liking a more worthier way   199
Than on a wretch whom nature is ashamed   200
Almost to acknowledge hers.
FRANCE   This is most strange,
That she that even but now was your best object,
The argument of your praise, balm of your age,   203
Most best, most dearest, should in this trice of time
Commit a thing so monstrous to dismantle   205
So many folds of favor. Sure her offense
Must be of such unnatural degree
That monsters it, or you fore-vouched affections   208
Fall'n into taint; which to believe of her   209
Must be a faith that reason without miracle   210
Could never plant in me.
CORDELIA   *[To Lear]*
I yet beseech your majesty,
If for I want that glib and oily art   213
To speak and purpose not – since what I well intend
I'll do't before I speak – that you may know   215
It is no vicious blot, murder, or foulness,
No unclean action or dishonored step

---

192 *strangered with* made a stranger by   194 *Election . . . conditions* choice is
impossible on such terms   197 *make . . . stray* stray so far as   199 *avert* turn
203 *argument* theme   205 *to dismantle* as to strip off   208 *monsters it* makes
it monstrous   208–9 *you . . . taint* you previously swore a love that must
now appear suspect   213 *for I want* because I lack   215 *you . . . know* (addressed to France – see textual note)

That hath deprived me of your grace and favor,
But even for want of that for which I am rich:
220 A still-soliciting eye, and such a tongue
As I am glad I have not, though not to have it
Hath lost me in your liking.

LEAR   Go to, go to.
Better thou hadst not been born than not to have
pleased me better.

FRANCE
Is it no more but this? A tardiness in nature,
That often leaves the history unspoke
That it intends to do? My lord of Burgundy,
What say you to the lady? Love is not love
228 When it is mingled with respects that stands
Aloof from the entire point. Will you have her?
230 She is herself a dower.

BURGUNDY   Royal Lear,
Give but that portion which yourself proposed,
And here I take Cordelia by the hand,
Duchess of Burgundy.

LEAR   Nothing; I have sworn.

BURGUNDY   *[To Cordelia]*
I am sorry, then, you have so lost a father
That you must lose a husband.

CORDELIA
Peace be with Burgundy.
237 Since that respects of fortune are his love,
I shall not be his wife.

FRANCE
Fairest Cordelia, that art most rich being poor,
240 Most choice forsaken, and most loved despised,
Thee and thy virtues here I seize upon.
Be it lawful I take up what's cast away.
Gods, gods! 'Tis strange that from their cold'st neglect

---

220 *still-soliciting* always begging   228–29 *respects . . . point* considerations
irrelevant to love   237 *respects . . . fortune* considerations of wealth

My love should kindle to inflamed respect.   244
Thy dowerless daughter, king, thrown to thy chance,
Is queen of us, of ours, and our fair France.
Not all the dukes in wat'rish Burgundy   247
Shall buy this unprized precious maid of me.   248
Bid them farewell, Cordelia, though unkind;
Thou losest here, a better where to find.   250

LEAR
Thou hast her, France. Let her be thine, for we
Have no such daughter, nor shall ever see
That face of hers again. Therefore be gone,
Without our grace, our love, our benison.   254
Come, noble Burgundy.
                Exeunt Lear and Burgundy [, Albany, Cornwall,
                        Gloucester, Edmund, and followers].

FRANCE   *[To Cordelia]*
Bid farewell to your sisters.

CORDELIA
The jewels of our father, with washed eyes   257
Cordelia leaves you. I know you what you are,
And, like a sister, am most loath to call
Your faults as they are named. Use well our father.   260
To your professèd bosoms I commit him;   261
But yet, alas, stood I within his grace,
I would prefer him to a better place.   263
So, farewell to you both.

GONERIL
Prescribe not us our duties.

REGAN   Let your study
Be to content your lord, who hath received you

---

244 *inflamed respect* ardent admiration   247 *wat'rish* (1) well-irrigated, (2)
weak, wishy-washy   248 *unprized* unappreciated   250 *where* elsewhere
254 *benison* blessing   257 *washed* tearful   260 *as . . . named* by their real
names   261 *professèd bosoms* proclaimed love   263 *prefer* promote

267   At fortune's alms. You have obedience scanted,
268   And well are worth the worth that you have wanted.
CORDELIA
        Time shall unfold what pleated cunning hides;
270   Who covers faults, at last shame them derides.
        Well may you prosper.
FRANCE   Come, fair Cordelia.
                        Exeunt France and Cordelia.
GONERIL   Sister, it is not a little I have to say of what
        most nearly appertains to us both. I think our father
        will hence tonight.
REGAN   That's most certain, and with you; next month
        with us.
GONERIL   You see how full of changes his age is. The ob-
        servation we have made of it hath not been little. He al-
        ways loved our sister most, and with what poor
280   judgment he hath now cast her off appears too gross.
REGAN   'Tis the infirmity of his age; yet he hath ever but
        slenderly known himself.
283   GONERIL   The best and soundest of his time hath been
284   but rash; then must we look to receive from his age not
285   alone the imperfection of long-engrafted condition,
286   but therewithal unruly waywardness that infirm and
        choleric years bring with them.
288   REGAN   Such unconstant starts are we like to have from
        him as this of Kent's banishment.
290   GONERIL   There is further compliment of leave-taking
291   between France and him. Pray, let's hit together. If our
        father carry authority with such dispositions as he
293   bears, this last surrender of his will but offend us.

---

267 *At . . . alms* as charity from fortune 268 *well . . . wanted* are properly
deprived of what you yourself have lacked 270 *Who . . . derides* i.e., time finally exposes hidden faults to shame 280 *gross* obvious 283 *The . . . been*
even at his best he was 284 *then* therefore 285 *long-engrafted* deep-seated
286 *therewithal* along with that 288 *unconstant starts* fits of impulsiveness
290 *compliment* formality 291 *hit* consult 293 *last surrender* recent abdication

REGAN   We shall further think on't.
GONERIL   We must do something, and i' th' heat.   295
                                                      Exeunt.

                              *

∾ **I.2** *Enter Bastard [Edmund] solus.*

EDMUND
  Thou, Nature, art my goddess. To thy law
  My services are bound. Wherefore should I
  Stand in the plague of custom and permit   3
  The curiosity of nations to deprive me   4
  For that I am some twelve or fourteen moonshines   5
  Lag of a brother? Why bastard? Wherefore base,   6
  When my dimensions are as well compact,   7
  My mind as generous, and my shape as true   8
  As honest madam's issue?   9
  Why brand they us with base, base bastardy,   *10*
  Who in the lusty stealth of nature take   11
  More composition and fierce quality   12
  Than doth within a stale, dull-eyed bed
  Go to the creating of a whole tribe of fops   14
  Got 'tween asleep and wake? Well then,   15
  Legitimate Edgar, I must have your land.   16
  Our father's love is to the bastard Edmund
  As to the legitimate. Well, my legitimate, if
  This letter speed and my invention thrive,   19

---

295 *i' th' heat* immediately ("while the iron is hot")
     I.2 Gloucester's house   **s.d.** *solus* alone   **3** *Stand . . . custom* submit to
the affliction of convention (whereby the eldest son inherits everything, and
illegitimate sons have no claim on the estate)   **4** *curiosity* (legal) technicalities   **5** *For that* because; *moonshines* months   **6** *Lag of* younger than   **7**
compact composed   **8** *My . . . generous* I am as well supplied with intelligence · **9** *honest* chaste (i.e., married)   **11** *the . . . nature* natural lust practiced in secret   **12** *composition* physical excellence; *fierce* vigorous   **14** *fops*
fools, sissies   **15** *Got* begotten   **16** *land* i.e., inheritance   **19** *speed* succeed;
invention scheme

20   Edmund the base shall to th' legitimate.
      I grow, I prosper. Now gods, stand up for bastards!
      Enter Gloucester. [Edmund reads a letter.]
      GLOUCESTER
22   Kent banished thus, and France in choler parted,
23   And the king gone tonight, subscribed his power,
24   Confined to exhibition – all this done
25   Upon the gad? – Edmund, how now? What news?
      EDMUND   So please your lordship, none.
      GLOUCESTER   Why so earnestly seek you to put up that
      letter?
      EDMUND   I know no news, my lord.
30   GLOUCESTER   What paper were you reading?
      EDMUND   Nothing, my lord.
32   GLOUCESTER   No? What needs then that terrible dis-
      patch of it into your pocket? The quality of nothing
      hath not such need to hide itself. Let's see. Come, if it
      be nothing I shall not need spectacles.
      EDMUND   I beseech you, sir, pardon me. It is a letter
      from my brother that I have not all o'er-read; for so
      much as I have perused, I find it not fit for your liking.
      GLOUCESTER   Give me the letter, sir.
40   EDMUND   I shall offend either to detain or give it. The
41   contents, as in part I understand them, are to blame.
      GLOUCESTER   Let's see, let's see.
      EDMUND   I hope for my brother's justification he wrote
44   this but as an essay or taste of my virtue.
      [He gives Gloucester] a letter.
      GLOUCESTER   *Reads.* "This policy of age makes the world
46   bitter to the best of our times, keeps our fortunes from
      us till our oldness cannot relish them. I begin to find an
48   idle and fond bondage in the oppression of aged

---

20 *to* rise to, equal   22 *in . . . parted* departed in anger   23 *tonight* i.e., last
night; *subscribed* given up   24 *Confined . . . exhibition* limited to an allowance   25 *Upon . . . gad* suddenly, impulsively   32 *terrible* frightened
41 *to blame* blameworthy   44 *essay or taste* (both words mean "test")   46
to . . . times in the prime of our lives   48 *idle . . . fond* worthless and foolish

tyranny, who sways not as it hath power but as it is suf-   49
fered. Come to me, that of this I may speak more. If   50
our father would sleep till I waked him, you should
enjoy half his revenue forever, and live the beloved of
your brother Edgar."
Hum, conspiracy! "Slept till I waked him, you should
enjoy half his revenue"– my son Edgar! Had he a hand
to write this, a heart and brain to breed it in? When
came this to you? Who brought it?

EDMUND   It was not brought me, my lord, there's the
cunning of it. I found it thrown in at the casement of   59
my closet.   60

GLOUCESTER   You know the character to be your   61
brother's?

EDMUND   If the matter were good, my lord, I durst swear   63
it were his; but in respect of that, I would fain think it   64
were not.

GLOUCESTER   It is his.

EDMUND   It is his hand, my lord, but I hope his heart is
not in the contents.

GLOUCESTER   Hath he never heretofore sounded you in   69
this business?   70

EDMUND   Never, my lord; but I have often heard him
maintain it to be fit that, sons at perfect age and fathers   72
declining, his father should be as ward to the son, and   73
the son manage the revenue.

GLOUCESTER   O villain, villain – his very opinion in the
letter. Abhorred villain, unnatural, detested, brutish villain – worse than brutish! Go, sir, seek him. I apprehend him, abominable villain! Where is he?

EDMUND   I do not well know, my lord. If it shall please
you to suspend your indignation against my brother till   80

49–50 *suffered* allowed to do so   59–60 *casement . . . closet* window of my
bedroom   61 *character* handwriting   63 *matter* substance   64 *in . . . that*
i.e., considering the content; *fain* prefer to   69 *sounded you* sounded you out
72 *sons . . . age* when sons are mature   73 *as . . . to* placed under the
guardianship of

you can derive from him better testimony of this in-
82 tent, you should run a certain course; where if you violently proceed against him, mistaking his purpose, it
would make a great gap in your own honor and shake
85 in pieces the heart of his obedience. I dare pawn down
86 my life for him he hath wrote this to feel my affection
87 to your honor, and to no further pretense of danger.
GLOUCESTER Think you so?
89 EDMUND If your honor judge it meet, I will place you
90 where you shall hear us confer of this, and by an auric-
ular assurance have your satisfaction, and that without
any further delay than this very evening.
GLOUCESTER He cannot be such a monster.
EDMUND Nor is not, sure.
GLOUCESTER To his father, that so tenderly and entirely
loves him. Heaven and earth! Edmund, seek him out,
97 wind me into him. I pray you, frame your business
98 after your own wisdom. I would unstate myself to be in
a due resolution.
100 EDMUND I shall seek him, sir, presently, convey the busi-
101 ness as I shall see means, and acquaint you withal.
102 GLOUCESTER These late eclipses in the sun and moon
103 portend no good to us. Though the wisdom of nature
104 can reason thus and thus, yet nature finds itself
scourged by the sequent effects. Love cools, friendship
106 falls off, brothers divide; in cities mutinies, in countries
discords, palaces treason, the bond cracked between
son and father. Find out this villain, Edmund. It shall

---

82 *run . . . course* be sure of your course of action; *where* whereas 85 *pawn down* stake 86 *feel* test 87 *pretense of danger* intent to do harm 89 *meet* appropriate 90–91 *an . . . assurance* the testimony of your own ears 97 *wind . . . him* worm your way into his confidence for me; *frame* arrange 98–99 *unstate . . . resolution* give up everything to resolve my doubts 100 *presently* immediately; *convey* conduct 101 *withal* with the result 102 *late* recent 103–4 *wisdom . . . thus* natural science can supply various explanations 104–5 *nature . . . effects* humanity ("nature") suffers the consequences 106 *mutinies* rebellions

lose thee nothing. Do it carefully. And the noble and
true-hearted Kent banished, his offense honesty –   110
strange, strange.   *[Exit.]*
EDMUND   This is the excellent foppery of the world, that   112
when we are sick in fortune – often the surfeit of our   113
own behavior – we make guilty of our disasters the sun,
the moon, and the stars, as if we were villains by necessity, fools by heavenly compulsion, knaves, thieves, and
treacherers by spherical predominance, drunkards,   117
liars, and adulterers by an enforced obedience of plane-   118
tary influence; and all that we are evil in by a divine
thrusting on. An admirable evasion of whoremaster   120
man, to lay his goatish disposition to the charge of   121
stars! My father compounded with my mother under   122
the Dragon's tail, and my nativity was under Ursa   123
Major, so that it follows I am rough and lecherous. Fut!
I should have been that I am had the maidenliest star of
the firmament twinkled on my bastardy. Edgar –
      Enter Edgar.
and out he comes, like the catastrophe of the old com-   127
edy; mine is villainous melancholy, with a sigh like   128
them of Bedlam. O these eclipses do portend these di-   129
visions –   130
EDGAR   How now, brother Edmund, what serious con-
templation are you in?
EDMUND   I am thinking, brother, of a prediction I read
this other day, what should follow these eclipses.
EDGAR   Do you busy yourself about that?

---

112 *foppery* foolishness   113 *surfeit* overindulgence   117 *treacherers* traitors;
spherical predominance astrological influence   118 *of* to   120 *thrusting on*
enforcement;   *admirable* astonishing   121 *goatish* lecherous   122 *compounded* had sex   123–24 *Dragon's tail, Ursa Major* the constellations of
Draco and the Great Bear   127–28 *catastrophe . . . comedy* conclusion in
early comedy (i.e., often arbitrary or unmotivated, but at the appointed
time)   128 *mine* my role; *villainous* severe   129 *Bedlam* Bedlam (Bethlehem) Hospital, the London madhouse   129–30 *divisions* (1) conflicts, (2)
musical phrases

136 EDMUND   I promise you the effects he writ of succeed
unhappily, as of unnaturalness between the child and
the parent, death, dearth, dissolutions of ancient ami-
ties, divisions in state, menaces and maledictions
140 against king and nobles, needless diffidences, banish-
141 ment of friends, dissipation of cohorts, nuptial
breaches, and I know not what.
143 EDGAR   How long have you been a sectary astronomical?
EDMUND   Come, come, when saw you my father last?
EDGAR   Why, the night gone by.
EDMUND   Spake you with him?
EDGAR   Two hours together.
EDMUND   Parted you in good terms? Found you no dis-
149 pleasure in him by word or countenance?
150 EDGAR   None at all.
EDMUND   Bethink yourself wherein you may have offended him, and at my entreaty forbear his presence till
153 some little time hath qualified the heat of his displeasure, which at this instant so rageth in him that with
155 the mischief of your person it would scarce allay.
EDGAR   Some villain hath done me wrong.
EDMUND   That's my fear, brother. I advise you to the
best. Go armed. I am no honest man if there be any
good meaning towards you. I have told you what I have
160 seen and heard but faintly, nothing like the image and
horror of it. Pray you, away.
EDGAR   Shall I hear from you anon?
EDMUND   I do serve you in this business.

Exit Edgar.

A credulous father, and a brother noble,
Whose nature is so far from doing harms

---

136 *succeed* conclude   **140** *diffidences* mistrust   **141** *dissipation of cohorts*
disbanding of armies   **143** *sectary astronomical* astrological expert   **149**
countenance look   **153** *qualified* moderated   **155** *the mischief of* injury to;
allay be allayed   **160–61** *image . . . it* as horrible as it seemed

That he suspects none, on whose foolish honesty
My practices ride easy. I see the business.   167
Let me, if not by birth, have lands by wit.   168
All with me's meet that I can fashion fit.   *Exit.*   169

*

∿ **I.3** *Enter Goneril and Steward [Oswald].*

GONERIL
Did my father strike my gentleman
For chiding of his fool?
OSWALD   Yes, madam.
GONERIL
By day and night he wrongs me. Every hour
He flashes into one gross crime or other   4
That sets us all at odds. I'll not endure it.
His knights grow riotous, and himself upbraids us
On every trifle. When he returns from hunting
I will not speak with him. Say I am sick.
If you come slack of former services   9
You shall do well; the fault of it I'll answer.   10
    [Horns within.]
OSWALD   He's coming, madam, I hear him.
GONERIL
Put on what weary negligence you please,
You and your fellow servants. I'd have it come in ques-   13
tion.
If he dislike it, let him to our sister,
Whose mind and mine I know in that are one,
Not to be overruled. Idle old man,
That still would manage those authorities

---

167 *practices* plots; *I . . . business* the plan is now clear   **168** *wit* intelligence
169 *with . . . meet* suits me; *fashion fit* shape to serve my purpose
    I.3 Albany's castle   **4** *crime* offense   **9** *come . . . services* serve him less
well than usual   **10** *answer* answer for   **13** *come . . . question* made an issue

That he hath given away! Now, by my life,
Old fools are babes again, and must be used
20   With checks as flatteries, when they are seen abused.
Remember what I tell you.
OSWALD   Very well, madam.
GONERIL
And let his knights have colder looks among you;
What grows of it, no matter. Advise your fellows so.
25   I would breed from hence occasions, and I shall
26   That I may speak. I'll write straight to my sister
27   To hold my very course. Go prepare for dinner.
                                                  [Exeunt separately.]

                              *

∾ **I.4** *Enter Kent [disguised].*

KENT
1   If but as well I other accents borrow
2   That can my speech defuse, my good intent
3   May carry through itself to that full issue
4   For which I razed my likeness. Now, banished Kent,
     If thou canst serve where thou dost stand condemned,
6   Thy master, whom thou lov'st, shall find thee full of
     labor.
         Enter Lear [and Knights from hunting].
7   LEAR   Let me not stay a jot for dinner. Go get it ready.
                                                  [Exit Knight.]
8   How now, what art thou?
     KENT   A man, sir.

---

20 *checks . . . flatteries* rebukes as well as compliments; *they . . . seen* the compliments are   25 *breed . . . occasions* use this to provoke scenes   26 *speak* speak my mind   27 *hold . . . course* pursue the same course I do
    I.4   1 *If . . . borrow* i.e., if I disguise my voice as effectively as I do my appearance   **2** *defuse* confuse, disguise   **3** *issue* outcome   **4** *razed . . . likeness* erased my appearance (including "razoring" his beard)   **6** *full . . . labor* i.e., hard at work   **7** *stay* wait   **8** *what* who

LEAR   What dost thou profess? What wouldst thou with   10
us?

KENT   I do profess to be no less than I seem, to serve him
truly that will put me in trust, to love him that is honest, to converse with him that is wise and says little, to   14
fear judgment, to fight when I cannot choose, and to   15
eat no fish.   16

LEAR   What art thou?

KENT   A very honest-hearted fellow, and as poor as the
king.

LEAR   If thou be as poor for a subject as he is for a king,   20
thou'rt poor enough. What wouldst thou?

KENT   Service.

LEAR   Who wouldst thou serve?

KENT   You.

LEAR   Dost thou know me, fellow?

KENT   No, sir, but you have that in your countenance
which I would fain call master.   27

LEAR   What's that?

KENT   Authority.

LEAR   What services canst do?   30

KENT   I can keep honest counsel, ride, run, mar a curi-   31
ous tale in telling it, and deliver a plain message
bluntly. That which ordinary men are fit for I am qualified in, and the best of me is diligence.

LEAR   How old art thou?

KENT   Not so young to love a woman for singing nor so
old to dote on her for anything. I have years on my
back forty-eight.

LEAR   Follow me. Thou shalt serve me. If I like thee no
worse after dinner, I will not part from thee yet. Din-   40

---

10 *dost . . . profess* is your trade   14 *converse* associate   15 *fear judgment*
show respect for authority; *choose* avoid it   16 *eat no fish* (A joke whose point
has obviously been lost: not to be Catholic, and thus forbidden to eat meat
on Fridays? To be a meat-eater only – i.e., manly?)   27 *fain* like to   31
keep . . . counsel respect confidences   31–32 *curious* complicated

41   ner, ho, dinner! Where's my knave, my fool? Go you
and call my fool hither.   *[Exit Knight.]*
    Enter Steward [Oswald].

43   You, sirrah, where's my daughter?
OSWALD   So please you.   *[Exit.]*

45   LEAR   What says the fellow there? Call the clotpoll back.
                  [Exeunt Kent and Knight.]
    Where's my fool, ho! I think the world's asleep.
    [Reenter Kent and Knight.]
    How now, where's that mongrel?
KENT   He says, my lord, your daughter is not well.
LEAR   Why came not the slave back to me when I called

50   him?

51   KNIGHT   Sir, he answered me in the roundest manner he
would not.

53   LEAR   A would not?
KNIGHT   My lord, I know not what the matter is, but to

55   my judgment your highness is not entertained with

56   that ceremonious affection as you were wont. There's a

57   great abatement appears as well in the general dependents, as in the duke himself also, and your daughter.
LEAR   Ha, sayst thou so?

60   KNIGHT   I beseech you pardon me, my lord, if I be mis-
taken, for my duty cannot be silent when I think your
highness wronged.

63   LEAR   Thou but rememb'rest me of mine own conception. I have perceived a most faint neglect of late,

65   which I have rather blamed as mine own jealous curiosity than as a very pretense and purport of unkindness. I
will look further into't. But where's this fool? I have not
seen him this two days.

---

41 *knave* boy (the term could be affectionate)   43 *sirrah* (term of address
used to a social inferior)   45 *clotpoll* blockhead   51 *roundest* rudest   53 *A*
he   55 *entertained* treated   56 *wont* accustomed to   57–58 *the . . . dependents* all the servants   63 *rememb'rest* remind   63–64 *conception* perception
65–66 *jealous curiosity* hypersensitiveness; *very pretense* real intention

KNIGHT   Since my young lady's going into France, sir,
the fool hath much pined away.   70
LEAR   No more of that, I have noted it. Go you and tell
my daughter I would speak with her.
                                          [Exit Knight.]
Go you, call hither my fool.
                                    [Exit another Knight.]
     [Enter Oswald.]
O, you sir, you sir, come you hither. Who am I, sir?
OSWALD   My lady's father.
LEAR   My lady's father? My lord's knave, you whoreson
dog, you slave, you cur!
OSWALD   I am none of this, my lord; I beseech you, par-
don me.
LEAR   Do you bandy looks with me, you rascal? *[Strikes*   80
him.]
OSWALD   I'll not be struck, my lord.
KENT   *[Tripping him]* Nor tripped neither, you base foot-   82
ball player.
LEAR   *[To Kent]* I thank thee, fellow; thou serv'st me, and
I'll love thee.
KENT   *[To Oswald]* Come, sir, I'll teach you differences.   86
Away, away. If you will measure your lubber's length   87
again, tarry; but away, if you have wisdom.
                                          [Exit Oswald.]
LEAR   Now, friendly knave, I thank thee. There's earnest   89
of thy service.   90
     [Lear gives Kent money.] Enter Fool.
FOOL   Let me hire him, too. *[To Kent]* Here's my cox-   91
comb.
LEAR   How now, my pretty knave, how dost thou?
FOOL   Sirrah, you were best take my coxcomb.
KENT   Why, fool?

82–83 *football player* (football was a lower-class street game)   86 *differences*
distinctions of rank   87 *measure . . . length* i.e., have me trip you up again;
lubber oaf   89–90 *earnest of* a down payment on   91–92 *coxcomb* fool's cap

FOOL   Why, for taking one's part that's out of favor. Nay,
97   an thou canst not smile as the wind sits, thou'lt catch
cold shortly. There, take my coxcomb. Why, this fellow
99   hath banished two on's daughters and done the third a
100   blessing against his will. If thou follow him, thou must
101   needs wear my coxcomb. How now, nuncle? Would I
had two coxcombs and two daughters.

LEAR   Why, my boy ?

104   FOOL   If I gave them my living I'd keep my coxcombs
myself. There's mine; beg another of thy daughters.

LEAR   Take heed, sirrah: the whip.

FOOL   Truth is a dog that must to kennel. He must be
108   whipped out when lady the brach may stand by the fire
and stink.

110   LEAR   A pestilent gall to me!

FOOL   Sirrah, I'll teach thee a speech.

LEAR   Do.

FOOL   Mark it, uncle:
Have more than thou showest,
Speak less than thou knowest,
116   Lend less than thou owest,
117   Ride more than thou goest,
118   Learn more than thou trowest,
119   Set less than thou throwest,
120   Leave thy drink and thy whore,
And keep in-a-door,
And thou shalt have more
123   Than two tens to a score.

---

97 *an* if   97–98 *an . . . shortly* if you can't please those in power, you'll soon
be out in the cold   99 *banished* (as Kent says, "banishment is here,"
(I.1.169); *on's* of his   101 *nuncle* (mine) uncle   104 *living* possessions
104–5 *I'd . . . myself* I'd be a double fool   108 *out* out of doors; *brach* bitch
108–9 *when . . . stink* i.e., as Goneril and Regan are favored and the truthful
Cordelia exiled   110 *gall* bitterness, sore   116 *owest* own   117 *goest* walk
118 *trowest* believe (i.e., don't believe everything you hear)   119 *Set . . .
throwest* bet less than you win (at dice)   123 *score* twenty (i.e., you'll do better than break even)

LEAR   This is nothing, fool.

FOOL   Then, like the breath of an unfeed lawyer, you   125
gave me nothing for't. Can you make no use of nothing, uncle?

LEAR   Why no, boy. Nothing can be made out of nothing.

FOOL   *[To Kent]* Prithee, tell him so much the rent of his   130
land comes to. He will not believe a fool.

LEAR   A bitter fool.

FOOL   Dost know the difference, my boy, between a bitter fool and a sweet fool?

LEAR   No, lad, teach me.

FOOL

> That lord that counseled thee
> To give away thy land,
> Come, place him here by me;
> Do thou for him stand.
> The sweet and bitter fool   *140*
> Will presently appear,   141
> The one in motley here,   142
> The other found out there.

LEAR   Dost thou call me fool, boy?

FOOL   All thy other titles thou hast given away; that
thou wast born with.

KENT   This is not altogether fool, my lord.

FOOL   No, faith, lords and great men will not let me. If   148
I had a monopoly out, they would have part on't, and
ladies too: they will not let me have all the fool to my-   *150*
self; they'll be snatching. Give me an egg, nuncle, and
I'll give thee two crowns.

LEAR   What two crowns shall they be?

---

125 *breath* speech; *unfeed* unpaid (lawyers proverbially will not plead without a fee)   130–31 *so . . . to* i.e., he no longer has any land, and therefore no
income from it   141 *Will . . . appear* i.e., it will be immediately apparent
which is which   142 *motley* the jester's parti-colored costume   148 *let me*
i.e., let me have all the foolishness, be "altogether fool"

FOOL Why, after I have cut the egg in the middle and
155 eat up the meat, the two crowns of the egg. When thou
clovest thy crown i' th' middle and gavest away both
157 parts, thou borest thy ass at th' back o'er the dirt. Thou
hadst little wit in thy bald crown when thou gavest thy
159 golden one away. If I speak like myself in this, let him
160 be whipped that first finds it so.
[Sings.]
161   Fools had ne'er less wit in a year,
162   For wise men are grown foppish,
163   They know not how their wits do wear,
164   Their manners are so apish.
165 LEAR When were you wont to be so full of songs, sirrah?
FOOL I have used it, nuncle, ever since thou madest thy
daughters thy mother; for when thou gavest them the
rod and putt'st down thine own breeches,
[Sings.]
       Then they for sudden joy did weep,
170   And I for sorrow sung,
171   That such a king should play bopeep
         And go the fools among.
Prithee, nuncle, keep a schoolmaster that can teach thy
174 fool to lie. I would fain learn to lie.
175 LEAR An you lie, we'll have you whipped.
FOOL I marvel what kin thou and thy daughters are.
They'll have me whipped for speaking true, thou wilt
have me whipped for lying, and sometime I am
whipped for holding my peace. I had rather be any
180 kind of thing than a fool; and yet I would not be thee,
nuncle. Thou hast pared thy wit o' both sides, and left
nothing in the middle.
Enter Goneril.

---

155 *two . . . egg* i.e., the empty shell   157 *at* on   159 *like myself* i.e., like a
fool   160 *that . . . so* i.e., for being a fool himself   161 *had . . . year* are now
out of fashion   162 *foppish* foolish   163 *their . . . wear* to use their heads
164 *apish* (1) stupid, (2) imitative   165 *wont* accustomed   171 *play bopeep*
i.e., act like a child   174 *fain* gladly   175 *An* if

Here comes one of the parings.

LEAR

How now, daughter, what makes that frontlet on? 184
Methinks you are too much o' late i' th' frown.

FOOL   Thou wast a pretty fellow when thou hadst no
need to care for her frown. Now thou art an O without 187
a figure. I am better than thou art now; I am a fool,
thou art nothing. *[To Goneril]* Yes, forsooth, I will hold
my tongue; so your face bids me, though you say noth- 190
ing.

Mum, mum.
He that keeps neither crust nor crumb,
Weary of all, shall want some.
That's a shelled peasecod. 195

GONERIL

Not only, sir, this your all-licensed fool, 196
But other of your insolent retinue
Do hourly carp and quarrel, breaking forth
In rank and not-to-be-endurèd riots. 199
Sir, I had thought by making this well known unto you 200
To have found a safe redress, but now grow fearful, 201
By what yourself too late have spoke and done, 202
That you protect this course, and put on 203
By your allowance; which if you should, the fault
Would not scape censure nor the redress sleep, 205
Which in the tender of a wholesome weal 206
Might in their working do you that offense
That else were shame, that then necessity 208
Must call discreet proceedings. 209

---

184 *what . . . on* why are you wearing such a face; *frontlet* forehead or a
headband worn on it   **187–88** *an . . . figure* a zero with no number in front
of it – i.e., nothing   **195** *shelled peasecod* empty pea pod   **196** *all-licensed* allowed to do anything   **199** *rank* gross   **201** *safe redress* sure remedy   **202**
too late lately   **203** *put on* encourage it   **205** *redress sleep* punishment lie dormant   **206** *tender . . . weal* government of a healthy commonwealth   **208**
necessity what the situation demands   **209** *Must . . . proceedings* might humiliate you, but, being necessary, would be merely prudent

210 FOOL   For you trow, nuncle,
211   The hedge-sparrow fed the cuckoo so long
212   That it had it head bit off by it young;
213   So out went the candle, and we were left darkling.
    LEAR   Are you our daughter?
    GONERIL
       Come, sir, I would you would make use of that good
         wisdom
216   Whereof I know you are fraught, and put away
217   These dispositions that of late transform you
       From what you rightly are.
    FOOL   May not an ass know when the cart draws the
220   horse? *[Sings.]* Whoop, Jug, I love thee.
    LEAR
       Doth any here know me? Why, this is not Lear.
       Doth Lear walk thus? Speak thus? Where are his eyes?
223   Either his notion weakens, or his discernings
224   Are lethargied. Sleeping or waking, ha?
       Sure 'tis not so.
       Who is it that can tell me who I am?
       Lear's shadow? I would learn that, for by the marks
       Of sovereignty, knowledge, and reason
       I should be false persuaded I had daughters.
230 FOOL   Which they will make an obedient father.
    LEAR
       Your name, fair gentlewoman?
    GONERIL   Come, sir,
232   This admiration is much of the savor
       Of other your new pranks. I do beseech you
       Understand my purposes aright.
       As you are old and reverend, should be wise.

211–12 *The . . . young* (the cuckoo lays its eggs in other birds' nests; the young cuckoos eventually destroy the sparrow that has been feeding them) 212 *it . . . it* its . . . its   213 *darkling* in darkness   216 *fraught* full   217 *dispositions* moods   220 *Jug* Joan (generic name for a whore)   223 *notion* mind; *discernings* perceptions   224 *Sleeping or waking* am I asleep or awake   232 *admiration* spectacle (something to be wondered at)

Here do you keep a hundred knights and squires,
Men so disordered, so debauched and bold   237
That this our court, infected with their manners,
Shows like a riotous inn, epicurism   239
And lust make more like a tavern or brothel   240
Than a great palace. The shame itself doth speak
For instant remedy. Be thou desired
By her that else will take the thing she begs
A little to disquantity your train,   244
And the remainder that shall still depend   245
To be such men as may besort your age,   246
That know themselves and you.

LEAR   Darkness and devils!
Saddle my horses, call my train together!   248
Degenerate bastard, I'll not trouble thee;
Yet have I left a daughter.   250

GONERIL
You strike my people, and your disordered rabble
Make servants of their betters.
    Enter Albany.

LEAR
Woe that too late repents – O, sir, are you come?
Is it your will that we – prepare my horses!
Ingratitude, thou marble-hearted fiend,
More hideous when thou showest thee in a child
Than the sea monster. *[To Goneril]* Detested kite, thou   257
    liest.
My train are men of choice and rarest parts,   258
That all particulars of duty know,
And in the most exact regard support   260

---

237 *bold* impudent 239 *Shows* looks; *epicurism* gluttony 244 *disquantity . . . train* reduce the size of your retinue 245 *depend* be your dependents
246 *besort* befit 248 *Saddle . . . together* (Most editors send some knights
off to do Lear's bidding, but it is more likely that everyone is immobilized
with astonishment: he has to order the horses saddled again at l. 254.) 257
Detested kite detestable bird of prey 258 *parts* qualities 260 *in . . . regard*
with the most scrupulous attention

261   The worships of their name. O most small fault,
       How ugly didst thou in Cordelia show,
263   That, like an engine, wrenched my frame of nature
       From the fixed place, drew from my heart all love
       And added to the gall. O Lear, Lear!
266   Beat at this gate that let thy folly in
       And thy dear judgment out. Go, go, my people!

ALBANY
       My lord, I am guiltless as I am ignorant –

LEAR
       It may be so, my lord. Hark, Nature; hear,
270   Dear goddess: suspend thy purpose if
       Thou didst intend to make this creature fruitful.
       Into her womb convey sterility;
       Dry up in her the organs of increase,
274   And from her derogate body never spring
275   A babe to honor her. If she must teem,
276   Create her child of spleen, that it may live
277   And be a thwart disnatured torment to her.
       Let it stamp wrinkles in her brow of youth,
279   With cadent tears fret channels in her cheeks,
280   Turn all her mother's pains and benefits
       To laughter and contempt, that she may feel –
       That she may feel
       How sharper than a serpent's tooth it is
284   To have a thankless child. Go, go, my people!
                      [Exeunt Lear, Kent, and Attendants.]

ALBANY
       Now gods that we adore, whereof comes this?

GONERIL
       Never afflict yourself to know the cause,

---

261 *worships* honor   263 *engine* machine   263–64 *my . . . place* the structure of my being from its foundations   266 *this gate* (presumably his head)
274 *derogate* debased   275 *teem* breed   276 *spleen* malice   277 *thwart disnatured* perverse unnatural   279 *cadent* falling; *fret* wear   280 *pains* care
284 **s.d.** The Fool apparently remains onstage.

But let his disposition have that scope   287
That dotage gives it.
[Reenter Lear.]

LEAR
What, fifty of my followers at a clap,
Within a fortnight?   *290*

ALBANY   What is the matter, sir?

LEAR
I'll tell thee. *[To Goneril]* Life and death! I am ashamed
That thou hast power to shake my manhood thus,
That these hot tears that break from me perforce,   293
Should make – the worst blasts and fogs upon thee!
Untented woundings of a father's curse   295
Pierce every sense about thee! Old fond eyes,   296
Beweep this cause again I'll pluck you out   297
And you cast with the waters that you make
To temper clay. Yea, is't come to this?   299
Yet have I left a daughter   *300*
Whom, I am sure, is kind and comfortable.   301
When she shall hear this of thee, with her nails
She'll flay thy wolvish visage. Thou shalt find
That I'll resume the shape which thou dost think
I have cast off forever; thou shalt, I warrant thee.
                              [Exit Lear.]

GONERIL
Do you mark that, my lord?

ALBANY
I cannot be so partial, Goneril,   307
To the great love I bear you –

GONERIL   Come, sir, no more.
[To Fool]
You, more knave than fool, after your master!

---

287 *disposition* mood   293 *perforce* i.e., against my will   295 *Untented woundings* wounds too deep to be probed   296 *fond* foolish   297 *Beweep* if you weep over   299 *temper* soften   301 *comfortable* comforting   307–8 *partial . . . To* biased . . . by

310 FOOL   Nuncle Lear, nuncle Lear, tarry, and take the fool
with.

            A fox, when one has caught her,
            And such a daughter,
314   Should sure to the slaughter,
315   If my cap would buy a halter.
            So the fool follows after.   *[Exit.]*

    GONERIL What, Oswald, ho!
    [Enter Oswald.]
    OSWALD Here, madam.
    GONERIL What, have you writ this letter to my sister?
320 OSWALD Yes, madam.
    GONERIL
    Take you some company, and away to horse.
    Inform her full of my particular fears,
    And thereto add such reasons of your own
324 As may compact it more. Get you gone,
    And hasten your return.
                         [Exit Oswald.]
                Now, my lord,
326 This milky gentleness and course of yours,
327 Though I dislike not, yet under pardon,
328 You're much more atasked for want of wisdom
    Than praised for harmful mildness.
    ALBANY
330 How far your eyes may pierce I cannot tell;
    Striving to better aught, we mar what's well.
332 GONERIL Nay, then –
    ALBANY   Well, well, the event.   *Exeunt.*

                       *

---

314 *sure* surely be sent 315 *halter* noose 324 *compact* confirm 326
milky . . . course mild and gentle way 327 *under pardon* if you'll pardon me
328 *atasked* taken to task 332 *the event* let's await the outcome

∾ **I.5** *Enter Lear [, Kent disguised, and Fool].*

LEAR   *[To Kent]* Go you before to Gloucester with these   1
letters. Acquaint my daughter no further with anything
you know than comes from her demand out of the let-   3
ter. If your diligence be not speedy, I shall be there before you.

KENT   I will not sleep, my lord, till I have delivered your
letter.   *Exit.*

FOOL   If a man's brains were in his heels, were't not in
danger of kibes?   9

LEAR   Ay, boy.   10

FOOL   Then I prithee be merry; thy wit shall ne'er go   11
slipshod.

LEAR   Ha, ha, ha!

FOOL   Shalt see thy other daughter will use thee kindly,   14
for though she's as like this as a crab is like an apple, yet   15
I con what I can tell.   16

LEAR   Why, what canst thou tell, my boy?

FOOL   She'll taste as like this as a crab doth to a crab.
Thou canst not tell why one's nose stand in the middle
of his face ?   20

LEAR   No.

FOOL   Why, to keep his eyes on either side's nose, that
what a man cannot smell out, a may spy into.   23

LEAR   I did her wrong.   24

FOOL   Canst tell how an oyster makes his shell?

LEAR   No.

I.5   1 *before* ahead of me; *Gloucester* (apparently not the earl but the town,
which would therefore be the location of Regan and Cornwall's castle)   **1–2**
these letters this letter (i.e., the letters that constitute one message; cf. "these
words")   **3** *demand . . . of* questions prompted by   **9** *kibes* chilblains
11–12 *shall . . . slipshod* will not have to wear slippers because of chilblains
(the point is that feet with brains would not make this journey)   **14** *Shalt*
thou shalt   **15** *crab* crab apple (proverbially sour)   **16** *con* know   **23** *a may*
he may   **24** *her* Cordelia

FOOL   Nor I neither; but I can tell why a snail has a
house.

LEAR   Why?

30 FOOL   Why, to put his head in, not to give it away to his
31   daughter and leave his horns without a case.

32 LEAR   I will forget my nature. So kind a father! Be my
horses ready?

FOOL   Thy asses are gone about them. The reason why
35   the seven stars are no more than seven is a pretty reason.

LEAR   Because they are not eight.

FOOL   Yes. Thou wouldst make a good fool.

39 LEAR   To take't again perforce! Monster ingratitude!

40 FOOL   If thou wert my fool, nuncle, I'd have thee beaten
for being old before thy time.

LEAR   How's that?

FOOL   Thou shouldst not have been old before thou
hadst been wise.

LEAR
O, let me not be mad, sweet heaven!
I would not be mad.
47   Keep me in temper; I would not be mad.
[Enter a Servant.]
Are the horses ready?

SERVANT   Ready, my lord.

50 LEAR   *[To Fool]* Come, boy.
                    [Exeunt Lear and Servant.]

FOOL
51   She that is maid now, and laughs at my departure,

---

31 *horns* (with a quibble on the cuckold's horns, implying that Goneril and
Regan are illegitimate)   32 *nature* paternal instincts   35 *the seven stars* the
constellation the Pleiades   39 *To . . . perforce* to take it back forcibly (Lear
either rages at Goneril's revocation of his privileges or contemplates reasserting his power)   47 *in temper* temperate, sane   51–52 *She . . . shorter* i.e., the
maid who laughed at my leaving would be a fool, and would not remain a
virgin unless men were castrated

Shall not be a maid long, except things be cut shorter.
Exit.

*

∾ **II.1** *Enter Bastard [Edmund] and Curan, meeting.*

EDMUND   Save thee, Curan.   1
CURAN   And you, sir. I have been with your father, and
    given him notice that the Duke of Cornwall and his
    duchess will be here with him tonight.
EDMUND   How comes that?
CURAN   Nay, I know not. You have heard of the news
    abroad? I mean, the whispered ones, for there are yet
    but ear-bussing arguments.   8
EDMUND   Not I. Pray you, what are they?
CURAN   Have you heard of no likely wars towards 'twixt   10
    the two Dukes of Cornwall and Albany?
EDMUND   Not a word.
CURAN   You may then in time. Fare you well, sir. *[Exit.]*
EDMUND
    The duke be here tonight! The better best.   14
    This weaves itself perforce into my business.   15
    My father hath set guard to take my brother,
    And I have one thing of a queasy question   17
    Which must ask briefness and fortune help.   18
    Brother, a word! Descend, brother, I say.   19
        Enter Edgar.
    My father watches. O, fly this place!   20
    Intelligence is given where you are hid.   21
    You have now the good advantage of the night.

II.1 Gloucester's house   **1** *Save thee* God save thee (a casual greeting like
"good day")   **8** *ear-bussing arguments* ear-kissing (i.e., whispered) matters
10 *towards* impending   **14** *better best* very best   **15** *perforce* necessarily   **17**
queasy question delicate problem   **18** *must . . . help* requires the aid of speed
and luck   **19** *Descend* (possibly Edgar has appeared on the upper-stage
gallery)   **21** *Intelligence* information

Have you not spoken 'gainst the Duke of Cornwall
  aught?
He's coming hither now, in the night, i' th' haste,
And Regan with him. Have you nothing said
26 Upon his party against the Duke of Albany?
27 Advise your –
EDGAR   I am sure on't, not a word.
EDMUND
I hear my father coming. Pardon me
In craving I must draw my sword upon you.
30 Seem to defend yourself. Now, quit you well.
    [They fight.]
Yield, come before my father! Light here, here!
(Fly, brother, fly!) Torches, torches! (So, farewell.)
                                    [Exit Edgar.]
33 Some blood drawn on me would beget opinion
Of my more fierce endeavor.
    [He cuts his arm.]
                     I have seen drunkards
Do more than this in sport. Father, father!
Stop, stop! No help?
    Enter Gloucester [and Servants].
GLOUCESTER   Now Edmund, where is the villain?
EDMUND
Here stood he in the dark, his sharp sword out,
Warbling of wicked charms, conjuring the moon
39 To stand's auspicious mistress.
GLOUCESTER   But where is he?
EDMUND
40 Look, sir, I bleed.
GLOUCESTER   Where is the villain, Edmund?

---

26 *Upon . . . against* relating to his quarrel with 27 *on't* of it 30 *quit you*
acquit yourself 33–34 *beget . . . endeavor* give the impression that I fought
fiercely 39 *stand's* act as his

EDMUND
   Fled this way, sir, when by no means he could –
GLOUCESTER
   Pursue him, go after.

                                    [Exeunt Servants.]
                          By no means what?
EDMUND
   Persuade me to the murder of your lordship,
   But that I told him the revengive gods   44
   'Gainst parricides did all their thunders bend,   45
   Spoke with how manifold and strong a bond
   The child was bound to the father. Sir, in fine,   47
   Seeing how loathly opposite I stood   48
   To his unnatural purpose, with fell motion   49
   With his preparèd sword he charges home   50
   My unprovided body, lanched mine arm;   51
   But when he saw my best alarumed spirits   52
   Bold in the quarrel's rights roused to the encounter,   53
   Or whether ghasted by the noise I made,   54
   But suddenly he fled.
GLOUCESTER   Let him fly far.
   Not in this land shall he remain uncaught;
   And found, dispatch! The noble duke my master,   57
   My worthy arch and patron, comes tonight.   58
   By his authority I will proclaim it
   That he which finds him shall deserve our thanks,   60
   Bringing the murderous caitiff to the stake;   61
   He that conceals him, death.
EDMUND
   When I dissuaded him from his intent,

---

44 *But that* however   45 *thunders bend* thunderbolts aim   47 *in fine* finally
48 *loathly opposite* loathingly opposed   49 *fell motion* deadly action   50
charges home thrusts directly at   51 *unprovided* unprotected; *lanched* lanced
52 *best alarumed* fully aroused   53 *quarrel's rights* justice of the cause   54
ghasted frightened   57 *found, dispatch!* once found, death!   58 *arch . . . patron* chief patron   61 *caitiff* villain, wretch

64   And found him pight to do it, with curst speech
65   I threatened to discover him. He replied,
66   "Thou unpossessing bastard, dost thou think
67   If I would stand against thee, could the reposure
     Of any trust, virtue, or worth in thee
69   Make thy words faithed? No, what I should deny –
70   As this I would, ay, though thou didst produce
71   My very character – I'd turn it all
72   To thy suggestion, plot, and damned pretense;
73   And thou must make a dullard of the world
     If they not thought the profits of my death
75   Were very pregnant and potential spurs
76   To make thee seek it."

GLOUCESTER   Strong and fastened villain!
77   Would he deny his letter? I never got him.
        [Tucket within.]
     Hark, the duke's trumpets. I know not why he comes.
79   All ports I'll bar; the villain shall not scape;
80   The duke must grant me that. Besides, his picture
     I will send far and near that all the kingdom
     May have note of him; and of my land,
     Loyal and natural boy, I'll work the means
84   To make thee capable.
        *Enter the Duke of Cornwall [, Regan, and
        Attendants].*

CORNWALL
     How now, my noble friend? Since I came hither,
86   Which I can call but now, I have heard strange news.

---

64 *pight* determined; *curst* angry   65 *discover* expose   66 *unpossessing* un-
propertied, landless   67 *reposure* placing   69 *faithed* believed; *what . . .
should* whatever I would   71 *character* handwriting (i.e., evidence in my own
hand); *turn* ascribe   72 *pretense* evil schemes   73 *make . . . world* consider
everyone stupid   75 *pregnant . . . spurs* meaningful and powerful motives
76 *fastened* hardened   77 *got* fathered   77 **s.d.** *Tucket* trumpet signal   79
ports (1) seaports, (2) town gates   84 *capable* legally able to inherit   86 *call
but* say was only

REGAN
    If it be true, all vengeance comes too short
    Which can pursue the offender. How dost, my lord?
GLOUCESTER
    Madam, my old heart is cracked, is cracked.
REGAN
    What, did my father's godson seek your life?   *90*
    He whom my father named, your Edgar?
GLOUCESTER
    Ay, lady, lady, shame would have it hid.
REGAN
    Was he not companion with the riotous knights
    That tends upon my father?
GLOUCESTER
    I know not, madam. 'Tis too bad, too bad.
EDMUND   Yes, madam, he was.
REGAN
    No marvel then though he were ill affected.   *97*
    'Tis they have put him on the old man's death,   *98*
    To have the spoil and waste of his revenues.   *99*
    I have this present evening from my sister   *100*
    Been well informed of them, and with such cautions
    That if they come to sojourn at my house
    I'll not be there.
CORNWALL   Nor I, assure thee, Regan.
    Edmund, I heard that you have shown your father
    A childlike office.
EDMUND   'Twas my duty, sir.
GLOUCESTER
    He did betray his practice, and received   *107*
    This hurt you see striving to apprehend him.
CORNWALL
    Is he pursued?

---

97 *though* that; *ill affected* disposed to evil   98 *put* set   99 *waste* plunder
107 *betray . . . practice* expose Edgar's plot

110 GLOUCESTER Ay, my good lord.

CORNWALL
    If he be taken, he shall never more
112 Be feared of doing harm. Make your own purpose
    How in my strength you please. For you, Edmund,
    Whose virtue and obedience doth this instant
    So much commend itself, you shall be ours.
    Natures of such deep trust we shall much need.
    You we first seize on.

EDMUND   I shall serve you truly,
118 However else.

GLOUCESTER
    For him I thank your grace.

CORNWALL
120 You know not why we came to visit you?

REGAN
121 Thus out-of-season, threat'ning dark-eyed night?
122 Occasions, noble Gloucester, of some poise,
    Wherein we must have use of your advice.
    Our father he hath writ, so hath our sister,
125 Of differences which I least thought it fit
126 To answer from our home. The several messengers
127 From hence attend dispatch. Our good old friend,
    Lay comforts to your bosom, and bestow
129 Your needful counsel to our business
130 Which craves the instant use.

GLOUCESTER
                            I serve you, madam;
    Your graces are right welcome.   *Exeunt.*

112–13 *Make . . . please* carry out your intentions making what use you wish
of my powers   118 *However else* if nothing else   121 *out-of-season* untimely (i.e., traveling at night); *threat'ning . . . night* with the dark night
threatening us   122 *poise* weight   125 *differences* quarrels   125–26
least . . . home i.e., thought it best to respond by being away from home
126 *several* various   127 *attend* await   129 *needful* needed   130 *the . . . use*
immediate action

*

ᖫ **II.2** *Enter Kent [disguised] and Steward [Oswald].*

OSWALD   Good even to thee, friend. Art of the house?   1
KENT   Ay.   2
OSWALD   Where may we set our horses?
KENT   I' th' mire.
OSWALD   Prithee, if thou love me, tell me.   5
KENT   I love thee not.
OSWALD   Why then, I care not for thee.
KENT   If I had thee in Lipsbury Pinfold I would make   8
thee care for me.
OSWALD   Why dost thou use me thus? I know thee not.   10
KENT   Fellow, I know thee.
OSWALD   What dost thou know me for?
KENT   A knave, a rascal, an eater of broken meats, a base,   13
proud, shallow, beggarly, three-suited, hundred-pound,   14
filthy worsted-stocking knave; a lily-livered, action-   15
taking knave; a whoreson, glass-gazing, superfinical   16
rogue; one-trunk-inheriting slave; one that wouldst be   17
a bawd in way of good service, and art nothing but the   18
composition of a knave, beggar, coward, pander, and   19
the son and heir of a mongrel bitch, whom I will beat   20

II.2   1 *even* evening; *Art of* are you a servant in   2 *Ay* (since the house is Gloucester's, Kent is lying, presumably as a way of picking a fight with Oswald)   5 *if . . . me* i.e., be kind enough to   8 *Lipsbury Pinfold* in the pen of my lips (i.e., between my teeth – treated jocularly as a place-name)   10 *use* treat   13 *broken meats* leftover food, fit for menials   14 *three-suited* (male household servants were furnished with three suits per year: Kent attacks Oswald's pretensions to gentility); *hundred-pound* (the minimum annual income for a gentleman)   15 *worsted-stocking* coarse wool stocking (a gentleman would wear silk); *lily-livered* cowardly   15–16 *action-taking* litigious (resorting to legal action instead of fighting)   16 *glass-gazing, . . . superfinical* vain, toadying, fussy   17 *one-trunk-inheriting* owning no more than will fit in a single trunk   18 *a bawd . . . service* a pimp if asked   19 *composition* composite

into clamorous whining if thou deny the least syllable
22   of the addition.

OSWALD   What a monstrous fellow art thou, thus to rail
on one that's neither known of thee nor knows thee!

25   KENT   What a brazen-faced varlet art thou, to deny thou
knowest me! Is it two days ago since I beat thee and
tripped up thy heels before the king? Draw, you rogue,
for though it be night, the moon shines. *[Kent draws his*
29   *sword.]* I'll make a sop of the moonshine o' you. Draw,
30   you whoreson, cullionly barbermonger, draw!

OSWALD   Away, I have nothing to do with thee.

KENT   Draw, you rascal. You bring letters against the
33   king, and take Vanity the puppet's part against the roy-
34   alty of her father. Draw, you rogue, or I'll so carbonado
35   your shanks – draw, you rascal, come your ways!

OSWALD   Help, ho, murder, help!
[Kent attacks Oswald, who tries to escape.]

37   KENT   Strike, you slave! Stand, rogue! Stand, you neat
slave, strike!

OSWALD   Help, ho, murder, help!
Enter Edmund with his rapier drawn, Gloucester,
[Servants, then] the duke [Cornwall] and duchess
[Regan].

40   EDMUND   How now, what's the matter?

41   KENT   With you, goodman boy. An you please come, I'll
42   flesh you. Come on, young master.

GLOUCESTER   Weapons? Arms? What's the matter here?

---

22 *addition* title (i.e., the names I have just called you)   **25** *varlet* rogue   **29**
make . . . moonshine fill you with holes so your body will sop up moonshine
30 *cullionly* despicable (cullions are testicles; the insult is analogous to calling
someone a prick); *barbermonger* (a particularly inventive insult: on the model
of whoremonger, a pimp for barbers, one who supplies them with clients,
hence who caters to the needs of effeminate men)   **33** *take . . . part* support
the vain, overdressed Goneril   **34** *carbonado* slash   **35** *come . . . ways* come
on, get to it   **37** *neat* prissy   **41** *goodman boy* (both are deliberate insults to
Edmund as a gentleman); *goodman* yeoman or farmer   **42** *flesh you* give you
your first taste of blood

CORNWALL   Keep peace, upon your lives. He dies that
strikes again. What's the matter?

REGAN   The messengers from our sister and the king.

CORNWALL   What's your difference? Speak.   47

OSWALD   I am scarce in breath, my lord.

KENT   No marvel, you have so bestirred your valor, you
cowardly rascal. Nature disclaims in thee; a tailor made   50
thee.

CORNWALL   Thou art a strange fellow – a tailor make a
man?

KENT   Ay, a tailor, sir. A stonecutter or a painter could
not have made him so ill though he had been but two   55
hours at the trade.

GLOUCESTER   Speak yet; how grew your quarrel?

OSWALD   This ancient ruffian, sir, whose life I have
spared at suit of his gray beard –   59

KENT   Thou whoreson zed, thou unnecessary letter! My   60
lord, if you'll give me leave, I will tread this unbolted   61
villain into mortar and daub the walls of a jakes with   62
him. *[To Oswald]* Spare my gray beard, you wagtail?   63

CORNWALL   Peace, sir! You beastly knave, you have no
reverence.

KENT   Yes, sir, but anger has a privilege.

CORNWALL   Why art thou angry?

KENT
That such a slave as this should wear a sword,
That wears no honesty. Such smiling rogues as these,
Like rats, oft bite those cords in twain   70
Which are too entrenched to unloose; smooth every   71
passion

---

47 *difference* quarrel   50 *disclaims in* disowns   55 *ill* badly   59 *at suit* at the
plea   60 *zed* the letter *z* ("unnecessary" because its sound is also represented
by *s*, and because it is not used in Latin)   61 *unbolted* unsifted (as flour or
plaster)   62 *jakes* toilet   63 *wagtail* (a bird that constantly wags its tail;
hence a nervous or effeminate person)   70 *cords* bonds   71 *entrenched* intertwined; *smooth* flatter

72   That in the natures of their lords rebel,
      Bring oil to fire, snow to their colder moods,
74   Renege, affirm, and turn their halcyon beaks
75   With every gale and vary of their masters,
      Knowing naught, like dogs, but following.
      [To Oswald]
77   A plague upon your epileptic visage!
78   Smile you my speeches as I were a fool?
79   Goose, an I had you upon Sarum Plain
80   I'd send you cackling home to Camelot.
      CORNWALL   What, art thou mad, old fellow?
      GLOUCESTER   How fell you out? Say that.
      KENT
83   No contraries hold more antipathy
      Than I and such a knave.
      CORNWALL
      Why dost thou call him knave? What's his offense?
      KENT
86   His countenance likes me not.
      CORNWALL
      No more perchance does mine, or his, or hers.
      KENT
      Sir, 'tis my occupation to be plain:
      I have seen better faces in my time
90   Than stands on any shoulder that I see
      Before me at this instant.
      CORNWALL   This is a fellow
92   Who, having been praised for bluntness, doth affect

---

72 *rebel* i.e., against reason   74 *Renege* deny; *halcyon* kingfisher (its beak was said to be usable as a weather vane)   75 *gale . . . vary* changing wind   77 *epileptic* grinning   78 *Smile you* do you smile at; *as* as if;   79 *an* if; *Sarum Plain* Salisbury Plain, near Winchester (Oswald is a goose because he is laughing, but it is not clear why Shakespeare associates geese with Salisbury Plain)   80 *Camelot* (legendary capital of King Arthur, thought to have been on the site of Winchester)   83 *contraries* opposites   86 *His . . . not* I don't like his face   92 *affect* adopt

A saucy roughness, and constrains the garb   93
Quite from his nature. He cannot flatter, he;   94
He must be plain, he must speak truth.
An they will take't, so; if not, he's plain.   96
These kind of knaves I know, which in this plainness
Harbor more craft and more corrupter ends
Than twenty silly-ducking observants   99
That stretch their duties nicely.   100

KENT
Sir, in good sooth, or in sincere verity,
Under the allowance of your grand aspect,
Whose influence, like the wreath of radiant fire
In flickering Phoebus' front –   104

CORNWALL   What mean'st thou by this?

KENT   To go out of my dialect, which you discommend   105
so much. I know, sir, I am no flatterer. He that beguiled   106
you in a plain accent was a plain knave, which for my
part I will not be, though I should win your displeasure
to entreat me to't.   109

CORNWALL   *[To Oswald]*
What's the offense you gave him?   *110*

OSWALD
I never gave him any.
It pleased the king his master very late   112
To strike at me upon his misconstruction,   113
When he, conjunct, and flattering his displeasure,   114
Tripped me behind; being down, insulted, railed,
And put upon him such a deal of man   116

93–94 *constrains . . . nature* forces plain speaking away from its proper function   93 *garb* style of speech   94 *his* its   96 *so* well and good; *he's plain* his
excuse is his bluntness   99 *silly . . . observants* bowing attendants   100
nicely excessively   104 *Phoebus' front* the sun god's forehead   105 *go . . . dialect* depart from my usual way of speaking   106–7 *He . . . you* whoever deceived you   109 *to . . . to't* i.e., even if you begged me to be a knave   112
very late recently   113 *misconstruction* misunderstanding me   114 *conjunct*
in league with (the king)   116 *deal . . . man* macho act

117   That worthied him, got praises of the king
118   For him attempting who was self-subdued,
119   And in the fleshment of this dread exploit,
120   Drew on me here again.

KENT
121   None of these rogues and cowards
    But Ajax is their fool.

CORNWALL   Bring forth the stocks, ho!
    You stubborn, ancient knave, you reverend braggart,
    We'll teach you.

KENT   I am too old to learn.
    Call not your stocks for me; I serve the king,
    On whose employments I was sent to you.
    You should do small respect, show too bold malice
    Against the grace and person of my master,
    Stocking his messenger.

CORNWALL   Fetch forth the stocks!
130   As I have life and honor, there shall he sit till noon.

REGAN
    Till noon? Till night, my lord, and all night too.

KENT
    Why, madam, if I were your father's dog
    You could not use me so.

REGAN
134   Sir, being his knave, I will.
    [Stocks brought out.]

CORNWALL
    This is a fellow of the selfsame nature
136   Our sister speaks of. Come, bring away the stocks.

GLOUCESTER
    Let me beseech your grace not to do so.
    His fault is much, and the good king his master

---

117 *worthied him* made him a hero   118 *For . . . self-subdued* for attacking a man who refused to fight   119 *fleshment* excitement   121–22 *None . . . fool* i.e., Oswald is making a fool out of Cornwall, whom Kent identifies with the dull-witted and boastful Greek hero Ajax   134 *being* as you are   136 *away* forward

Will check him for't. Your purposed low correction
Is such as basest and contemned'st wretches   *140*
For pilf'rings and most common trespasses
Are punished with. The king must take it ill
That he's so slightly valued in his messenger,
Should have him thus restrained.   144
CORNWALL   I'll answer that.
REGAN
My sister may receive it much more worse
To have her gentlemen abused, assaulted,
For following her affairs. Put in his legs.
  [Kent is put in the stocks.]
  [To Gloucester]
Come, my good lord, away!
                  [Exeunt all but Kent and Gloucester.]
GLOUCESTER
I am sorry for thee, friend. 'Tis the duke's pleasure,
Whose disposition, all the world well knows,   *150*
Will not be rubbed nor stopped. I'll entreat for thee.   151
KENT
Pray you, do not, sir. I have watched and traveled hard. 152
Some time I shall sleep out; the rest I'll whistle.
A good man's fortune may grow out at heels.   154
Give you good morrow.
GLOUCESTER
The duke's to blame in this; 'twill be ill took.   *[Exit.]*
KENT
Good king, that must approve the common saw: 157
Thou out of heaven's benediction comest   158
To the warm sun.
Approach, thou beacon to this under globe,   160

---

144 *answer* answer for   **151** *rubbed* deflected (term from the game of bowls)
152 *watched* stayed awake   **154** *grow . . . heels* wear thin   **157** *approve . . .*
saw prove the truth of the old saying   **158–59** *Thou . . . sun* you go from
God's blessing into the hot sun (i.e., you go from good to bad)   **160** *beacon*
(presumably the moon, since it is night)

161 That by thy comfortable beams I may
162 Peruse this letter. Nothing almost sees miracles
     But misery. I know 'tis from Cordelia,
     Who hath most fortunately been informed
165 Of my obscurèd course. "– And shall find time
166 From this enormous state, seeking to give
167 Losses their remedies." All weary and overwatched,
168 Take vantage, heavy eyes, not to behold
     This shameful lodging. Fortune, good night;
170 Smile; once more turn thy wheel.   *Sleeps.*

*

❧ **II.3** *Enter Edgar.*

EDGAR
1   I hear myself proclaimed,
2   And by the happy hollow of a tree
     Escaped the hunt. No port is free, no place
     That guard and most unusual vigilance
5   Does not attend my taking. While I may scape
6   I will preserve myself, and am bethought
     To take the basest and most poorest shape
8   That ever penury in contempt of man
     Brought near to beast. My face I'll grime with filth,
10   Blanket my loins, elf all my hair with knots,

---

161 *comfortable* comforting   **162–63** *Nothing . . . misery* miracles are rarely seen by any but the miserable   **165** *obscurèd* disguised   **165–67** *And . . . remedies* (a famously incoherent crux: is Kent reading a bit of Cordelia's letter?)   **166** *enormous state* terrible situation   **167** *overwatched* too long without sleep   **168** *Take vantage* take advantage (by falling asleep)   **170** *turn . . . wheel* change my luck (The goddess Fortuna is depicted with a large vertical wheel, which she turns arbitrarily; Kent is now at the bottom.) **II.3 s.d.** Kent remains onstage in the stocks, asleep, but he and Edgar are clearly not part of the same scene   **1** *proclaimed* i.e., as an outlaw   **2** *happy hollow* i.e., lucky hiding place   **5** *attend . . . taking* prepare to arrest me   **6** *am bethought* have a plan   **8** *of* for   **10** *elf* tangle (into "elf locks")

And with presented nakedness outface   11
The wind and persecution of the sky.
The country gives me proof and precedent   13
Of Bedlam beggars who with roaring voices   14
Strike in their numbed and mortified bare arms   15
Pins, wooden pricks, nails, sprigs of rosemary,
And with this horrible object from low service,   17
Poor pelting villages, sheepcotes, and mills   18
Sometime with lunatic bans, sometime with prayers   19
Enforce their charity. "Poor Turlygod! poor Tom!"   20
That's something yet. Edgar I nothing am.   *Exit.*   21

*

∾ **II.4** *Enter Lear [, Fool, and Knight. Kent still in the*
stocks].

LEAR
'Tis strange that they should so depart from home
And not send back my messenger.
KNIGHT   As I learned,
The night before there was no purpose   3
Of his remove.
KENT   Hail to thee, noble master.
LEAR
How! Mak'st thou this shame thy pastime?
FOOL   Ha, ha, look, he wears cruel garters. Horses are   6
tied by the heads, dogs and bears by th' neck, monkeys
by th' loins, and men by th' legs. When a man's over-   8
lusty at legs, then he wears wooden netherstocks.   9

---

11 *presented* the show of   13 *proof* experience   14 *Bedlam beggars* (see
I.2.129)   15 *Strike* stick; *mortified* dead to pain   17 *object* spectacle; *low
service* menial servants   18 *pelting* paltry   19 *bans* curses   20 *Turlygod* (unexplained, but evidently another name for a Bedlam beggar)   21 *Edgar* i.e.,
as Edgar   II.4   3–4 *there . . . remove* the duke had no intention of leaving
6 *cruel* (punning on "crewel," worsted cloth)   8–9 *overlusty . . . legs* too
eager to run   9 *netherstocks* stockings

LEAR

10   What's he that hath so much thy place mistook
To set thee here?

KENT

It is both he and she,

13   Your son and daughter.

LEAR   No.

KENT   Yes.

LEAR   No, I say.

KENT

I say yea.

LEAR   No, no, they would not.

KENT   Yes, they have.

LEAR

By Jupiter, I swear no. They durst not do't,
They would not, could not do't. 'Tis worse than murder

17   To do upon respect such violent outrage.

18   Resolve me with all modest haste which way
Thou mayst deserve or they purpose this usage,

20   Coming from us.

KENT   My lord, when at their home

21   I did commend your highness' letters to them,
Ere I was risen from the place that showed

23   My duty kneeling, came there a reeking post
Stewed in his haste, half breathless, panting forth
From Goneril his mistress salutations;

26   Delivered letters spite of intermission,

27   Which presently they read, on whose contents
They summoned up their men, straight took horse,
Commanded me to follow and attend

30   The leisure of their answer, gave me cold looks;
And meeting here the other messenger,

---

13 *son* i.e., son-in-law   17 *upon respect* to one who should be respected (as the king's messenger)   18 *Resolve* explain to; *modest* decent   21 *commend* deliver   23–24 *reeking . . . Stewed* hot and sweaty messenger   26 *spite . . . intermission* though he was interrupting me   27 *presently* immediately

Whose welcome I perceived had poisoned mine,
Being the very fellow that of late
Displayed so saucily against your highness,   34
Having more man than wit about me, drew.   35
He raised the house with loud and coward cries.
Your son and daughter found this trespass worth
This shame which here it suffers.

LEAR
O, how this mother swells up toward my heart!   39
Hysterica passio, down, thou climbing sorrow,   40
Thy element's below. Where is this daughter?   41

KENT
With the earl, sir, within.

LEAR
[To Attendants]
Follow me not; stay there.   *[Exit.]*

KNIGHT Made you no more offense than what you
speak of?

KENT No. How chance the king comes with so small a
train?

FOOL An thou hadst been set in the stocks for that ques-   48
tion, thou hadst well deserved it.

KENT Why, fool?   50

FOOL We'll set thee to school to an ant, to teach thee   51
there's no laboring in the winter. All that follow their
noses are led by their eyes but blind men, and there's
not a nose among a hundred but can smell him that's
stinking. Let go thy hold when a great wheel runs down
a hill, lest it break thy neck with following it; but the
great one that goes up the hill, let him draw thee after.
When a wise man gives thee better counsel, give me

---

34 *Displayed* behaved 35 *wit* sense; *drew* drew my sword 39 *mother* hysteria 40 *Hysterica passio* (the medical term for hysteria) 41 *Thy . . . below*
(hysteria's natural place, "element," was said to be the abdomen or, in
women, the womb) 48 *An* if 51–52 *We'll . . . winter* (ants proverbially do
not work in winter – implying that working for Lear is now unprofitable)

59 mine again. I would have none but knaves follow it,
60 since a fool gives it.
                    That sir that serves for gain
62   And follows but for form,
63   Will pack when it begin to rain,
                    And leave thee in the storm.
                    But I will tarry, the fool will stay,
                    And let the wise man fly.
67   The knave turns fool that runs away,
68   The fool no knave, perdy.
     KENT   Where learnt you this, fool?
70   FOOL   Not in the stocks.
            Enter Lear and Gloucester.
     LEAR
        Deny to speak with me? They're sick, they're weary,
72   They traveled hard tonight? Mere justice?
73   Ay, the images of revolt and flying off.
        Fetch me a better answer.
     GLOUCESTER   My dear lord,
75   You know the fiery quality of the duke,
        How unremovable and fixed he is
        In his own course.
     LEAR
        Vengeance, death, plague, confusion!
        What "fiery quality"? Why, Gloucester, Gloucester,
80   I'd speak with the Duke of Cornwall and his wife.
     GLOUCESTER   Ay, my good lord.
     LEAR
        The king would speak with Cornwall; the dear father
        Would with his daughter speak, commands her service.
        Fiery duke? Tell the hot duke that Lear –
        No, but not yet; maybe he is not well.

---

59 *again* back   62 *form* show   63 *pack* leave   67 *knave . . . away* i.e., dis-
loyalty is the real folly   68 *perdy* by God (*par Dieu*)   72 *Mere justice* (presumably Cornwall's explanation for why Kent is in the stocks)   73 *images*
signs; *flying off* insurrection   75 *quality* disposition

Infirmity doth still neglect all office   86
Whereto our health is bound. We are not ourselves   87
When nature, being oppressed, commands the mind
To suffer with the body. I'll forbear,
And am fallen out with my more headier will,   90
To take the indisposed and sickly fit   91
For the sound man. – Death on my state! wherefore   92
Should he sit here? This act persuades me   93
That this remotion of the duke and her   94
Is practice only. Give me my servant forth.   95
Tell the duke and's wife I'll speak with them,
Now, presently. Bid them come forth and hear me,   97
Or at their chamber door I'll beat the drum
Till it cry sleep to death.   99
GLOUCESTER   I would have all well betwixt you.   *[Exit.]*   100
LEAR   O, my heart, my heart!
FOOL   Cry to it, nuncle, as the cockney did to the eels   102
when she put 'em i' th' paste alive. She rapped 'em o' th'   103
coxcombs with a stick, and cried "Down, wantons,   104
down!" 'Twas her brother that, in pure kindness to his
horse, buttered his hay.   106
        Enter Cornwall and Regan [, followed by Gloucester
        and Servants].
LEAR   Good morrow to you both.
CORNWALL   Hail to your grace.
REGAN
        I am glad to see your highness.
        [Kent is set free.]

---

86 *still . . . office* always neglects duty   87 *Whereto . . . bound* which in
health we are bound to obey   90 *fallen out* angry; *headier* headstrong   91
To take that mistook   92 *Death . . . state* (the expletive is ironic: "Let my
royal power die")   93 *he* Kent   94 *remotion* (1) removal (from their home),
(2) aloofness (from Lear)   95 *practice* trickery; *Give . . . forth* release my servant   97 *presently* instantly   99 *Till . . . death* till it kills sleep with the noise
102 *cockney* Londoner (i.e., a city dweller)   103 *paste* pastry   104 *coxcombs*
heads; *wantons* rascals (with a quibble on lechers, and on deflating erections)
106 *buttered . . . hay* (misguided kindness: horses will not eat grease)

LEAR
Regan, I think you are. I know what reason
110 I have to think so. If thou shouldst not be glad
I would divorce me from thy mother's tomb,
112 Sepulch'ring an adult'ress. *[To Kent]* Yea, are you free?
Some other time for that. Belovèd Regan,
114 Thy sister is naught. O, Regan, she hath tied
Sharp-toothed unkindness like a vulture here.
I can scarce speak to thee. Thou'lt not believe
Of how depraved a quality – O Regan!

REGAN
I pray, sir, take patience. I have hope
119 You less know how to value her desert
120 Than she to slack her duty.

LEAR
My curses on her.

REGAN   O, sir, you are old;
122 Nature in you stands on the very verge
Of her confine. You should be ruled and led
124 By some discretion that discerns your state
Better than you yourself. Therefore I pray
That to our sister you do make return;
Say you have wronged her, sir.

LEAR   Ask her forgiveness?
128 Do you mark how this becomes the house?
[Kneels.]
"Dear daughter, I confess that I am old;
130 Age is unnecessary. On my knees I beg
That you'll vouchsafe me raiment, bed, and food."

---

112 *Sepulch'ring . . . adult'ress* i.e., it would prove you were not my daughter
114 *naught* wicked (cf. "naughty") 119–20 *You . . . duty* the problem is
that you are unable to evaluate her merit rather than that she has failed in her
duty 122–23 *Nature . . . confine* your life stands at the very edge of its allotted space 124 *discretion . . . state* discerning person who understands
your condition 128 *house* family 130 *Age is* old people are

REGAN
> Good sir, no more. These are unsightly tricks.
> Return you to my sister.
LEAR   *[Rising]*   No, Regan.
> She hath abated me of half my train,   134
> Looked black upon me, struck me with her tongue
> Most serpentlike upon the very heart.
> All the stored vengeances of heaven fall
> On her ingrateful top! Strike her young bones,   138
> You taking airs, with lameness.   139
CORNWALL   Fie, fie, sir.
LEAR
> You nimble lightnings, dart your blinding flames   *140*
> Into her scornful eyes. Infect her beauty,
> You fen-sucked fogs drawn by the pow'rful sun   142
> To fall and blast her pride.
REGAN   O the blest gods!
> So will you wish on me when the rash mood –
LEAR
> No, Regan, thou shalt never have my curse.
> Thy tender-hefted nature shall not give   146
> Thee o'er to harshness. Her eyes are fierce, but thine
> Do comfort and not burn. 'Tis not in thee
> To grudge my pleasures, to cut off my train,
> To bandy hasty words, to scant my sizes,   150
> And, in conclusion, to oppose the bolt   151
> Against my coming in. Thou better knowest
> The offices of nature, bond of childhood,   153
> Effects of courtesy, dues of gratitude;   154
> Thy half of the kingdom hast thou not forgot,
> Wherein I thee endowed.

---

134 *abated* deprived   138 *top* head   139 *taking airs* infectious vapors   142 *fen-sucked . . . sun* (the sun was believed to draw infectious vapors from swamps)   146 *tender-hefted* gently disposed   150 *sizes* allowance   151 *oppose the bolt* bolt the door   153 *offices* duties   154 *Effects* obligations

REGAN   Good sir, to th' purpose.

LEAR
Who put my man i' th' stocks?
[Tucket within.]
CORNWALL   What trumpet's that?
Enter Steward [Oswald].

REGAN
158   I know't, my sister's. This approves her letters
That she would soon be here. *[To Oswald]* Is your lady
come?

LEAR
160   This is a slave whose easy, borrowed pride
161   Dwells in the fickle grace of her a follows.
[Strikes Oswald.]
162   Out, varlet, from my sight!
CORNWALL   What means your grace?
Enter Goneril.

GONERIL
Who struck my servant? Regan, I have good hope
164   Thou didst not know on't.
LEAR   Who comes here? O heavens,
165   If you do love old men, if you sweet sway
Allow obedience, if yourselves are old,
Make it your cause; send down and take my part.
[To Goneril]
Art not ashamed to look upon this beard?
O Regan, wilt thou take her by the hand?

GONERIL
170   Why not by the hand, sir? How have I offended?
171   All's not offense that indiscretion finds
And dotage terms so.

---

156 *to . . . purpose* get to the point   158 *approves* confirms   160 *easy* impudent; *borrowed* assumed   161 *a* he   162 *varlet* scoundrel   164 *on't* of it
165–66 *If . . . obedience* if you permit gentle rule to be obeyed   171 *indiscretion* poor judgment

LEAR   O sides, you are too tough!
  Will you yet hold? How came my man i' th' stocks?
CORNWALL
  I set him there, sir, but his own disorders
  Deserved much less advancement.   175
LEAR   You? Did you?
REGAN
  I pray you, father, being weak, seem so.
  If till the expiration of your month
  You will return and sojourn with my sister,
  Dismissing half your train, come then to me.
  I am now from home, and out of that provision   180
  Which shall be needful for your entertainment.   181
LEAR
  Return to her, and fifty men dismissed?
  No, rather I abjure all roofs, and choose
  To wage against the enmity of the air,   184
  To be a comrade with the wolf and owl –
  Necessity's sharp pinch. Return with her?
  Why, the hot-blood in France that dowerless took
  Our youngest born – I could as well be brought
  To knee his throne and, squirelike, pension beg   189
  To keep base life afoot. Return with her?   190
  Persuade me rather to be slave and sumpter   191
  To this detested groom.   *[Points at Oswald.]*
GONERIL   At your choice, sir.
LEAR
  Now I prithee, daughter, do not make me mad.
  I will not trouble thee, my child. Farewell;
  We'll no more meet, no more see one another.
  But yet thou art my flesh, my blood, my daughter,

---

172 *sides* breast (which should burst with grief)   175 *less advancement* less of
a promotion (i.e., a worse punishment)   180 *from* away from   181 *enter-tainment* reception   184 *wage* fight   189 *knee* kneel to   191 *sumpter* pack-horse

Or rather a disease that lies within my flesh,
Which I must needs call mine. Thou art a boil,
199   A plague-sore, an embossèd carbuncle
200   In my corrupted blood. But I'll not chide thee.
Let shame come when it will, I do not call it.
202   I do not bid the thunder-bearer shoot,
Nor tell tales of thee to high-judging Jove.
Mend when thou canst; be better at thy leisure.
I can be patient, I can stay with Regan,
I and my hundred knights.

REGAN
Not altogether so, sir;
I look not for you yet, nor am provided
For your fit welcome. Give ear, sir, to my sister;
210   For those that mingle reason with your passion
Must be content to think you are old, and so –
But she knows what she does.

LEAR
Is this well spoken now?

REGAN
214   I dare avouch it, sir. What, fifty followers?
Is it not well? What should you need of more,
216   Yea, or so many, sith that both charge and danger
Speaks 'gainst so great a number? How in a house
Should many people under two commands
Hold amity? 'Tis hard, almost impossible.

GONERIL
220   Why might not you, my lord, receive attendance
From those that she calls servants, or from mine?

REGAN
222   Why not, my lord? If then they chanced to slack you,
We could control them. If you will come to me,
For now I spy a danger, I entreat you

---

199 *embossèd carbuncle* swollen tumor   202 *the thunder-bearer* Jove   210
mingle . . . passion deal rationally with your intemperate behavior   214 *avouch*
swear   216 *sith that* since; *charge* expense   222 *slack* neglect

To bring but five-and-twenty; to no more
Will I give place or notice.   226
LEAR
I gave you all.
REGAN   And in good time you gave it.
LEAR
Made you my guardians, my depositaries,   228
But kept a reservation to be followed   229
With such a number. What, must I come to you   230
With five-and-twenty, Regan? Said you so?
REGAN
And speak't again, my lord. No more with me.
LEAR
Those wicked creatures yet do seem well favored   233
When others are more wicked. Not being the worst
Stands in some rank of praise. *[To Goneril]* I'll go with   235
    thee.
Thy fifty yet doth double five-and-twenty,
And thou art twice her love.   237
GONERIL   Hear me, my lord:
What need you five-and-twenty, ten, or five,
To follow in a house where twice so many
Have a command to tend you?   240
REGAN   ,   What needs one?
LEAR
O reason not the need! Our basest beggars   241
Are in the poorest thing superfluous.   242
Allow not nature more than nature needs,   243
Man's life is cheap as beasts'. Thou art a lady;
If only to go warm were gorgeous,   245
Why, nature needs not what thou gorgeous wearest,

---

226 *notice* recognition   228 *depositaries* trustees   229 *kept . . . be* stipulated
that I be   233 *well favored* attractive   235 *Stands . . . of* deserves at least some
237 *twice . . . love* twice as loving as she   241 *reason* calculate   242 *Are . . . superfluous* have something more than is absolutely necessary   243 *Allow not* if
you do not grant   245 *If . . . gorgeous* if warmth were the measure of fashionable dress

Which scarcely keeps thee warm. But for true need –
You heavens, give me that patience, patience I need.
You see me here, you gods, a poor old fellow,
250   As full of grief as age, wretched in both.
If it be you that stirs these daughters' hearts
252   Against their father, fool me not so much
To bear it tamely. Touch me with noble anger.
O, let not women's weapons, waterdrops,
Stain my man's cheeks! No, you unnatural hags,
I will have such revenges on you both
That all the world shall – I will do such things,
What they are, yet I know not; but they shall be
The terrors of the earth. You think I'll weep:
260   No, I'll not weep.
          [Storm and tempest.]
I have full cause of weeping, but this heart
262   Shall break in a hundred thousand flaws
263   Or ere I'll weep. O fool, I shall go mad!
               Exeunt Lear, Gloucester, Kent, [Knight,] and Fool.

CORNWALL
Let us withdraw; 'twill be a storm.

REGAN
This house is little: the old man and his people
Cannot be well bestowed.

GONERIL
'Tis his own blame hath put himself from rest,
And must needs taste his folly.

REGAN
269   For his particular I'll receive him gladly,
270   But not one follower.

CORNWALL   So am I purposed.
Where is my lord of Gloucester?

REGAN
Followed the old man forth.

252–53 *fool . . . To* don't make me such a fool as to   262 *flaws* fragments
263 *Or ere* before   269 *his particular* himself alone

Enter Gloucester.
                              He is returned.
GLOUCESTER
The king is in high rage, and will I know not whither.
REGAN
'Tis good to give him way. He leads himself.
GONERIL
My lord, entreat him by no means to stay.
GLOUCESTER
Alack, the night comes on, and the bleak winds
Do sorely ruffle. For many miles about   277
There's not a bush.
REGAN   O sir, to willful men
The injuries that they themselves procure
Must be their schoolmasters. Shut up your doors.   280
He is attended with a desperate train,   281
And what they may incense him to, being apt   282
To have his ear abused, wisdom bids fear.
CORNWALL
Shut up your doors, my lord; 'tis a wild night.
My Regan counsels well. Come out o' th' storm.
                                        Exeunt.

                              ✳

∾ **III.1** *[Storm still.] Enter Kent [disguised] and a*
    Gentleman at several doors.

KENT
What's here beside foul weather?
GENTLEMAN
One minded like the weather, most unquietly.
KENT
I know you. Where's the king?

---

277 *ruffle* rage   281 *desperate train* violent troop   282–83 *apt . . . abused*
i.e., likely to be misled
   III.1 A heath   **s.d.** *several* different

GENTLEMAN

4   Contending with the fretful element;
    Bids the wind blow the earth into the sea
6   Or quell the curlèd waters 'bove the main,
    That things might change or cease; tears his white hair,
8   Which the impetuous blasts, with eyeless rage,
    Catch in their fury and make nothing of;
10   Strives in his little world of man to outscorn
    The to-and-fro conflicting wind and rain.
12   This night, wherein the cub-drawn bear would couch,
13   The lion and the belly-pinchèd wolf
    Keep their fur dry, unbonneted he runs,
15   And bids what will take all.

KENT   But who is with him?

GENTLEMAN

16   None but the fool, who labors to outjest
    His heart-struck injuries.

KENT   Sir, I do know you,

18   And dare upon the warrant of my art
19   Commend a dear thing to you. There is division,
20   Although as yet the face of it be covered
    With mutual cunning, 'twixt Albany and Cornwall;
    But true it is. From France there comes a power
    Into this scattered kingdom, who already,
24   Wise in our negligence, have secret feet
25   In some of our best ports, and are at point
    To show their open banner. Now to you:
27   If on my credit you dare build so far
    To make your speed to Dover, you shall find
    Some that will thank you, making just report

---

4 *fretful element* angry sky   6 *main* mainland   8 *eyeless* blind   12 *cub-drawn* sucked dry by her cubs, and therefore ravenous; *couch* stay inside   13 *belly-pinchèd* starving   15 *bids . . . will* commands whatever wishes to   16 *outjest* overcome with jesting   18 *art* judgment   19 *Commend . . . thing* entrust a precious matter; *division* dissension   24 *Wise in* knowing of; *secret feet* secretly set foot   25 *at point* ready   27 *If . . . build* if you trust me

Of how unnatural and bemadding sorrow   *30*
The king hath cause to plain.   *31*
I am a gentleman of blood and breeding,
And from some knowledge and assurance offer
This office to you.   *34*

GENTLEMAN
I will talk farther with you.

KENT   No, do not.
For confirmation that I am much more
Than my outwall, open this purse and take   *37*
What it contains. If you shall see Cordelia,
As fear not but you shall, show her this ring,
And she will tell you who your fellow is   *40*
That yet you do not know. Fie on this storm!
I will go seek the king.

GENTLEMAN
Give me your hand. Have you no more to say?

KENT
Few words, but to effect more than all yet: *44*
That when we have found the king – I'll this way,
You that – he that first lights on him
Holla the other.   *Exeunt [in different directions].*
                            ✳

∾ **III.2** *[Storm still.] Enter Lear and Fool.*

LEAR
Blow, wind, and crack your cheeks! Rage, blow,   *1*
You cataracts and hurricanoes, spout   *2*
Till you have drenched the steeples, drowned the cocks! *3*

---

31 *plain* complain **34** *office* undertaking **37** *outwall* outward appearance
40 *who . . . is* i.e., who I am **44** *to effect* in importance
   III.2 Elsewhere on the heath **1** *crack . . . cheeks* (as winds are represented
on old maps, heads with cheeks puffed out) **2** *cataracts . . . hurricanoes* torrential rains and hurricanes **3** *cocks* weather vanes

4   You sulphurous and thought-executing fires,
5   Vaunt-couriers to oak-cleaving thunderbolts,
     Singe my white head; and thou all-shaking thunder,
     Smite flat the thick rotundity of the world,
8   Crack nature's mold, all germens spill at once
     That make ingrateful man.
10   FOOL   O nuncle, court holy water in a dry house is bet-
     ter than this rainwater out o' door. Good nuncle, in,
     and ask thy daughters' blessing. Here's a night pities
     neither wise man nor fool.
     LEAR
     Rumble thy bellyful! Spit, fire; spout, rain!
     Nor rain, wind, thunder, fire are my daughters.
16   I tax not you, you elements, with unkindness.
     I never gave you kingdom, called you children.
18   You owe me no subscription. Why then, let fall
     Your horrible pleasure. Here I stand your slave,
20   A poor, infirm, weak, and despised old man,
21   But yet I call you servile ministers,
     That have with two pernicious daughters joined
23   Your high-engendered battle 'gainst a head
     So old and white as this. O, 'tis foul!
     FOOL   He that has a house to put his head in has a good
26   headpiece.
27   The codpiece that will house
                Before the head has any,
29   The head and he shall louse,
30   So beggars marry many.

---

4 *thought-executing* either annihilating thought or acting as fast as thought
5 *Vaunt-couriers* heralds   8 *nature's mold* (in which life is given form); *germens* seeds   10 *court holy water* flattery   16 *tax* charge   18 *subscription* deference   21 *ministers* agents   23 *high-engendered battle* heavenly battalion
26 *headpiece* (1) helmet, (2) brain   27 *codpiece* the pouch for the genitals on
men's breeches (here used for the penis); *house* lodge (in copulation)   29–30
The . . . many will infest both the head and the codpiece with lice, and end
in married poverty

> The man that makes his toe   31
> What he his heart should make
> Shall have a corn, cry woe,
> And turn his sleep to wake.
> For there was never yet fair woman but she made   35
> mouths in a glass.

LEAR
No, I will be the pattern of all patience.
   Enter Kent [disguised].
I will say nothing. *[He sits.]*

KENT   Who's there?

FOOL   Marry, here's grace and a codpiece, that's a wise   40
man and a fool.

KENT
Alas, sir, sit you here? Things that love night
Love not such nights as these. The wrathful skies
Gallow the very wanderers of the dark   44
And makes them keep their caves. Since I was man   45
Such sheets of fire, such bursts of horrid thunder,
Such groans of roaring wind and rain I ne'er
Remember to have heard. Man's nature cannot carry 48
The affliction nor the force.

LEAR   Let the great gods,
That keep this dreadful pother o'er our heads,   50
Find out their enemies now. Tremble, thou wretch
That hast within thee undivulgèd crimes
Unwhipped of justice; hide thee, thou bloody hand, 53
Thou perjured and thou simular man of virtue   54
That art incestuous; caitiff, in pieces shake,   55
That under covert and convenient seeming   56

31–32 *The . . . make* (a parallel instance of preferring the lower part to the higher)   35–36 *made . . . glass* practiced smiling in a mirror (i.e., was afflicted with vanity)   40 *Marry* (a mild exclamation, originally an oath on the name of the Virgin)   44 *Gallow* frighten   45 *keep* stay inside   48 *carry* endure   50 *pother* tumult   53 *of* by   54 *simular . . . of* pretender to   55 *caitiff* wretch   56 *seeming* hypocrisy

57 Hast practiced on man's life;
58 Close pent-up guilts, rive your concealèd centers,
59 And cry these dreadful summoners grace.
60 I am a man more sinned against than sinning.

KENT
Alack, bareheaded?
62 Gracious my lord, hard by here is a hovel.
Some friendship will it lend you 'gainst the tempest.
Repose you there whilst I to this hard house –
More hard than is the stone whereof 'tis raised,
66 Which even but now, demanding after you,
Denied me to come in – return and force
68 Their scanted courtesy.

LEAR
My wit begins to turn.
70 Come on, my boy. How dost, my boy? Art cold?
I am cold myself. Where is this straw, my fellow?
The art of our necessities is strange,
That can make vile things precious. Come, your hovel.
Poor fool and knave, I have one part of my heart
That sorrows yet for thee.

FOOL
He that has a little tiny wit,
With heigh-ho, the wind and the rain,
78 Must make content with his fortunes fit,
79 For the rain it raineth every day.

LEAR
80 True, my good boy. Come, bring us to this hovel.
[Exeunt.]

＊

---

57 *practiced on* plotted against 58 *Close* secret; *rive* split open 59 *cry . . .
grace* beg for mercy from these terrible agents of justice (summoners are officers of church courts) 62 *hard* close 66 *demanding* as I was asking 68
scanted deficient 78 *make . . . fit* be content with his lot 79 (the song re-
figures Feste's song at the end of *Twelfth Night*)

∾ **III.3** *Enter Gloucester and the Bastard [Edmund]*
with lights.

GLOUCESTER   Alack, alack, Edmund, I like not this unnatural dealing. When I desired their leave that I might
pity him, they took from me the use of mine own   3
house, charged me on pain of their displeasure neither
to speak of him, entreat for him, nor any way sustain
him.

EDMUND   Most savage and unnatural!

GLOUCESTER   Go to, say you nothing. There's a division   8
betwixt the dukes, and a worse matter than that. I have
received a letter this night − 'tis dangerous to be spo-   10
ken. I have locked the letter in my closet. These injuries 11
the king now bears will be revenged home. There's part   12
of a power already landed. We must incline to the king.   13
I will seek him and privily relieve him. Go you and   14
maintain talk with the duke, that my charity be not of   15
him perceived. If he ask for me, I am ill and gone to
bed. Though I die for't − as no less is threatened me −
the king my old master must be relieved. There is some
strange thing toward, Edmund. Pray you, be careful.   19
                                              Exit.

EDMUND
This courtesy, forbid thee, shall the duke   20
Instantly know, and of that letter too.
This seems a fair deserving, and must draw me   22
That which my father loses: no less than all.
Then younger rises when the old do fall.   *Exit.*

                        *

III.3 Gloucester's house   3 *pity* take pity on   8 *Go to* be quiet   11 *closet*
(any private room: study, bedroom)   12 *home* thoroughly   13 *power* army;
incline to side with   14 *privily* secretly   15 *of* by   19 *toward* impending
20 *courtesy . . . thee* kindness you have been forbidden to show   22 *fair de-*
serving action that would deserve a fair reward

∾ **III.4** *[Storm still.] Enter Lear, Kent [disguised], and Fool.*

KENT
Here is the place, my lord; good my lord, enter.
The tyranny of the open night's too rough
3 For nature to endure.
LEAR   Let me alone.
KENT
Good my lord, enter.
LEAR
Wilt break my heart?
KENT
I had rather break mine own. Good my lord, enter.
LEAR
Thou think'st 'tis much that this contentious storm
Invades us to the skin; so 'tis to thee,
9 But where the greater malady is fixed,
10 The lesser is scarce felt. Thou'dst shun a bear,
But if thy flight lay toward the roaring sea
12 Thou'dst meet the bear i' th' mouth. When the mind's
free,
13 The body's delicate. This tempest in my mind
Doth from my senses take all feeling else
Save what beats there: filial ingratitude.
16 Is it not as this mouth should tear this hand
For lifting food to't? But I will punish sure.
No, I will weep no more. – In such a night as this!
O Regan, Goneril, your old kind father,
20 Whose frank heart gave you all. – O, that way mad-
ness lies.
Let me shun that; no more of that.

III.4 Before a hovel on the heath   **3** *nature* humanity, human frailty   **9**
fixed lodged   **12** *i' th' mouth* head-on; *When . . . free* only when the mind is
untroubled   **13** *delicate* sensitive to pain   **16** *as* as if

KENT
    Good my lord, enter.
LEAR
    Prithee, go in thyself; seek thy own ease.
    This tempest will not give me leave to ponder
    On things would hurt me more; but I'll go in.   25
                                              [Exit Fool.]
    Poor naked wretches, wheresoe'er you are,
    That bide the pelting of this pitiless night,   27
    How shall your houseless heads and unfed sides,
    Your looped and windowed raggedness, defend you   29
    From seasons such as these? O, I have ta'en   30
    Too little care of this. Take physic, pomp,   31
    Expose thyself to feel what wretches feel,
    That thou mayst shake the superflux to them   33
    And show the heavens more just.
        [Enter Fool.]
FOOL   Come not in here, nuncle; here's a spirit! Help
    me, help me!
KENT   Give me thy hand. Who's there?
FOOL   A spirit. He says his name's Poor Tom.
KENT
    What art thou that dost grumble there in the straw?
    Come forth.   40
        [Enter Edgar disguised as a madman.]
EDGAR   Away, the foul fiend follows me. "Through the   41
    sharp hawthorn blows the cold wind." Go to thy cold
    bed and warm thee.
LEAR   Hast thou given all to thy two daughters, and art
    thou come to this?
EDGAR   Who gives anything to Poor Tom, whom the
    foul fiend hath led through fire and through ford and

---

25 *would* that would   **27** *bide* endure, wait out   **29** *looped, windowed* (both
mean "full of holes")   **30** *seasons* weather   **31** *Take . . . pomp* grandeur,
purge yourself   **33** *shake . . . superflux* pour out your surplus   **41–42**
Through . . . wind (apparently a fragment of a ballad, quoted again at ll.
90–91)

48 whirlypool, o'er bog and quagmire; that has laid knives
49 under his pillow and halters in his pew, set ratsbane by
50 his pottage, made him proud of heart to ride on a bay
51 trotting horse over four-inched bridges, to course his
52 own shadow for a traitor. Bless thy five wits, Tom's
53 acold! Bless thee from whirlwinds, star-blasting, and
54 taking. Do Poor Tom some charity, whom the foul
fiend vexes. There could I have him now – and there –
and there again.

LEAR
What, his daughters brought him to this pass?
[To Edgar]
Couldst thou save nothing? Didst thou give them all?

FOOL   Nay, he reserved a blanket, else we had been all
60 shamed.

LEAR   *[To Edgar]*
61 Now all the plagues that in the pendulous air
62 Hang fated o'er men's faults fall on thy daughters!

KENT   He hath no daughters, sir.

LEAR
Death, traitor! Nothing could have subdued nature
To such a lowness but his unkind daughters.
Is it the fashion that discarded fathers
Should have thus little mercy on their flesh?
Judicious punishment: 'twas this flesh begot
69 Those pelican daughters.

70 EDGAR   Pillicock sat on pillicock's hill, a lo, lo, lo.

48-49 *knives, halters, ratsbane* (all temptations to suicide)   49 *halters...*
pew nooses on his balcony   50–51 *made... bridges* i.e., made him take mad
risks   51–52 *course... traitor* hunt his own shadow as if it were an enemy
52 *five wits* (the constituent parts of intelligence in Renaissance theories of
cognition: common wit, imagination, fantasy, estimation, memory)   53 *star-*
blasting malignant stars   54 *taking* infection   61 *pendulous* overhanging
62 *fated* ominously   69 *pelican* cannibalistic (young pelicans were said to
feed on their mother's blood)   70 *Pillicock... lo* (a fragment of a nursery
rhyme) *Pillicock* (1) an endearment, (2) baby talk for penis

FOOL   This cold night will turn us all to fools and mad-
men.

EDGAR   Take heed o' th' foul fiend; obey thy parents;   73
keep thy words justly; swear not; commit not with   74
man's sworn spouse; set not thy sweet heart on proud   75
array. Tom's acold.

LEAR   What hast thou been?

EDGAR   A servingman proud in heart and mind, that
curled my hair, wore gloves in my cap, served the lust of   79
my mistress' heart, and did the act of darkness with her;   80
swore as many oaths as I spake words, and broke them
in the sweet face of heaven; one that slept in the con-   82
triving of lust, and waked to do it. Wine loved I deeply,
dice dearly, and in woman out-paramoured the Turk.   84
False of heart, light of ear, bloody of hand; hog in sloth,   85
fox in stealth, wolf in greediness, dog in madness, lion
in prey. Let not the creaking of shoes nor the rustlings of   87
silks betray thy poor heart to women. Keep thy foot out
of brothel, thy hand out of placket, thy pen from   89
lender's book, and defy the foul fiend. "Still through the   90
hawthorn blows the cold wind. Heigh no nonny." Dol-   91
phin my boy, my boy! cease, let him trot by.

LEAR   Why, thou wert better in thy grave than to answer   93
with thy uncovered body this extremity of the skies. Is
man no more but this? Consider him well. Thou owest

---

73 *Take heed* beware; *obey . . . parents* (this and the following injunctions are
from the Ten Commandments)   74 *keep . . . justly* i.e., do not lie; *commit
not* i.e., do not commit adultery   75–76 *proud array* luxurious clothing   79
wore . . . cap (as courtly lovers did with tokens from their mistresses)   82-83
slept . . . lust went to sleep planning acts of lechery   84 *out-paramoured . . .
Turk* had more lovers than the sultan has in his harem   85 *light of ear* attentive to gossip and slander   87–88 *creaking . . . silks* (both fashionable in
women)   89 *placket* a slit in women's skirts (hence, the vagina)   89–90
pen . . . book i.e., stay out of debt   91–92 *Dolphin . . . cease* (Unexplained;
possibly a bit of a ballad, possibly a hunting call. Dolphin is usually taken to
refer to the French crown prince, the dauphin, but it sounds more like a
hunting dog's name.)   93 *answer* experience

the worm no silk, the beast no hide, the sheep no wool,
97   the cat no perfume. Here's three on's are sophisticated.
98   Thou art the thing itself. Unaccommodated man is no
more but such a poor, bare, forked animal as thou art.
100   *[Removing his clothes]* Off, off, you lendings, come on.
101   FOOL   Prithee, nuncle, be content. This is a naughty
night to swim in. Now a little fire in a wild field were
like an old lecher's heart, a small spark, all the rest in
body cold. Look, here comes a walking fire.
        Enter Gloucester [with a torch].
105   EDGAR   This is the foul fiend Flibbertigibbet. He begins
106   at curfew and walks till the first cock. He gives the web
107   and the pin, squinies the eye, and makes the harelip;
108   mildews the white wheat, and hurts the poor creature
of earth.
110   Swithold footed thrice the wold,
111   He met the night mare and her ninefold;
112   Bid her alight
113   And her troth plight,
114   And aroint thee, witch, aroint thee!
      KENT   How fares your grace?
      LEAR   *[Pointing to Gloucester]* What's he?
      KENT   *[To Gloucester]* Who's there? What is't you seek?
      GLOUCESTER   What are you there? Your names?
      EDGAR   Poor Tom, that eats the swimming frog, the
120   toad, the tadpole, the wall newt and the water; that in
the fury of his heart, when the foul fiend rages, eats cow

---

97 *cat* civet cat (from whose secretions perfume was made); *on's* of us; *sophisticated* artificial **98** *Unaccommodated* unadorned, unfurnished **100** *lendings* borrowed articles (because not part of his body) **101** *naughty* evil **105** *Flibbertigibbet* (in Elizabethan folklore, a dancing devil) **106** *curfew* 9 P.M.; *first cock* midnight **106–07** *the web . . . pin* eye cataracts **107** *squinies* makes squint **108** *white* almost ripe **110** *Swithold* Saint Withold (invoked as a general protector against harm); *footed . . . wold* walked the plain three times **111** *night mare* incubus, female demon; *ninefold* nine offspring **112** *Bid . . . alight* ordered her to get off (the sleeper's chest) **113** *her troth plight* give her promise (not to do it again) **114** *aroint thee* be gone **120** *wall newt* lizard; *water* i.e., water newt

dung for sallets, swallows the old rat and the ditch dog,   122
drinks the green mantle of the standing pool; who is   123
whipped from tithing to tithing, and stock-punished,   124
and imprisoned; who hath had three suits to his back,
six shirts to his body,
      Horse to ride, and weapon to wear,
      But mice and rats and such small deer   128
      Hath been Tom's food for seven long year.
Beware my follower. Peace, Smulkin; peace, thou   130
fiend!

GLOUCESTER
What, hath your grace no better company?

EDGAR
The Prince of Darkness is a gentleman;
Modo he's called, and Mahu –

GLOUCESTER   *[To Lear]*
Our flesh and blood is grown so vile, my lord,
That it doth hate what gets it.   136

EDGAR   Poor Tom's acold.

GLOUCESTER
Go in with me. My duty cannot suffer   138
To obey in all your daughters' hard commands.
Though their injunction be to bar my doors   *140*
And let this tyrannous night take hold upon you,
Yet have I ventured to come seek you out
And bring you where both food and fire is ready.

LEAR
First let me talk with this philosopher.
What is the cause of thunder?

KENT   My good lord,
Take his offer; go into the house.

---

122 *sallets* delicacies; *ditch dog* dead dog thrown in a ditch   123 *green mantle* scum; *standing* stagnant   124 *tithing* parish; *stock-punished* put in the stocks   128 *deer* game (the jingle is adapted from the popular romance *Bevis of Hampton*)   130 *Smulkin* (like Modo and Mahu below, devils identified in Samuel Harsnett's *Declaration of Egregious Popish Impostures*, 1603)   136 *gets* begets   138 *suffer* allow me

LEAR
147   I'll talk a word with this most learnèd Theban.
148   What is your study?
EDGAR
149   How to prevent the fiend, and to kill vermin.
150 LEAR   Let me ask you one word in private.
        [They talk aside.]
KENT
        Importune him to go, my lord;
        His wits begin to unsettle.
GLOUCESTER   Canst thou blame him?
        His daughters seek his death. O, that good Kent,
        He said it would be thus, poor banished man!
        Thou sayest the king grows mad; I'll tell thee, friend,
        I am almost mad myself. I had a son,
157 · Now outlawed from my blood; a sought my life
158   But lately, very late. I loved him, friend;
        No father his son dearer. True to tell thee,
160   The grief hath crazed my wits. What a night's this!
161   I do beseech your grace –
LEAR   O, cry you mercy!
        [To Edgar]
        Noble philosopher, your company.
EDGAR   Tom's acold.
GLOUCESTER
        In, fellow, there in t' hovel; keep thee warm.
LEAR
        Come, let's in all.
KENT   This way, my lord.
LEAR   With him;
        I will keep still with my philosopher.

---

147 *learnèd Theban* Greek scholar **148** *study* field of study **149** *prevent*
thwart **157** *outlawed . . . blood* disowned, disinherited; *a* he **158** *late* recently **161** *cry . . . mercy* I beg your pardon

KENT   Good my lord, soothe him; let him take the fellow.   167
GLOUCESTER   Take him you on.   168
KENT   Sirrah, come on. Go along with us.
LEAR   Come, good Athenian.   170
GLOUCESTER   No words, no words, hush!
EDGAR

    Child Roland to the dark tower come,   171
    His word was still "Fie, fo, and fum;   172
    I smell the blood of a British man."

                               Exeunt.

             ✳

∾ **III.5**   *Enter Cornwall and Bastard [Edmund].*

CORNWALL   I will have my revenge ere I depart the house.
EDMUND   How, my lord, I may be censured that nature   2
    thus gives way to loyalty, something fears me to think of.   3
CORNWALL   I now perceive it was not altogether your
    brother's evil disposition made him seek his death, but   5
    a provoking merit set awork by a reprovable badness in   6
    himself.   7
EDMUND   How malicious is my fortune that I must re-
    pent to be just! This is the letter he spoke of, which ap-   9
    proves him an intelligent party to the advantages of   10
    France. O heavens, that his treason were not, or not I
    the detector!
CORNWALL   Go with me to the duchess.

---

167 *soothe* humor   168 *you on* along with you   170 *Athenian* philosopher
171 *Child . . . come* (presumably from a ballad about the hero of *La Chanson
de Roland*); *Child* a knight in training   172–73 *His . . . man* (Edgar switches
to a ballad about Jack the Giant Killer)   172 *word* motto; *still* always
    III.5 Gloucester's house   2 *censured* criticized   2–3 *nature . . . loyalty*
(the contrast is between familial and political bonds)   3 *something . . . me* I
am almost afraid   5 *his* Gloucester's   6 *a . . . awork* a virtue incited to work
7 *himself* Gloucester (i.e., however wicked parricide is, Gloucester got what
he deserved)   9–10 *approves* proves   10 *intelligent . . . of* spy on behalf of

EDMUND   If the matter of this paper be certain, you have
mighty business in hand.

CORNWALL   True or false, it hath made thee Earl of
Gloucester. Seek out where thy father is, that he may be
18   ready for our apprehension.

19   EDMUND   *[Aside]* If I find him comforting the king, it
20   will stuff his suspicion more fully. *[To Cornwall]* I will
persever in my course of loyalty, though the conflict be
22   sore between that and my blood.

CORNWALL   I will lay trust upon thee, and thou shalt
find a dearer father in my love.   *Exeunt.*

*

∾ **III.6**   *Enter Gloucester and Lear, Kent [disguised],*
Fool, and [Edgar as] Tom.

GLOUCESTER   Here is better than the open air; take it
2   thankfully. I will piece out the comfort with what addition I can. I will not be long from you.

4   KENT   All the power of his wits have given way to impa-
5   tience; the gods deserve your kindness!
                                        [Exit Gloucester.]

6   EDGAR   Frateretto calls me, and tells me Nero is an an-
gler in the Lake of Darkness. Pray, innocent; beware
the foul fiend.

FOOL   Prithee, nuncle, tell me whether a madman be a
10   gentleman or a yeoman.

LEAR   A king, a king! To have a thousand with red burning spits come hissing in upon them!

EDGAR   The foul fiend bites my back.

---

18 *apprehension* arrest   19 *comforting* abetting   22 *blood* family ties
   III.6 Within the hovel   2 *piece out* augment   4–5 *impatience* passion,
rage   5 *deserve . . . kindness* give your kindness what it deserves   6 *Frateretto*
(another devil from Harsnett's *Declaration*; see III.4.130); *Nero* (the diabolical
Roman emperor, here condemned, following Chaucer's "Monk's Tale," to fish
in the lake of Hell)   10 *yeoman* a landowner, but not a gentleman

FOOL   He's mad that trusts in the tameness of a wolf, a horse's health, a boy's love, or a whore's oath.

LEAR

It shall be done. I will arraign them straight.   16

[To Edgar]

Come, sit thou here, most learnèd justicer.

[To Fool]

Thou sapient sir, sit here. – No, you she-foxes –

EDGAR   Look where he stands and glares. Want'st thou   19
eyes at trial, madam?   20

[Sings.]

　　　Come o'er the burn, Bessy, to me.   21

FOOL

[Sings.]

　　　Her boat hath a leak,   22
　　　And she must not speak
　　　Why she dares not come over to thee.

EDGAR   The foul fiend haunts Poor Tom in the voice of a
nightingale. Hoppedance cries in Tom's belly for two   26
white herring. Croak not, black angel: I have no food   27
for thee.

KENT

How do you, sir? Stand you not so amazed.   29

Will you lie down and rest upon the cushions?   30

LEAR

I'll see their trial first. Bring in their evidence.

[To Edgar]

Thou robèd man of justice, take thy place;

---

16 *arraign . . . straight* put them on trial immediately   19–20 *Want'st . . . eyes* do you lack for spectators (?); are you blind (?)   21 *Come . . . me* (From a popular ballad; *burn* stream. The Fool's continuation is an obscene parody, punning on "burn" as the pain of venereal disease.)   22 *Her boat . . . leak* i.e., (1) from the effects of the disease, (2) because women are proverbially "leaky vessels"   26 *Hoppedance* (another devil from Harsnett)   27 *white* fresh; *Croak not* i.e., stop rumbling, belly   29 *amazed* bewildered

[To Fool]

33   And thou, his yokefellow of equity,
34   Bench by his side. *[To Kent]* You are o' th' commission,
     Sit you, too.
     EDGAR   Let us deal justly.
     [Sings.]
         Sleepest or wakest thou, jolly shepherd?
38   Thy sheep be in the corn,
39   And for one blast of thy minikin mouth
40   Thy sheep shall take no harm.
41   Pur the cat is gray.
     LEAR   Arraign her first. 'Tis Goneril. I here take my oath
     before this honorable assembly she kicked the poor
     king her father.
     FOOL   Come hither, mistress. Is your name Goneril?
     LEAR   She cannot deny it.
47   FOOL   Cry you mercy, I took you for a joint stool.
     LEAR
     And here's another, whose warped looks proclaim
49   What store her heart is made on. Stop her there!
50   Arms, arms, sword, fire! Corruption in the place!
     False justicer, why hast thou let her scape?
     EDGAR   Bless thy five wits.
     KENT
     O pity, sir, where is the patience now
     That you so oft have boasted to retain?
     EDGAR   *[Aside]*
     My tears begin to take his part so much
     They'll mar my counterfeiting.

---

33 *yokefellow . . . equity* fellow judge   34 *Bench* preside; *o' th' commission* i.e.,
presiding as a judge   38 *corn* wheat   39 *minikin* pretty little   41 *Pur the cat*
(another Harsnett devil, here taking the form of a cat)   47 *Cry . . . stool* I
beg your pardon, I mistook you for a stool – i.e., I didn't notice you (but the
stool here is standing in for Goneril)   49 *store* material; *on* of   50 *Corrup-*
tion . . . place i.e., there's bribery in the court

LEAR
The little dogs and all,   57
Trey, Blanch, and Sweetheart, see, they bark at me.
EDGAR   Tom will throw his head at them. Avaunt, you   59
curs!   60
                    Be thy mouth or black or white,   61
                    Tooth that poisons if it bite,
                    Mastiff, greyhound, mongrel grim,
                    Hound or spaniel, brach or him,   64
                    Bobtail tyke or trundle-tail,   65
                    Tom will make them weep and wail;
                    For with throwing thus my head,
                    Dogs leap the hatch, and all are fled.   68
Loudla, doodla! Come, march to wakes and fairs   69
And market towns. Poor Tom, thy horn is dry.   70
LEAR   Then let them anatomize Regan, see what breeds   71
about her heart. Is there any cause in nature that makes
this hardness? *[To Edgar]* You, sir, I entertain you for   73
one of my hundred, only I do not like the fashion of
your garments. You'll say they are Persian attire; but let   75
them be changed.
KENT   Now, good my lord, lie here awhile.
LEAR   Make no noise, make no noise; draw the curtains.   78
So, so, so. We'll go to supper i' th' morning. So, so, so.
    Enter Gloucester.
GLOUCESTER
    [To Kent]
Come hither, friend. Where is the king my master?   80

---

57 *The . . . all* even the lapdogs   59 *throw* shake; *Avaunt* get away   61 *or* either   64 *brach . . . him* bitch or male   65 *Bobtail . . . trundle-tail* short- or long-tailed mongrel   68 *hatch* (lower half of a Dutch door)   69 *wakes* festivals   70 *horn is dry* drinking horn is empty (i.e., "I've run out of steam")   71 *anatomize* dissect   73 **s.d.** or perhaps addressed to Kent, who has, ironically, been in Lear's service; *entertain* employ   75 *Persian* luxurious   78 *curtains* i.e., about an imaginary four-poster bed

KENT
>   Here, sir, but trouble him not; his wits are gone.

GLOUCESTER
>   Good friend, I prithee take him in thy arms.
> 83 I have o'erheard a plot of death upon him.
>   There is a litter ready. Lay him in't
>   And drive towards Dover, friend, where thou shalt meet
>   Both welcome and protection. Take up thy master.
>   If thou shouldst dally half an hour, his life,
>   With thine and all that offer to defend him,
> 89 Stand in assurèd loss. Take up the king,
> 90 And follow me, that will to some provision
>   Give thee quick conduct.

KENT   Oppressèd nature sleeps.
>   This rest might yet have balmed thy broken sinews
> 93 Which, if convenience will not allow,
> 94 Stand in hard cure. *[To Fool]* Come, help to bear thy
>   master.
>   Thou must not stay behind.

GLOUCESTER   Come, come away.
>   *Exeunt [carrying Lear. Edgar remains].*

EDGAR
> 96 When we our betters see bearing our woes,
>   We scarcely think our miseries our foes.
>   Who alone suffers, suffers most i' th' mind,
> 99 Leaving free things and happy shows behind.
> *100* But then the mind much sufferance doth o'erskip
> 101 When grief hath mates, and bearing fellowship.
> 102 How light and portable my pain seems now,
>   When that which makes me bend makes the king bow.
> 104 He childed as I fathered. Tom, away.

---

83 *upon* against   89 *Stand . . . loss* will surely be lost   90–91 *to . . . conduct* will quickly lead you to provisions for the journey   93 *convenience* circumstances   94 *Stand . . . cure* will be hard to cure   96 *bearing . . . woes* enduring the same suffering as we do   99 *free* carefree; *shows* scenes   101 *bearing fellowship* endurance has company   102 *portable* bearable   104 *He* he is

Mark the high noises, and thyself bewray   105
When false opinion, whose wrong thoughts defile thee,   106
In thy just proof repeals and reconciles thee.
What will hap more tonight, safe scape the king!   108
Lurk, lurk.   *[Exit.]*

*

∿ **III.7** *Enter Cornwall and Regan, and Goneril, and
Bastard [Edmund, and Servants].*

CORNWALL   *[To Goneril]* Post speedily to my lord your   1
husband; show him this letter. The army of France is
landed. *[To servants]* Seek out the villain Gloucester.
                              [Exeunt some Servants.]
REGAN   Hang him instantly!
GONERIL   Pluck out his eyes!
CORNWALL   Leave him to my displeasure. Edmund, keep
you our sister company. The revenges we are bound to   7
take upon your traitorous father are not fit for your be-
holding. Advise the duke where you are going to a most   9
festinate preparation; we are bound to the like. Our   10
post shall be swift, and intelligence betwixt us.   11
Farewell, dear sister. Farewell, my lord of Gloucester.   12
    Enter Steward [Oswald].
How now, where's the king?
OSWALD
My lord of Gloucester hath conveyed him hence.
Some five or six and thirty of his knights,
Hot questrists after him, met him at gate,   16
Who, with some other of the lord's dependents,

---

105 *Mark . . . noises* follow the news of those in power; *bewray* reveal
106–7 *When . . . repeals* when proof of your innocence vindicates **108**
What . . . more whatever more happens
    III.7 Gloucester's house   **1** *Post* ride   **7** *sister* i.e., Goneril   **9–10** *to . . .
preparation* to prepare himself quickly   **10** *are . . . to* must do   **11** *post* messenger; *intelligence* i.e., information will pass swiftly   **12** *my . . . Gloucester*
(Edmund has been given his father's title)   **16** *questrists* searchers

Are gone with him towards Dover, where they boast
To have well-armèd friends.
CORNWALL
20   Get horses for your mistress.   *[Exit Oswald.]*
GONERIL
Farewell, sweet lord, and sister.
CORNWALL   Edmund, farewell.
                              Exeunt Goneril and Edmund.
Go, seek the traitor Gloucester.
23   Pinion him like a thief; bring him before us.
                                      [Exeunt Servants.]
24   Though we may not pass upon his life
Without the form of justice, yet our power
26   Shall do a curtsy to our wrath, which men
May blame but not control.
                Enter Gloucester brought in by two or three [Servants].
                                      Who's there? The traitor?

REGAN
Ingrateful fox, 'tis he.
CORNWALL   *[To Servants]*
29   Bind fast his corky arms.
GLOUCESTER
30   What means your graces? Good my friends, consider
You are my guests. Do me no foul play, friends.
CORNWALL   *[To Servants]*
Bind him, I say.
REGAN   Hard, hard! O filthy traitor!
GLOUCESTER
33   Unmerciful lady as you are, I am true.
CORNWALL
To this chair bind him. *[To Gloucester]* Villain, thou
shalt find –
                [Regan plucks Gloucester's beard.]

---

23 *Pinion him* tie him up   **24** *pass* pass sentence   **26** *do . . . to* defer to   **29** *corky* dry, withered   **33** *true* loyal

GLOUCESTER
  By the kind gods, 'tis most ignobly done
  To pluck me by the beard.   36
REGAN
  So white, and such a traitor!   37
GLOUCESTER   Naughty lady,
  These hairs which thou dost ravish from my chin
  Will quicken and accuse thee. I am your host.   39
  With robbers' hands my hospitable favors   40
  You should not ruffle thus. What will you do?   41
CORNWALL
  Come, sir, what letters had you late from France?   42
REGAN
  Be simple, answerer, for we know the truth.   43
CORNWALL
  And what confederacy have you with the traitors
  Late footed in the kingdom?   45
REGAN   To whose hands
  You have sent the lunatic king, speak!
GLOUCESTER
  I have a letter guessingly set down,   47
  Which came from one that's of a neutral heart,
  And not from one opposed.
CORNWALL   Cunning.
REGAN   And false.
CORNWALL   Where hast thou sent the king?   50
GLOUCESTER   To Dover.
REGAN   Wherefore to Dover? Wast thou not charged at   52
  peril –
CORNWALL   Wherefore to Dover? Let him first answer
  that.

---

36 *To . . . beard* (considered an extreme insult) **37** *Naughty* evil **39** *quicken* come to life **40** *hospitable favors* welcoming face **41** *ruffle* tear at **42** *late* lately **43** *Be simple, answerer* answer plainly **45** *Late footed* lately landed **47** *guessingly* speculatively **52–53** *charged at peril* ordered at peril of your life

56 GLOUCESTER   I am tied to th' stake, and I must stand the
    course.
REGAN   Wherefore to Dover, sir?
GLOUCESTER
    Because I would not see thy cruel nails
60   Pluck out his poor old eyes, nor thy fierce sister
61   In his anointed flesh rash boarish fangs.
    The sea, with such a storm on his bowed head
63   In hell-black night endured, would have buoyed up
64   And quenched the stellèd fires.
65   Yet, poor old heart, he holped the heavens to rage.
66   If wolves had at thy gate howled that dern time,
67   Thou shouldst have said "Good porter, turn the key" –
68   All cruels else subscribe. But I shall see
69   The wingèd vengeance overtake such children.
CORNWALL
70   See't shalt thou never. Fellows, hold the chair.
    Upon those eyes of thine I'll set my foot.
GLOUCESTER
    He that will think to live till he be old
    Give me some help. O, cruel! O ye gods!
    [Cornwall puts out one of Gloucester's eyes.]
REGAN
    One side will mock another; t'other too.
CORNWALL
    If you see vengeance –
SERVANT   Hold your hand, my lord.
    I have served ever since I was a child,
    But better service have I never done you
    Than now to bid you hold.
REGAN   How now, you dog!

56–57 *I . . . course* (the image is from bearbaiting, in which the animal is tied
to a stake and attacked by dogs)   **61** *anointed* consecrated; *rash* tear   **63**
buoyed swelled   **64** *stellèd* stellar   **65** *holped* helped   **66** *dern* dreadful   **67**
turn the key open the door   **68** *All . . . subscribe* all other cruel creatures submit (to feelings of compassion) (?)   **69** *wingèd vengeance* avenging Furies

SERVANT
    If you did wear a beard upon your chin
    I'd shake it on this quarrel. What do you mean?   80
CORNWALL   My villain!   81
SERVANT
    Why then, come on, and take the chance of anger.   82
    [They] draw and fight. [Cornwall is wounded.]
REGAN
    [To another servant]
    Give me thy sword. A peasant stand up thus!
    She takes a sword and runs at him behind.
SERVANT
    O, I am slain! My lord, yet have you one eye left
    To see some mischief on him. Oh!   *[He dies.]*
CORNWALL
    Lest it see more, prevent it. Out, vile jelly!
    [He puts out Gloucester's other eye.]
    Where is thy luster now?
GLOUCESTER
    All dark and comfortless. Where's my son Edmund?
    Edmund, unbridle all the sparks of nature
    To quit this horrid act.   90
REGAN   Out, villain!
    Thou call'st on him that hates thee. It was he
    That made the overture of thy treasons to us,   92
    Who is too good to pity thee.
GLOUCESTER
    O my follies! Then Edgar was abused.   94
    Kind gods, forgive me that and prosper him!
REGAN
    Go thrust him out at gates, and let him smell
    His way to Dover.

---

80 *shake . . . quarrel* pluck it in this cause; *What . . . mean* i.e., how dare you
81 *villain* (the word retained some of its original meaning of "serf" or "servant") 82 *chance . . . anger* risk of an angry fight 90 *quit* avenge 92
made . . . of revealed 94 *abused* wronged

                              [Exit a Servant with Gloucester.]
98   How is't, my lord, how look you?
CORNWALL
        I have received a hurt. Follow me, lady.
        [To Servants]
100   Turn out that eyeless villain. Throw this slave
        Upon the dunghill. Regan, I bleed apace.
        Untimely comes this hurt. Give me your arm.
                              Exeunt [Cornwall and Regan].
SECOND SERVANT
        I'll never care what wickedness I do
        If this man come to good.
THIRD SERVANT   If she live long
105   And in the end meet the old course of death,
        Women will all turn monsters.
SECOND SERVANT
        Let's follow the old earl and get the Bedlam
        To lead him where he would. His roguish madness
        Allows itself to anything.
THIRD SERVANT
110   Go thou. I'll fetch some flax and whites of eggs
        To apply to his bleeding face. Now heaven help him!
                                                  Exeunt.

                              *

∾ **IV.1**   *Enter Edgar [as Poor Tom].*

EDGAR
1   Yet better thus and known to be contemned
2   Than still contemned and flattered. To be worst,
        The lowest and most dejected thing of fortune,
4   Stands still in esperance, lives not in fear.

---

98 *How . . . you* how do you feel   **105** *meet . . . death* i.e., die a natural death
    IV.1 Open country   **1** *contemned* despised   **2** *still* always   **4** *Stands . . .*
esperance always has hope (because he has no fear of falling lower)

The lamentable change is from the best,
The worst returns to laughter.   6
    Enter Gloucester led by an Old Man.
Who's here? My father parti-eyed? World, world, O   7
world!
But that thy strange mutations make us hate thee,   8
Life would not yield to age.   *[Stands aside.]*   9

OLD MAN   O my good lord,
I have been your tenant and your father's tenant   10
This fourscore –

GLOUCESTER
Away, get thee away, good friend, begone.
Thy comforts can do me no good at all,
Thee they may hurt.

OLD MAN
Alack, sir, you cannot see your way.

GLOUCESTER
I have no way, and therefore want no eyes.
I stumbled when I saw. Full oft 'tis seen
Our means secure us, and our mere defects   18
Prove our commodities. Ah dear son Edgar,   19
The food of thy abusèd father's wrath,   20
Might I but live to see thee in my touch,
I'd say I had eyes again.

OLD MAN   How now, who's there?

EDGAR   *[Aside]*
O gods, who is't can say "I am at the worst"?
I am worse than e'er I was.

OLD MAN   'Tis poor mad Tom.

EDGAR   *[Aside]*
And worse I may be yet. The worst is not
As long as we can say "This is the worst."

---

6 *returns to laughter* i.e., can only get better   **7** *parti-eyed* with parti-colored
eyes (because of the blood on the bandages)   **8** *But* except   **9** *yield to age* be
reconciled to growing old   **18** *Our . . . us* our prosperity makes us overconfident; *mere defects* utter deprivation   **19** *commodities* advantages   **20** *food*
prey

OLD MAN
    Fellow, where goest?
GLOUCESTER   Is it a beggarman?
OLD MAN   Madman and beggar too.
GLOUCESTER
29   A has some reason, else he could not beg.
30   In the last night's storm I such a fellow saw,
    Which made me think a man a worm. My son
    Came then into my mind, and yet my mind
    Was then scarce friends with him. I have heard more
        since.
34   As flies are to th' wanton boys are we to th' gods:
    They kill us for their sport.
EDGAR   *[Aside]*   How should this be?
36   Bad is the trade that must play the fool to sorrow,
    Ang'ring itself and others. – Bless thee, master.
GLOUCESTER
    Is that the naked fellow?
OLD MAN   Ay, my lord.
GLOUCESTER
    Then, prithee, get thee gone. If for my sake
40   Thou wilt o'ertake us here a mile or twain,
41   I' th' way toward Dover, do it for ancient love,
    And bring some covering for this naked soul,
    Who I'll entreat to lead me.
OLD MAN
    Alack, sir, he is mad.
GLOUCESTER
45   'Tis the times' plague when madmen lead the blind.
    Do as I bid thee, or rather do thy pleasure.
47   Above the rest, begone.

---

29 *A* he; *reason* sanity   **34** *wanton* playful, irresponsible   **36** *Bad . . . sorrow*
playing the fool in the presence of grief is a bad business   **41** *ancient love* our
long relationship (as lord and tenant)   **45** *times' plague* sickness of the times
47 *Above . . . rest* above all

OLD MAN
     I'll bring him the best 'parel that I have,   48
     Come on't what will.   *[Exit.]*   49
GLOUCESTER   Sirrah, naked fellow!
EDGAR   Poor Tom's acold. *[Aside]* I cannot dance it far-   50
     ther.
GLOUCESTER   Come hither, fellow.
EDGAR   Bless thy sweet eyes, they bleed.
GLOUCESTER   Know'st thou the way to Dover?
EDGAR   Both stile and gate, horseway and footpath. Poor
     Tom hath been scared out of his good wits. Bless thee,
     goodman, from the foul fiend. Five fiends have been in
     Poor Tom at once, of lust as Obidicut, Hobbididence,
     prince of dumbness, Mahu of stealing, Modo of mur-
     der, Flibbertigibbet of mopping and mowing, who   60
     since possesses chambermaids and waiting-women. So
     bless thee, master.
GLOUCESTER
     Here, take this purse, thou whom the heavens' plagues
     Have humbled to all strokes. That I am wretched   64
     Makes thee the happier. Heavens deal so still.
     Let the superfluous and lust-dieted man   66
     That stands your ordinance, that will not see   67
     Because he does not feel, feel your power quickly.
     So distribution should undo excess,
     And each man have enough. Dost thou know Dover?   70
EDGAR   Ay, master.
GLOUCESTER
     There is a cliff whose high and bending head   72
     Looks firmly in the confinèd deep.   73

---

48 *'parel* apparel 49 *Come . . . will* whatever may come of it **50–51**
dance . . . farther continue the masquerade 60 *mopping . . . mowing* making
faces 64 *humbled to* reduced to bearing meekly 66 *superfluous . . . man*
man who has too much and feeds his desires 67 *stands . . . ordinance* resists
(*stands*) heaven's command (to give to the poor) 72 *bending* overhanging
73 *in . . . deep* over the straits (of the English Channel) below

Bring me but to the very brim of it
And I'll repair the misery thou dost bear
With something rich about me. From that place
I shall no leading need.

EDGAR   Give me thy arm;
Poor Tom shall lead thee.   *[Exeunt.]*

*

∾ **IV.2** *Enter Goneril and Bastard [Edmund].*

GONERIL
    Welcome, my lord. I marvel our mild husband
2   Not met us on the way.
        Enter Steward [Oswald].
                            Now, where's your master?

OSWALD
    Madam, within; but never man so changed.
    I told him of the army that was landed;
    He smiled at it. I told him you were coming;
    His answer was "The worse." Of Gloucester's treachery
    And of the loyal service of his son
8   When I informed him, then he called me sot,
    And told me I had turned the wrong side out.
10 What he should most dislike seems pleasant to him;
    What like, offensive.

GONERIL   *[To Edmund]*
    Then shall you go no further.
13 It is the cowish terror of his spirit
14 That dares not undertake. He'll not feel wrongs
    Which tie him to an answer. Our wishes on the way
16 May prove effects. Back, Edmund, to my brother.
17 Hasten his musters and conduct his powers.

IV.2 Before Albany's castle   **2** *Not* has not   **8** *sot* fool   **13** *cowish* cowardly
14 *undertake* commit himself to action   **14–15** *He'll . . . answer* he'll ignore
injuries that require him to retaliate   **16** *prove effects* be fulfilled; *brother*
brother-in-law, Cornwall   **17** *musters* the muster of his troops; *conduct . . .*
powers guide his forces

I must change arms at home, and give the distaff   18
Into my husband's hands. This trusty servant
Shall pass between us. Ere long you are like to hear,   20
If you dare venture in your own behalf,
A mistress's command. Wear this. Spare speech.   22
Decline your head. This kiss, if it durst speak,
Would stretch thy spirits up into the air.
Conceive, and fare you well.   25

EDMUND
Yours in the ranks of death.   26

GONERIL   My most dear Gloucester!
                                   [Exit Edmund.]
To thee a woman's services are due;
A fool usurps my bed.   28

OSWALD
Madam, here comes my lord.   *Exit Steward [Oswald].*
  [Enter Albany.]

GONERIL
I have been worth the whistling.   30

ALBANY   O Goneril,
You are not worth the dust which the rude wind
Blows in your face. I fear your disposition.
That nature which contemns it origin   33
Cannot be bordered certain in itself.   34
She that herself will sliver and disbranch   35
From her material sap perforce must wither,
And come to deadly use.   37

GONERIL
No more, the text is foolish.

18–19 *give . . . hands* give my husband the housewife's spinning staff   20
like likely   22 *Wear this* (Goneril gives Edmund a lover's token, such as a
handkerchief or a glove)   25 *Conceive* understand me   26 *in the ranks of*
even up to   28 *A . . . bed* i.e., my fool of a husband wrongfully possesses me
30 *I . . . whistling* I used to be worth welcoming home (alluding to the
proverbial poor dog who is "not worth the whistling")   33 *contemns it* de-
spises its   34 *Cannot . . . certain* can have no secure boundaries   35 *sliver
and disbranch* cut herself off and split away   37 *deadly use* destructiveness

ALBANY
        Wisdom and goodness to the vile seem vile;
40   Filths savor but themselves. What have you done?
        Tigers, not daughters, what have you performed?
        A father, and a gracious agèd man,
43   Whose reverence even the head-lugged bear would lick,
44   Most barbarous, most degenerate, have you madded.
45   Could my good brother suffer you to do it,
        A man, a prince, by him so benefited?
        If that the heavens do not their visible spirits
        Send quickly down to tame these vile offenses,
        It will come –
50   Humanity must perforce prey on itself
51   Like monsters of the deep.
        GONERIL   Milk-livered man,
52   That bear'st a cheek for blows, a head for wrongs;
53   Who hast not in thy brows an eye discerning
        Thine honor from thy suffering; that not know'st
55   Fools do those villains pity who are punished
56   Ere they have done their mischief. Where's thy drum?
57   France spreads his banners in our noiseless land,
58   With plumèd helm; thy state begins thereat,
59   Whilst thou, a moral fool, sits still and cries
60   "Alack, why does he so?"
        ALBANY   See thyself, devil.
61   Proper deformity shows not in the fiend
62   So horrid as in woman.
        GONERIL   O vain fool!

---

43 *head-lugged* dragged by a chain around its neck (and thus ill-tempered)
44 *madded* driven mad   45 *brother* brother-in-law   51 *Milk-livered* cowardly   52 *for* fit for   53–54 *discerning . . . suffering* that can distinguish
what affects your honor (and thus must be resisted) from what must be endured   55 *Fools* i.e., only fools   56 *drum* i.e., why are you not mustering
your army   57 *France* the King of France; *noiseless* silent (without the sound
of military drums)   58 *thy . . . thereat* i.e., this is where the exercise of your
power should begin (a famous crux, much emended)   59 *moral* moralizing
61 *Proper . . . not* a deformed nature does not appear   62 *vain* silly, worthless

ALBANY
  Thou changèd and self-covered thing, for shame,   63
  Bemonster not thy feature. Were't my fitness   64
  To let these hands obey my blood,   65
  They are apt enough to dislocate and tear
  Thy flesh and bones. Howe'er thou art a fiend,   67
  A woman's shape doth shield thee.
GONERIL
  Marry, your manhood mew –   69
  Enter a Gentleman.
ALBANY   What news?   70
GENTLEMAN
  O my good lord, the Duke of Cornwall's dead,
  Slain by his servant, going to put out
  The other eye of Gloucester.
ALBANY   Gloucester's eyes?
GENTLEMAN
  A servant that he bred, thralled with remorse,   74
  Opposed against the act, bending his sword
  To his great master, who thereat enraged
  Flew on him, and amongst them felled him dead,
  But not without that harmful stroke which since
  Hath plucked him after.
ALBANY   This shows you are above,
  You justicers, that these our nether crimes   80
  So speedily can venge. But O, poor Gloucester,
  Lost he his other eye?
GENTLEMAN   Both, both, my lord.
  This letter, madam, craves a speedy answer.
  'Tis from your sister.
GONERIL   *[Aside]*   One way I like this well;
  But being widow, and my Gloucester with her,   85

---

63 *self-covered* hiding your true nature   **64** *Were't . . . fitness* if it were appropriate for me   **65** *blood* passion   **67** *Howe'er* although   **69** *Marry* (an interjection, originally an oath on the name of the Virgin); *your manhood mew* lock up your manhood   **74** *thralled . . . remorse* seized with pity   **80** *justicers* (heavenly) judges   **85** *being* she being

86   May all the building on my fancy pluck
87   Upon my hateful life. Another way
88   The news is not so took. I'll read and answer.   *Exit.*

ALBANY
Where was his son when they did take his eyes?

GENTLEMAN
90   Come with my lady hither.

ALBANY   He is not here.

GENTLEMAN
91   No, my good lord, I met him back again.

ALBANY
Knows he the wickedness?

GENTLEMAN
Ay, my good lord; 'twas he informed against him,
And quit the house on purpose that their punishment
Might have the freer course.

ALBANY   Gloucester, I live
To thank thee for the love thou showed'st the king,
And to revenge thy eyes. Come hither, friend,
Tell me what more thou knowest.   *Exeunt.*

∗

∾ **IV.3a** *Enter Kent [disguised] and a Gentleman.*

KENT   Why the King of France is so suddenly gone back
know you no reason?
3   GENTLEMAN   Something he left imperfect in the state
4   which since his coming forth is thought of, which imports to the kingdom so much fear and danger that his
personal return was most required and necessary.
KENT   Who hath he left behind him general?
GENTLEMAN   The Marshal of France, Monsieur La Far.

---

86 *all . . . pluck* pull down my dream castles   87 *Another way* i.e., returning
to the "One way" of l. 84   88 *not . . . took* may be taken differently   91
back returning
   IV.3a Near Dover   3 *imperfect* incomplete   4–5 *imports* threatens

KENT   Did your letters pierce the queen to any demon-
stration of grief?   *10*

GENTLEMAN

Ay, sir. She took them, read them in my presence,
And now and then an ample tear trilled down
Her delicate cheek. It seemed she was a queen
Over her passion who, most rebel-like,   *14*
Sought to be king o'er her.

KENT   O, then it moved her.

GENTLEMAN

Not to a rage. Patience and sorrow strove
Who should express her goodliest. You have seen   *17*
Sunshine and rain at once; her smiles and tears
Were like, a better way. Those happy smilets   *19*
That played on her ripe lip seem not to know   *20*
What guests were in her eyes, which parted thence
As pearls from diamonds dropped. In brief,
Sorrow would be a rarity most beloved   *23*
If all could so become it.   *24*

KENT

Made she no verbal question?

GENTLEMAN

Faith, once or twice she heaved the name of father
Pantingly forth, as if it pressed her heart,
Cried "Sisters, sisters, shame of ladies, sisters,
Kent, father, sisters, what, i' th' storm, i' th' night?
Let pity not be believed!" There she shook   *30*
The holy water from her heavenly eyes
And clamor moistened; then away she started   *32*
To deal with grief alone.

KENT   It is the stars,
The stars above us govern our conditions,

---

14 *who* which   **17** *Who . . . goodliest* which should best express her feelings
19 *like . . . way* like that, only better   **23** *rarity* jewel   **24** *all . . . it* everyone
wore it so well   **30** *Let . . . believed* never trust in pity (or, how can pity be
believed to exist)   **32** *clamor moistened* moistened her grief with tears

35   Else one self mate and make could not beget
36   Such different issues. You spoke not with her since?
GENTLEMAN   No.
KENT
    Was this before the king returned?
GENTLEMAN   No, since.
KENT
    Well, sir, the poor distressèd Lear's i' th' town,
40   Who sometime in his better tune remembers
    What we are come about, and by no means
    Will yield to see his daughter.
GENTLEMAN   Why, good sir?
KENT
    A sovereign shame so elbows him: his own unkindness,
    That stripped her from his benediction, turned her
45   To foreign casualties, gave her dear rights
    To his dog-hearted daughters, these things sting
    His mind so venomously that burning shame
    Detains him from Cordelia.
GENTLEMAN
    Alack, poor gentleman.
KENT
50   Of Albany's and Cornwall's powers you heard not?
GENTLEMAN
    'Tis so, they are afoot.
KENT
    Well, sir, I'll bring you to our master Lear,
53   And leave you to attend him. Some dear cause
    Will in concealment wrap me up awhile.
55   When I am known aright you shall not grieve
    Lending me this acquaintance. I pray you go
    Along with me.   *Exeunt.*

                    *

---

35 *one . . . make* one married couple ("mate" and "make" both mean "spouse")
36 *issues* offspring   40 *better tune* more rational state   45 *casualties* dangers;
dear valuable   50 *powers* forces   53 *dear* important   55 *grieve* regret

∾ **IV.3b** *Enter Cordelia, Doctor, and others.*

CORDELIA
Alack, 'tis he. Why, he was met even now,
As mad as the vexed sea, singing aloud,
Crowned with rank fumiter and furrow weeds,   3
With hardocks, hemlock, nettles, cuckooflowers,
Darnel, and all the idle weeds that grow   5
In our sustaining corn. A century is sent forth.   6
Search every acre in the high-grown field,
And bring him to our eye. What can man's wisdom   8
In the restoring his bereavèd sense,
He that can help him, take all my outward worth.   10
DOCTOR
There is means, madam.
Our foster nurse of nature is repose,   12
The which he lacks; that to provoke in him   13
Are many simples operative, whose power   14
Will close the eye of anguish.
CORDELIA   All blest secrets,
All you unpublished virtues of the earth,   16
Spring with my tears, be aidant and remediate   17
In the good man's distress! Seek, seek for him,
Lest his ungoverned rage dissolve the life
That wants the means to lead it.   20
       Enter Messenger.
MESSENGER   News, madam.
The British powers are marching hitherward.
CORDELIA
'Tis known before; our preparation stands

IV.3b The French camp   **3** *fumiter* fumitory (this and the following are all
field weeds)   **5** *idle* useless, uncultivated   **6** *sustaining corn* life-sustaining
wheat; *century* troop of one hundred soldiers   **8** *What... wisdom* whatever
man's wisdom can do   **10** *outward worth* material possessions   **12** *Our...
nature* what naturally cares for us   **13** *provoke* induce   **14** *simples operative*
herbal remedies   **16** *unpublished virtues* secret powers   **17** *be... remediate*
aid and heal   **20** *wants* lacks

In expectation of them. O dear father,
It is thy business that I go about;
25   Therefore great France
26   My mourning and important tears hath pitied.
27   No blown ambition doth our arms incite,
But love, dear love, and our agèd father's right.
Soon may I hear and see him!   *Exeunt.*

*

∾ **IV.4** *Enter Regan and Steward [Oswald].*

REGAN
1   But are my brother's powers set forth?
OSWALD   Ay, madam.
REGAN
2   Himself in person?
OSWALD   Madam with much ado.
Your sister is the better soldier.
REGAN   Lord Edmund spake not with your lady at
home?
OSWALD   No, madam.
REGAN   What might import my sister's letters to him?
OSWALD   I know not, lady.
REGAN
9   Faith, he is posted hence on serious matter.
10   It was great ignorance, Gloucester's eyes being out,
To let him live; where he arrives he moves
All hearts against us, and now, I think, is gone,
In pity of his misery, to dispatch
14   His nighted life; moreover to descry
The strength o' th' army.

---

25 *France* the King of France   26 *important* urgent, of great import   27
blown presumptuous
    IV.4 Gloucester's house   1 *brother's powers* Albany's forces   2 *ado* diffi-
culty   9 *is posted hence* rushed away from here   14 *nighted* (1) benighted,
(2) blind; *descry* spy out

OSWALD
　I must needs after him with my letters.
REGAN
　Our troop sets forth tomorrow. Stay with us.
　The ways are dangerous.
OSWALD　　　　　　　　　　I may not, madam;
　My lady charged my duty in this business.　　　　　　19
REGAN
　Why should she write to Edmund? Might not you　　20
　Transport her purposes by word? Belike –　　　　21
　Something, I know not what. I'll love thee much;
　Let me unseal the letter.
OSWALD　　　　　　　　　Madam I'd rather –
REGAN
　I know your lady does not love her husband;
　I am sure of that, and at her late being here　　　25
　She gave strange oeillades and most speaking looks　26
　To noble Edmund. I know you are of her bosom.　27
OSWALD　I, madam?
REGAN
　I speak in understanding, for I know't.　　　　　29
　Therefore I do advise you take this note.　　　　30
　My lord is dead; Edmund and I have talked,
　And more convenient is he for my hand　　　　　32
　Than for your lady's – you may gather more.　　　33
　If you do find him, pray you give him this;　　　34
　And when your mistress hears thus much from you,
　I pray desire her call her wisdom to her.　　　　36

---

19 *charged* strictly commanded　21 *Belike* perhaps　25 *late* recently　26 *oeillades* amorous glances　27 *of . . . bosom* in her confidence (with a sexual overtone)　29 *understanding* certain knowledge　30 *take . . . note* take note of this　32 *convenient* appropriate　33 *gather more* infer more (from what I say)　34 *this* (Perhaps a token; perhaps a letter: Edgar finds only Goneril's letter in Oswald's pockets in IV.5.253 ff., but Oswald, dying, speaks of "letters," so perhaps Edgar misses one. "Letters," on the other hand, could be singular.)　36 *wisdom to her* back to reason

So, farewell.
If you do chance to hear of that blind traitor,
39　Preferment falls on him that cuts him off.
OSWALD
40　Would I could meet him, madam. I would show
What lady I do follow.
REGAN　　　　　　　　　　　Fare thee well.　　　　*Exeunt.*

*

∾ **IV.5** *Enter Gloucester and Edgar [disguised as a peasant].*

GLOUCESTER
When shall we come to th' top of that same hill?
EDGAR
You do climb it up now; look how we labor!
GLOUCESTER
Methinks the ground is even.
EDGAR　　　　　　　　　　　Horrible steep.
Hark, do you hear the sea?
GLOUCESTER　　　　　　　No, truly.
EDGAR
Why then your other senses grow imperfect
By your eyes' anguish.
GLOUCESTER　　　　　So may it be indeed.
Methinks thy voice is altered, and thou speakest
With better phrase and matter than thou didst.
EDGAR
You're much deceived: in nothing am I changed
10　But in my garments.
GLOUCESTER　　　　　　Methinks you're better spoken.
EDGAR
Come on, sir, here's the place. Stand still. How fearful
And dizzy 'tis to cast one's eyes so low!

---

39 *cuts him off* cuts short his life
IV.5 Open country near Dover

The crows and choughs that wing the midway air   13
Show scarce so gross as beetles. Halfway down   14
Hangs one that gathers samphire, dreadful trade!   15
Methinks he seems no bigger than his head.
The fishermen that walk upon the beach
Appear like mice, and yon tall anchoring bark   18
Diminished to her cock, her cock a buoy   19
Almost too small for sight. The murmuring surge   20
That on the unnumbered idle pebble chafes   21
Cannot be heard, it's so high. I'll look no more,
Lest my brain turn and the deficient sight
Topple down headlong.   24
GLOUCESTER   Set me where you stand.
EDGAR
Give me your hand. You are now within a foot
Of th' extreme verge. For all beneath the moon
Would I not leap upright.   27
GLOUCESTER   Let go my hand.
Here, friend, 's another purse; in it a jewel
Well worth a poor man's taking. Fairies and gods
Prosper it with thee! Go thou farther off;   30
Bid me farewell, and let me hear thee going.
EDGAR
Now fare you well, good sir.
GLOUCESTER   With all my heart.
EDGAR *[Aside]*
Why I do trifle thus with his despair
Is done to cure it.
GLOUCESTER   O you mighty gods.
    He kneels.

---

13 *choughs* jackdaws (pronounced "chuffs") **14** *Show* appear; *gross* large
15 *samphire* (Saint Peter's herb, used in pickling; it grows on steep cliffs,
hence the danger in gathering it) **18** *bark* ship **19** *cock* dinghy **21** *unnumbered . . . pebble* barren reach of innumerable pebbles **24** *Topple* topple
me **27** *leap upright* jump upward (to jump forward would reveal to
Gloucester that he is not on the edge of a cliff) **30** *Prosper* increase

This world I do renounce, and in your sights
Shake patiently my great affliction off.
If I could bear it longer, and not fall
To quarrel with your great opposeless wills,
39   My snuff and loathèd part of nature should
40   Burn itself out. If Edgar live, O bless him!
Now, fellow, fare thee well.

EDGAR   Gone, sir, farewell.
        [Gloucester falls forward.]
        [Aside]
42   And yet I know not how conceit may rob
The treasury of life, when life itself
44   Yields to the theft. Had he been where he thought,
45   By this had thought been past. – Alive or dead?
Ho you, sir! Hear you, sir? Speak!
        [Aside]
47   Thus might he pass indeed. Yet he revives.
– What are you, sir?

GLOUCESTER   Away, and let me die.

EDGAR
49   Hadst thou been aught but gossamer, feathers, air,
50   So many fathom down precipitating,
51   Thou hadst shivered like an egg; but thou dost breathe,
Hast heavy substance, bleed'st not, speak'st, art sound.
53   Ten masts at each make not the altitude
Which thou hast perpendicularly fell.
Thy life's a miracle. Speak yet again.

GLOUCESTER
But have I fallen or no?

EDGAR
57   From the dread summit of this chalky bourn.

―――――――

39 *snuff* burnt-out candle end; *loathèd . . . nature* despised remnant of life
42 *conceit* illusion, imagination   **44** *Yields to* accedes to, welcomes   **45** *this*
this time   **47** *pass indeed* really die   **49** *aught* anything   **51** *shivered* shat-
tered   **53** *at each* placed end to end   **57** *chalky bourn* chalk cliff (the White
Cliffs of Dover)

Look up a-height. The shrill-gorged lark so far   58
Cannot be seen or heard. Do but look up.

GLOUCESTER

Alack, I have no eyes.   60
Is wretchedness deprived that benefit   61
To end itself by death? 'Twas yet some comfort
When misery could beguile the tyrant's rage   63
And frustrate his proud will.

EDGAR   Give me your arm.
Up; so. How feel you your legs? You stand.

GLOUCESTER

Too well, too well.

EDGAR   This is above all strangeness.
Upon the crown of the cliff what thing was that
Which parted from you?

GLOUCESTER   A poor unfortunate beggar.

EDGAR

As I stood here below, methoughts his eyes
Were two full moons. A had a thousand noses,   70
Horns whelked and waved like the enridgèd sea.   71
It was some fiend. Therefore, thou happy father,   72
Think that the clearest gods, who made their honors   73
Of men's impossibilities, have preserved thee.

GLOUCESTER

I do remember now. Henceforth I'll bear
Affliction till it do cry out itself
"Enough, enough," and die. That thing you speak of,
I took it for a man. Often would it say
"The fiend, the fiend." He led me to that place.

EDGAR

Bear free and patient thoughts.   80
          Enter Lear mad [, crowned with weeds].

---

58 *shrill-gorged* shrill-voiced 61 *deprived* denied 63 *beguile* cheat 70 *A*
he 71 *whelked* twisted 72 *happy father* lucky old man 73 *clearest* wisest,
most glorious 73–74 *who . . . impossibilities* whose glory consists in performing miracles

> But who comes here?

81 The safer sense will ne'er accommodate
His master thus.

83 LEAR   No, they cannot touch me for coining; I am the
king himself.

EDGAR   O thou side-piercing sight!

86 LEAR   Nature is above art in that respect. There's your
87 press money. That fellow handles his bow like a
88 crowkeeper. Draw me a clothier's yard. Look, look, a
89 mouse! Peace, peace, this toasted cheese will do it.
90 There's my gauntlet. I'll prove it on a giant. Bring up
91 the brown bills. O, well flown bird, in the air. Ha! Give
92 the word.

EDGAR   Sweet marjoram.

LEAR   Pass.

GLOUCESTER   I know that voice.

96 LEAR   Ha, Goneril! Ha, Regan! They flattered me like a
97 dog, and told me I had white hairs in my beard ere the
black ones were there. To say "ay" and "no" to every-
99 thing I said "ay" and "no" to was no good divinity.
100 When the rain came to wet me once, and the wind to
make me chatter, when the thunder would not peace at
102 my bidding, there I found them, there I smelt them
out. Go to, they are not men of their words. They told
104 me I was everything. 'Tis a lie; I am not ague-proof.

---

81 *The . . . sense* a sane mind; *accommodate* array   83 *touch* arrest; *coining*
counterfeiting (because minting money was a royal prerogative)   86
Nature . . . respect i.e., kings are born, not made   87 *press money* payment for
volunteering or being drafted to fight (Lear is conscripting an imaginary
army)   88 *crowkeeper* scarecrow; *Draw . . . yard* draw the bow out fully (a
clothier's yard, 37 inches, was the length of an arrow)   89 *do it* catch the
mouse   90 *gauntlet* armored glove (thrown down as a challenge); *prove it on*
uphold my cause against   91 *brown bills* pike carriers (Lear continues to assemble his army); *bird* arrow   92 *word* password   96–97 *like a dog* as a dog
does (i.e., they fawned on me)   97 *white . . . beard* i.e., the wisdom of age
99 *no . . . divinity* bad theology   102 *found them* found them out   104
ague-proof immune to fever

GLOUCESTER
    The trick of that voice I do well remember.   105
    Is't not the king?
LEAR   Ay, every inch a king.
    When I do stare, see how the subject quakes.
    I pardon that man's life. What was thy cause?   108
    Adultery? Thou shalt not die for adultery.
    No, the wren goes to't, and the small gilded fly   110
    Does lecher in my sight.
    Let copulation thrive, for Gloucester's bastard son
    Was kinder to his father than my daughters
    Got 'tween the lawful sheets. To't, luxury, pell-mell,   114
    For I lack soldiers. Behold yon simp'ring dame
    Whose face between her forks presageth snow,   116
    That minces virtue, and does shake the head   117
    To hear of pleasure's name:
    The fitchew nor the soilèd horse goes to't   119
    With a more riotous appetite. Down from the waist   120
    They're centaurs, though women all above;   121
    But to the girdle do the gods inherit,   122
    Beneath is all the fiend's: there's hell, there's darkness,
    There's the sulphury pit, burning, scalding;
    Stench, consummation. Fie, fie, fie; pah, pah!
    Give me an ounce of civet, good apothecary,   126
    To sweeten my imagination.
    There's money for thee.
GLOUCESTER   O, let me kiss that hand.
LEAR   Here, wipe it first; it smells of mortality.   130

---

105 *trick* special quality 108 *cause* offense 114 *Got* begotten; *luxury* lechery 116 *face . . . forks* (1) her face between the combs that hold her hair in place, (2) her genitals between her forked legs; *snow* sexual coldness, frigidity 117 *minces* affects 119 *fitchew* (1) polecat, (2) prostitute; *soilèd* pastured, well-fed 121 *centaurs* (the classical centaurs were men to the waist and horses below, and were notoriously lustful) 122 *But . . . girdle* only down to the waist; *inherit* possess 126 *civet* perfume

GLOUCESTER

131   O ruined piece of nature! This great world

132   Should so wear out to naught. Do you know me?

LEAR I remember thy eyes well enough. Dost thou

134   squiny on me? No, do thy worst, blind Cupid, I'll not
love. Read thou that challenge. Mark the penning of't.

GLOUCESTER
Were all the letters suns, I could not see one.

EDGAR

137   I would not take this from report. It is,
And my heart breaks at it.

LEAR Read.

140 GLOUCESTER What, with the case of eyes?

141 LEAR O, ho, are you there with me? No eyes in your
head, nor no money in your purse? Your eyes are in a

143   heavy case, your purse in a light; yet you see how this
world goes.

GLOUCESTER I see it feelingly.

LEAR What, art mad? A man may see how the world
goes with no eyes. Look with thy ears. See how yon jus-

148   tice rails upon yon simple thief. Hark in thy ear:

149   handy-dandy, which is the thief, which is the justice?

150   Thou hast seen a farmer's dog bark at a beggar?

GLOUCESTER Ay, sir.

152 LEAR And the creature run from the cur? There thou
mightst behold the great image of authority: a dog's

154   obeyed in office.

155   Thou rascal beadle, hold thy bloody hand.
Why dost thou lash that whore? Strip thine own back.

157   Thy blood hotly lusts to use her in that kind

---

131 *piece* masterpiece   132 *so . . . naught* decay to nothing in the same way
134 *squiny* squint   137 *take* believe; *is* is actually happening   140 *case* sockets   141 *are . . . me* is that what you mean (with an overtone of "Are we
both blind?")   143 *heavy case* sad situation   148 *simple* mere   149 *handy-
dandy* the child's game "choose a hand"   152 *creature* man   154 *in office* in
a position of power   155 *beadle* church constable   157 *kind* way

For which thou whipp'st her. The usurer hangs the   158
cozener.
Through tattered rags small vices do appear;
Robes and furred gowns hides all. Get thee glass eyes,   160
And like a scurvy politician seem   161
To see the things thou dost not. No. Now,   *[Sits.]*
Pull off my boots; harder, harder! So.

EDGAR   *[Aside]*
O matter and impertinency mixed,   164
Reason in madness.

LEAR
If thou wilt weep my fortune, take my eyes.
I know thee well enough; thy name is Gloucester.
Thou must be patient; we came crying hither.
Thou knowest the first time that we smell the air,
We wail and cry. I will preach to thee: mark me.   *170*

GLOUCESTER   Alack, alack, the day.

LEAR
When we are born, we cry that we are come
To this great stage of fools. This' a good block.   173
It were a delicate stratagem to shoe   174
A troop of horse with felt; and when I have stole upon
These son-in-laws, then kill, kill, kill, kill, kill, kill!
Enter three Gentlemen.

GENTLEMAN
O, here he is. Lay hands upon him, sirs.
[To Lear]
Your most dear —

LEAR
No rescue? What, a prisoner? I am e'en

---

158 *usurer . . . cozener* i.e., the big thief hangs the little one; *usurer* moneylender; *cozener* cheat   160 *glass eyes* eyeglasses   161 *scurvy politician* vile
Machiavel   164 *matter . . . impertinency* sense and nonsense   173 *This'* this
is; *block* felt hat (either the hat decked with weeds, which he removes to
begin his sermon, or an imaginary hat suggested by the crown of weeds)
174–75 *shoe . . . felt* (and thus enable them to approach silently)

180   The natural fool of fortune. Use me well.
      You shall have ransom. Let me have a surgeon;
      I am cut to the brains.
      GENTLEMAN   You shall have anything.
      LEAR
184   No seconds? all myself?
185   Why, this would make a man of salt,
186   To use his eyes for garden waterpots,
      Ay, and laying autumn's dust.
      GENTLEMAN   Good sir –
      LEAR
188   I will die bravely, like a bridegroom.
      What, I will be jovial. Come, come,
190   I am a king, my masters, know you that?
      GENTLEMAN
      You are a royal one, and we obey you.
192   LEAR   Then there's life in't. Nay, an you get it, you shall
      get it with running.
        Exit King [Lear] running [pursued by two Gentlemen].
      GENTLEMAN
      A sight most pitiful in the meanest wretch,
      Past speaking of in a king. Thou hast one daughter
196   Who redeems nature from the general curse
      Which twain hath brought her to.
      EDGAR   Hail, gentle sir.
      GENTLEMAN
198   Sir, speed you; what's your will?
      EDGAR
199   Do you hear aught of a battle toward?

---

180 *natural fool* born plaything; *Use* treat **184** *seconds* supporters **185** *salt* tears **186** *waterpots* watering cans **188** *die* (with a quibble on the sexual sense, have an orgasm); *bravely* (1) courageously (2) handsomely **192** *there's . . . in't* i.e., there's still hope; *an* if **196–97** *general . . . to* the universal disruption caused by your other two daughters (but also the original sin caused by the filial ingratitude of the original pair, Adam and Eve) **197** *gentle* noble **198** *speed* God prosper **199** *toward* impending

GENTLEMAN
　Most sure and vulgar; everyone hears that　　　　　200
　That can distinguish sense.　　　　　　　　　　　201
EDGAR　　　　　　　　　　But, by your favor,
　How near's the other army?
GENTLEMAN
　Near and on speed for't; the main descries　　　　203
　Stands on the hourly thoughts.
EDGAR
　I thank you, sir; that's all.
GENTLEMAN
　Though that the queen on special cause is here,　　206
　Her army is moved on.
EDGAR　　　　　　　　　I thank you, sir.
　　　　　　　　　　　　　　Exit [Gentleman].

GLOUCESTER
　You ever gentle gods, take my breath from me.
　Let not my worser spirit tempt me again　　　　　209
　To die before you please.　　　　　　　　　　　210
EDGAR　　　　　　　　　Well pray you, father.
GLOUCESTER
　Now, good sir, what are you?
EDGAR
　A most poor man made lame by fortune's blows,
　Who, by the art of known and feeling sorrows,　　213
　Am pregnant to good pity. Give me your hand,　　214
　I'll lead you to some biding.　　　　　　　　　　215
GLOUCESTER　　　　　　　Hearty thanks.
　The bounty and the benison of heaven　　　　　　216
　To boot, to boot.

---

200 *vulgar* common knowledge　**201** *That* who　**203** *on speed* in haste
203–4 *the . . . thoughts* the sight of the main body is expected hourly　**206**
Though that however; *on . . . cause* for a particular reason　**209** *worser spirit*
"bad side"　**210** *father* old man　**213** *art . . . sorrows* lesson of sorrows experienced and deeply felt　**214** *pregnant* prone　**215** *biding* dwelling　**216–17**
bounty . . . boot may it bring you the bounty and a blessing of heaven in addition

Enter Steward [Oswald].

OSWALD
218 A proclaimed prize! Most happy!
219 That eyeless head of thine was first framed flesh
220 To raise my fortunes. Thou most unhappy traitor,
221 Briefly thyself remember. The sword is out
     That must destroy thee.
     GLOUCESTER   Now let thy friendly hand
     Put strength enough to't.
          [Edgar interposes.]
     OSWALD   Wherefore, bold peasant,
224 Durst thou support a published traitor? Hence,
     Lest the infection of his fortune take
     Like hold on thee. Let go his arm.
227 EDGAR   'Chill not let go, sir, without 'cagion.
     OSWALD   Let go, slave, or thou diest.
229 EDGAR   Good gentleman, go your gate. Let poor volk
230 pass. An 'chud have been swaggered out of my life, it
     would not have been so long by a vortnight. Nay, come
232 not near the old man. Keep out, 'che vor' ye, or I'll try
233 whether your costard or my bat be the harder, I'll be
     plain with you.
     OSWALD   Out, dunghill!
          They fight.
236 EDGAR   'Chill pick your teeth, sir. Come, no matter for
237 your foins.
          [Oswald falls.]
     OSWALD
     Slave, thou hast slain me. Villain, take my purse.

---

218 *proclaimed prize* criminal with a price on his head; *happy* lucky **219**
framed flesh made human   **221** *thyself remember* i.e., remember your sins and
pray   **224** *published* proclaimed   **227** *'Chill* I'll (Edgar adopts a west country dialect); *'cagion* occasion, cause   **229** *go your gate* be on your way   **230**
An . . . swaggered if I could have been bullied   **232** *'che vor' ye* I warn you
233 *your . . . bat* your head or my cudgel   **236** *pick . . . teeth* i.e., with my
club   **237** *foins* sword thrusts

If ever thou wilt thrive, bury my body,
And give the letters which thou find'st about me   240
To Edmund, Earl of Gloucester. Seek him out
Upon the British party. O untimely death! Death –   242
He dies.

EDGAR
I know thee well: a serviceable villain,
As duteous to the vices of thy mistress
As badness would desire.

GLOUCESTER   What, is he dead?

EDGAR
Sit you down, father, rest you.
Let's see his pockets. These letters that he speaks of
May be my friends. He's dead; I am only sorrow   248
He had no other deathsman. Let us see.
Leave, gentle wax, and manners blame us not.   250
To know our enemies' minds we'd rip their hearts;
Their papers is more lawful.   252
[Reads] a letter.
"Let your reciprocal vows be remembered. You have
many opportunities to cut him off. If your will want   254
not, time and place will be fruitfully offered. There is   255
nothing done if he return the conqueror; then am I the   256
prisoner, and his bed my jail, from the loathed warmth
whereof deliver me, and supply the place for your   258
labor.
Your wife – so I would say – your affectionate ser-   260
vant, and for you her own for venture,
Goneril."

---

240 *letters* (Oswald has a letter for Edmund from Goneril; if he has indeed
been given one by Regan too, as is implied at IV.4.34, Edgar fails to find it.
But "letters" may be singular – the letters that together compose one letter –
as at I.5.2.)   242 *Upon* among   248 *I . . . sorrow* my only sorrow is   250
Leave . . . wax by your leave, kind seal   252 *Their* to rip their   254 *him* Albany   254–55 *If . . . not* if you do not lack the will   255 *fruitfully* i.e.,
promising success   256 *done* accomplished   258 *supply* fill

263   O indistinguished space of woman's wit!
       A plot upon her virtuous husband's life,
       And the exchange my brother! – Here in the sands
266   Thee I'll rake up, the post unsanctified
267   Of murderous lechers, and in the mature time
       With this ungracious paper strike the sight
269   Of the death-practiced duke. For him 'tis well
270   That of thy death and business I can tell.
                                    [Exit with Oswald's body.]

GLOUCESTER
271   The king is mad. How stiff is my vile sense,
272   That I stand up and have ingenious feeling
273   Of my huge sorrows! Better I were distract,
       So should my thoughts be fencèd from my griefs,
275   And woes by wrong imaginations lose
       The knowledge of themselves.
          [Enter Edgar.] A drum afar off.
EDGAR   Give me your hand.
       Far off, methinks, I hear the beaten drum.
       Come, father, I'll bestow you with a friend.   *Exeunt.*

                         *

∾ **IV.6** *Enter Cordelia, [and] Kent [disguised].*

CORDELIA
       O thou good Kent,
       How shall I live and work to match thy goodness?
       My life will be too short, and every measure fail me.

---

263 *indistinguished* unlimited; *wit* cunning   **266** *rake up* cover over; *post unsanctified* unholy messenger   **267** *in . . . time* when the time is ripe   **269** *death-practiced* whose death is plotted   **270 s.d.** None of the original texts makes any provision for the removal of Oswald's body. Editors since the eighteenth century have had Edgar exit here dragging it offstage, and then return six lines later. The very awkward alternative is for him to remove it while he is also leading Gloucester offstage.   **271** *How . . . sense* how obstinate is my hateful consciousness   **272** *ingenious* rational, intelligent   **273** *distract* mad   **275** *wrong imaginations* delusions
    IV.6 The French camp

KENT

To be acknowledged, madam, is o'erpaid. 4
All my reports go with the modest truth, 5
Nor more, nor clipped, but so. 6

CORDELIA Be better suited.

These weeds are memories of those worser hours; 7
I prithee put them off.

KENT Pardon me, dear madam.

Yet to be known shortens my made intent. 9
My boon I make it that you know me not 10
Till time and I think meet. 11

CORDELIA

Then be't so, my good lord.
    [Enter Doctor and Gentleman.]
            – How does the king?

DOCTOR Madam, sleeps still.

CORDELIA

O you kind gods,
Cure this great breach in his abusèd nature;
The untuned and jarring senses O wind up 16
Of this child-changèd father. 17

DOCTOR So please your majesty

That we may wake the king? He hath slept long.

CORDELIA

Be governed by your knowledge, and proceed
I' th' sway of your own will. Is he arrayed? 20

GENTLEMAN

Ay, madam. In the heaviness of his sleep
We put fresh garments on him.

---

4 *o'erpaid* more than sufficient 5 *go* accord 6 *clipped* less; *suited* dressed 7 *weeds* clothes; *memories* reminders 9 *Yet . . . intent* to reveal myself now would spoil my plan (for Lear to recognize him as Kent) 10 *My . . . it* I ask as my reward 11 *meet* suitable 16 *jarring* discordant; *wind up* put in tune 17 *child-changèd* (1) changed by his children, (2) changed into a child 20 *I' th' sway . . . will* as you see fit; *arrayed* properly dressed

DOCTOR
Good madam, be by when we do awake him.
24   I doubt not of his temperance.
CORDELIA   Very well.
  [Music.]
DOCTOR
Please you draw near. Louder the music there.
  [Lear is revealed asleep.]
CORDELIA
O my dear father, restoration hang
Thy medicine on my lips, and let this kiss
Repair those violent harms that my two sisters
29   Have in thy reverence made.
KENT   Kind and dear princess!
CORDELIA
30   Had you not been their father, these white flakes
31   Had challenged pity of them. Was this a face
To be exposed against the warring winds,
To stand against the deep dread-bolted thunder
In the most terrible and nimble stroke
35   Of quick cross-lightning, to watch, poor *perdu,*
36   With this thin helm? Mine injurious dog,
Though he had bit me, should have stood that night
38   Against my fire; and wast thou fain, poor father,
To hovel thee with swine and rogues forlorn
40   In short and musty straw? Alack, alack,
'Tis wonder that thy life and wits at once
Had not concluded all. – He wakes. Speak to him.
DOCTOR
Madam, do you; 'tis fittest.
CORDELIA
How does my royal lord? How fares your majesty?

---

24 *temperance* self-control   29 *in . . . reverence* on the dignity of your age
30 *flakes* hairs   31 *challenged* demanded   35 *watch* stand guard; *perdu* exposed (and expendable) sentry   36 *helm* helmet (i.e., his white hair)   38 *Against* beside; *fain* obliged   40 *short* broken

LEAR
You do me wrong to take me out o' th' grave.
Thou art a soul in bliss, but I am bound
Upon a wheel of fire, that mine own tears   47
Do scald like molten lead.
CORDELIA   Sir, know me.
LEAR
You're a spirit, I know. Where did you die?
CORDELIA
Still, still far wide.   50
DOCTOR
He's scarce awake. Let him alone awhile.
LEAR
Where have I been? Where am I? Fair daylight?
I am mightily abused. I should e'en die with pity   53
To see another thus. I know not what to say.
I will not swear these are my hands. Let's see:
I feel this pin prick. Would I were assured
Of my condition.
CORDELIA   O look upon me, sir,
And hold your hands in benediction o'er me.
No, sir, you must not kneel.
LEAR   Pray do not mock.
I am a very foolish fond old man,   60
Fourscore and upward, and, to deal plainly,
I fear I am not in my perfect mind.
Methinks I should know you, and know this man;
Yet I am doubtful, for I am mainly ignorant   64
What place this is; and all the skill I have
Remembers not these garments; nor I know not
Where I did lodge last night. Do not laugh at me,

---

47 *wheel of fire* (the image combines the wheel on which prisoners were
bound for beatings with the burning of heretics or of souls in hell)   50 *wide*
wide of the mark   53 *abused* ill-used, deceived   60 *fond* (the word also
means "foolish")   64 *mainly* entirely

For, as I am a man, I think this lady
To be my child Cordelia.

CORDELIA   And so I am.

LEAR

70   Be your tears wet? Yes, faith. I pray, weep not.
If you have poison for me, I will drink it.
I know you do not love me, for your sisters
Have, as I do remember, done me wrong.
You have some cause, they have not.

CORDELIA   No cause, no cause.

LEAR

Am I in France?

KENT   In your own kingdom, sir.

LEAR

76   Do not abuse me.

DOCTOR

Be comforted, good madam. The great rage,
You see, is cured in him, and yet it is danger

79   To make him even o'er the time he has lost.

80   Desire him to go in; trouble him no more

81   Till further settling.

CORDELIA

Will't please your highness walk?

LEAR   You must bear with me.
Pray now, forget and forgive. I am old and foolish.

Exeunt [Lear, Cordelia, and Doctor]. Kent and Gentle-
man remain.

GENTLEMAN   Holds it true, sir, that the Duke of Cornwall was so slain?

KENT   Most certain, sir.

87   GENTLEMAN   Who is conductor of his people?

KENT   As 'tis said, the bastard son of Gloucester.

---

76 *abuse* deceive   79 *even o'er* fill in   81 *settling* calm sets in   87 *conduc-*
tor . . . people commander of his forces

GENTLEMAN   They say Edgar, his banished son, is with
   the Earl of Kent in Germany.   *90*
KENT   Report is changeable. 'Tis time to look about. The   *91*
   powers of the kingdom approach apace.   *92*
GENTLEMAN   The arbitrament is like to be bloody. Fare   *93*
   you well, sir.   *[Exit.]*
KENT
   My point and period will be throughly wrought,   *95*
   Or well or ill, as this day's battle's fought.   *Exit.*   *96*

*

∾ **V.1** *Enter Edmund, Regan, and their powers.*

EDMUND   *[To a Gentleman]*
   Know of the duke if his last purpose hold,   *1*
   Or whether since he is advised by aught   *2*
   To change the course. He's full of alteration
   And self-reproving. Bring his constant pleasure.   *4*
                                   [Exit Gentleman.]
REGAN
   Our sister's man is certainly miscarried.   *5*
EDMUND
   'Tis to be doubted, madam.   *6*
REGAN   Now, sweet lord,
   You know the goodness I intend upon you.
   Tell me but truly, but then speak the truth,
   Do you not love my sister?   *9*
EDMUND   Ay, honored love.

---

91 *Report* rumor; *look about* see to our preparations   92 *powers* forces   93
arbitrament action   95 *My . . . wrought* my purpose and end will be fully
completed   96 *Or* either
      V.1 The British camp   1 *Know . . . hold* find out from Albany if his most
recent intention (to join in the fight against Cordelia's forces) still holds good
2 *since* since then   4 *constant pleasure* firm decision   5 *sister's man* Oswald;
is . . . miscarried has certainly met with an accident   6 *doubted* feared   9
honored honorable

REGAN

10 But have you never found my brother's way
11 To the forfended place?

EDMUND   That thought abuses you.

REGAN

12 I am doubtful that you have been conjunct
13 And bosomed with her, as far as we call hers.

EDMUND

No, by mine honor, madam.

REGAN

I never shall endure her. Dear my lord,
16 Be not familiar with her.

EDMUND   Fear me not.

She and the duke her husband –

Enter Albany and Goneril with troops.

GONERIL *[Aside]*

I had rather lose the battle than that sister
Should loosen him and me.

ALBANY

20 Our very loving sister, well bemet,
For this I hear: the king is come to his daughter,
22 With others whom the rigor of our state
23 Forced to cry out. Where I could not be honest
I never yet was valiant. For this business,
25 It touches us as France invades our land,
26 Not bolds the king, with others whom, I fear,
27 Most just and heavy causes make oppose.

EDMUND

28 Sir, you speak nobly.

REGAN   Why is this reasoned?

---

10 *brother's* Albany's 11 *forfended* forbidden; *abuses* is unworthy of 12
doubtful suspicious 12–13 *conjunct . . . her* in complicity with her, and her
lover 13 *as . . . hers* as completely hers as you can be 16 *familiar* intimate;
Fear doubt 22 *rigor . . . state* harshness of our rule 23 *be honest* behave
honorably 25 *touches* concerns 26 *Not bolds* not because he emboldens
27 *heavy* serious 28 *Why . . . reasoned?* i.e., why are you telling us this

GONERIL
   Combine together 'gainst the enemy,   29
   For these domestic door particulars   30
   Are not to question here.   31
ALBANY   Let us then determine
   With the ensign of war on our proceedings.   32
EDMUND
   I shall attend you presently at your tent.   *[Exit.]*
REGAN   Sister, you'll go with us?
GONERIL   No.
REGAN
   'Tis most convenient; pray you, go with us.   36
GONERIL   *[Aside]*
   O, ho, I know the riddle. I will go.   37
     Enter Edgar [disguised].
EDGAR
   If e'er your grace had speech with man so poor,
   Hear me one word.
            Exeunt [all except Edgar and Albany].
ALBANY   *[To the departing forces]*
   I'll overtake you. *[To Edgar]* Speak.   40
EDGAR
   Before you fight the battle, ope this letter.
   If you have victory, let the trumpet sound
   For him that brought it. Wretched though I seem,
   I can produce a champion that will prove   44
   What is avouchèd there. If you miscarry,   45
   Your business of the world hath so an end.
   Fortune love you.
ALBANY
   Stay till I have read the letter.

---

29 *Combine together* let us join our forces 30 *domestic . . . particulars* household matters 31 *to question* the issue 32 *ensign of war* experienced senior
officers 36 *convenient* proper that you do 37 *I . . . riddle* I get the point
(which is not to leave her alone with Edmund) 44 *prove* establish as true (in
a trial by single combat) 45 *avouchèd* asserted; *miscarry* lose the battle

EDGAR
I was forbid it.
50 When time shall serve, let but the herald cry,
And I'll appear again.   *Exit.*
ALBANY
52 Why, fare thee well. I will o'erlook the paper.
Enter Edmund.
EDMUND
The enemy's in view; draw up our powers.
54 Here is the guess of their great strength and forces
55 By diligent discovery; but your haste
56 Is now urged on you.
ALBANY   We will greet the time.   *Exit.*
EDMUND
To both these sisters have I sworn my love,
58 Each jealous of the other as the stung
Are of the adder. Which of them shall I take?
60 Both, one, or neither? Neither can be enjoyed
If both remain alive. To take the widow
Exasperates, makes mad, her sister Goneril,
63 And hardly shall I carry out my side,
Her husband being alive. Now then, we'll use
65 His countenance for the battle, which being done,
Let her that would be rid of him devise
67 His speedy taking off. As for his mercy
Which he intends to Lear and to Cordelia,
The battle done, and they within our power,
70 Shall never see his pardon; for my state
Stands on me to defend, not to debate.   *Exit.*

∗

---

52 s.d. presumably Albany has no time to read Oswald's letter before Edmund's entrance **54** *guess* estimate **55** *discovery* spying **56** *greet the time*
be ready when the time comes **58** *jealous* suspicious; *stung* those who have
been bitten **63** *carry . . . side* accomplish my plan **65** *countenance* authority, backing **67** *taking off* murder **70** *Shall* they shall **70–71** *state . . . me*
situation requires me

∾ **V.2** *Alarum. Enter the powers of France over the stage, Cordelia with her father in her hand. [Exeunt.] Enter Edgar [disguised] and Gloucester.*

EDGAR

Here, father, take the shadow of this bush   1
For your good host; pray that the right may thrive.   2
If ever I return to you again
I'll bring you comfort.

GLOUCESTER   Grace go with you, sir.
        Exit [Edgar]. Alarum and [sound of] retreat.
        [Enter Edgar.]

EDGAR

Away, old man – give me thy hand, away!
King Lear hath lost, he and his daughter ta'en.
Give me thy hand. Come on.

GLOUCESTER

No farther, sir; a man may rot even here.

EDGAR

What, in ill thoughts again? Men must endure
Their going hence even as their coming hither.   10
Ripeness is all. Come on.   *[Exeunt.]*   11

                                *

∾ **V.3** *Enter Edmund, with Lear and Cordelia prisoners [, a Captain, and Soldiers].*

EDMUND

Some officers take them away. Good guard,
Until their greater pleasures best be known   2
That are to censure them.   3

V.2 A field   **s.d.** *Alarum* trumpets; *with . . . hand* leading her father by the hand   **1** *father* old man (Edgar still has not revealed his identity to Gloucester)   **2** *host* shelter   **11** *Ripeness is all* i.e., the gods decree when fruit is ripe and falls; coming to that ripeness is all that matters

   V.3 The British camp   **2** *their . . . pleasures* the wishes of those in command   **3** *censure* pass judgment on

CORDELIA   We are not the first
4   Who with best meaning have incurred the worst.
     For thee, oppressèd king, am I cast down,
6   Myself could else outfrown false fortune's frown.
     Shall we not see these daughters and these sisters?

LEAR
     No, no. Come, let's away to prison.
     We two alone will sing like birds i' th' cage.
10   When thou dost ask me blessing, I'll kneel down
     And ask of thee forgiveness; so we'll live,
     And pray, and sing, and tell old tales, and laugh
     At gilded butterflies, and hear poor rogues
     Talk of court news, and we'll talk with them too,
     Who loses and who wins, who's in, who's out,
     And take upon's the mystery of things
17   As if we were God's spies; and we'll wear out
18   In a walled prison packs and sects of great ones
19   That ebb and flow by th' moon.

EDMUND   Take them away.

LEAR
20   Upon such sacrifices, my Cordelia,
21   The gods themselves throw incense. Have I caught thee?
22   He that parts us shall bring a brand from heaven
     And fire us hence like foxes. Wipe thine eyes.
24   The good years shall devour 'em, flesh and fell,
     Ere they shall make us weep. We'll see 'em starve first.
     Come.
                    [Exeunt Lear and Cordelia with Soldiers.]

EDMUND
     Come hither, captain, hark.
     Take thou this note; go follow them to prison.

---

4 *meaning* intentions   6 *else* otherwise   17 *wear out* outlast   18 *packs and sects* parties and factions   19 *That . . . moon* whose power changes monthly
21 *throw incense* are celebrants; *Have . . . thee?* i.e., do I really have you again
22 *brand* torch (i.e., it will take divine powers to separate us now)   24 *good years* passage of time, old age; *flesh . . . fell* meat and skin, entirely

One step I have advanced thee; if thou dost   28
As this instructs thee, thou dost make thy way
To noble fortunes. Know thou this, that men   30
Are as the time is; to be tender-minded   31
Does not become a sword. Thy great employment   32
Will not bear question. Either say thou'lt do't,   33
Or thrive by other means.
CAPTAIN   I'll do't, my lord.
EDMUND
About it; and write happy when thou hast done.   35
Mark, I say instantly, and carry it so   36
As I have set it down.
CAPTAIN
I cannot draw a cart,   38
Nor eat dried oats. If it be man's work, I'll do't. *[Exit.]*
   Enter Duke [Albany], the two ladies [Goneril and
   Regan] and Others [, Officers and Soldiers].
ALBANY
Sir, you have showed today your valiant strain,   40
And fortune led you well. You have the captives
That were the opposites of this day's strife.   42
We do require then of you so to use them   43
As we shall find their merits and our safety
May equally determine.
EDMUND   Sir, I thought it fit
To send the old and miserable king
To some retention and appointed guard;   47
Whose age has charms in it, whose title more,
To pluck the common bosom on his side   49
And turn our impressed lances in our eyes   50

---

28 *advanced* promoted **31** *Are . . . is* i.e., must seize their opportunities
32 *sword* i.e., soldier **33** *question* discussion **35** *write happy* call yourself
fortunate **36** *carry it* carry it out **38–39** *draw . . . oats* i.e., I'm a man, not
a horse **40** *strain* (1) qualities, (2) lineage **42** *opposites of* opponents in **43**
use treat **47** *retention* detention **49** *pluck . . . on* draw popular sympathy to
50 *turn . . . eyes* i.e., turn our soldiers against us; *impressed lances* drafted
pikemen

Which do command them. With him I sent the queen,
My reason all the same; and they are ready
53   Tomorrow, or at further space, to appear
54   Where you shall hold your session. At this time
We sweat and bleed. The friend hath lost his friend,
56   And the best quarrels in the heat are cursed
57   By those that feel their sharpness.
The question of Cordelia and her father
Requires a fitter place.
ALBANY   Sir, by your patience,
60   I hold you but a subject of this war,
61   Not as a brother.
REGAN   That's as we list to grace him.
62   Methinks our pleasure should have been demanded
Ere you had spoke so far. He led our powers,
64   Bore the commission of my place and person,
65   The which immediate may well stand up
66   And call itself your brother.
GONERIL   Not so hot.
67   In his own grace he doth exalt himself
68   More than in your advancement.
REGAN   In my right
69   By me invested, he compeers the best.
GONERIL
70   That were the most if he should husband you.
REGAN
Jesters do oft prove prophets.
GONERIL   Holla, holla –
72   That eye that told you so looked but asquint.

---

53 *further space* a later time   54 *session* court hearing   56 *best . . . heat* most
just wars in the heat of battle   57 *feel . . . sharpness* endure their pain   60
subject of subordinate in   61 *we list* I please   62 *pleasure . . . demanded*
wishes should have been consulted   64 *Bore . . . person* i.e., acted with my
authority   65 *immediate* present status (as my deputy)   66 *hot* fast   67
grace merit   68 *your advancement* the honors conferred by you   69 *compeers*
equals   70 *the most* i.e., the most complete investiture with your rights   72
asquint cross-eyed (i.e., jealously)

REGAN
    Lady, I am not well, else I should answer
    From a full-flowing stomach. *[To Edmund]* General,   74
    Take thou my soldiers, prisoners, patrimony.   75
    Witness the world that I create thee here
    My lord and master.
GONERIL   Mean you to enjoy him then?
ALBANY
    The let-alone lies not in your good will.   78
EDMUND
    Nor in thine, lord.   79
ALBANY   Half-blooded fellow, yes.
EDMUND
    Let the drum strike and prove my title good.   80
ALBANY
    Stay yet, hear reason. Edmund, I arrest thee
    On capital treason, and in thine attaint   82
        [Indicating Goneril]
    This gilded serpent. For your claim, fair sister,
    I bar it in the interest of my wife.
    'Tis she is subcontracted to this lord,   85
    And I, her husband, contradict the banns.   86
    If you will marry, make your love to me.   87
    My lady is bespoke. – Thou art armed, Gloucester.   88
    If none appear to prove upon thy head
    Thy heinous, manifest, and many treasons,   90
    There is my pledge. *[Throws down a glove.]* I'll prove it
    on thy heart,
    Ere I taste bread, thou art in nothing less   92
    Than I have here proclaimed thee.
REGAN   Sick, O sick!

---

74 *stomach* anger 75 *patrimony* inheritance 78 *let-alone* (1) permission,
(2) veto 79 *Half-blooded* illegitimate (and only half noble) 80 *drum strike*
(as a signal to prepare for battle) 82 *in . . . attaint* in complicity with your
crimes 85 *subcontracted* (because she is already contracted, by marriage, to
Albany) 86 *banns* declaration of an intention to marry 87 *make . . . to*
woo 88 *bespoke* already spoken for 92 *nothing less* no way less guilty

GONERIL   *[Aside]*
    If not, I'll ne'er trust poison.
EDMUND   *[Throws his glove.]*
95   There's my exchange. What in the world he is
    That names me traitor, villainlike he lies.
    Call by thy trumpet. He that dares approach,
    On him, on you – who not? – I will maintain
    My truth and honor firmly.
ALBANY   A herald, ho!
EDMUND
100 A herald, ho, a herald!
ALBANY
101 Trust to thy single virtue, for thy soldiers,
    All levied in my name, have in my name
    Took their discharge.
REGAN   This sickness grows upon me.
ALBANY
    She is not well. Convey her to my tent.
        [Regan is led out. Enter a Herald and a Trumpeter.]
    Come hither, herald. Let the trumpet sound,
    And read out this.
CAPTAIN   Sound, trumpet! *[Trumpet sounds.]*
HERALD   "If any man of quality or degree in the host of
    the army will maintain upon Edmund, supposed Earl
110 of Gloucester, that he's a manifold traitor, let him ap-
    pear at the third sound of the trumpet. He is bold in his
    defense."
113 EDMUND   Sound! *[Trumpet sounds.]* Again! *[Trumpet
    sounds.]*
        *Enter Edgar [armed] at the third sound, a
        Trumpet[er] before him.*
ALBANY
    Ask him his purposes, why he appears
    Upon this call o' th' trumpet.

---

95 *What . . . world* whoever   101 *single virtue* unaided strength   113 **s.d.**
armed (Edgar wears a helmet with the beaver down, covering his face)

HERALD   What are you?
  Your name and quality, and why you answer   116
  This present summons?
EDGAR   O, know my name is lost,
  By treason's tooth bare-gnawn and canker-bit.   118
  Yet ere I move't, where is the adversary   119
  I come to cope withal?   120
ALBANY   Which is that adversary?
EDGAR
  What's he that speaks for Edmund, Earl of Gloucester?
EDMUND
  Himself. What sayest thou to him?
EDGAR   Draw thy sword,
  That if my speech offend a noble heart
  Thy arm may do thee justice. Here is mine.
  Behold, it is the privilege of my tongue,
  My oath, and my profession. I protest,   126
  Maugre thy strength, youth, place, and eminence,   127
  Despite thy victor sword and fire-new fortune,   128
  Thy valor and thy heart, thou art a traitor,   129
  False to thy gods, thy brother, and thy father,   130
  Conspirant 'gainst this high illustrious prince,   131
  And from th' extremest upward of thy head   132
  To the descent and dust beneath thy feet   133
  A most toad-spotted traitor. Say thou no,   134
  This sword, this arm, and my best spirits are bent
  To prove upon thy heart, whereto I speak,
  Thou liest.   137
EDMUND   In wisdom I should ask thy name,
  But since thy outside looks so fair and warlike,

---

116 *quality* rank   118 *treason's* treachery's; *canker-bit* eaten away by worms
119 *ere . . . mov't* before I make my declaration   120 *cope* encounter   126
profession i.e., as a knight   127 *Maugre* despite   128 *fire-new* newly forged
129 *heart* courage   131 *Conspirant* conspirator   132 *upward* top   133 *descent* lowest part   134 *toad-spotted* venomous, reptilian   137 *In . . . name*
(because one was not obliged to fight with an inferior, nor with an unknown
adversary)

139   And that thy being some say of breeding breathes,
140   By right of knighthood I disdain and spurn.
      Here do I toss those treasons to thy head,
142   With the hell-hated lie o'erturn thy heart,
143   Which, for they yet glance by and scarcely bruise,
144   This sword of mine shall give them instant way
      Where they shall rest forever. Trumpets, speak!
      [Alarums. They fight. Edmund falls.]
ALBANY
146   Save him, save him.
GONERIL   This is mere practice, Gloucester.
      By the law of arms thou art not bound to answer
148   An unknown opposite. Thou art not vanquished,
149   But cozened and beguiled.
ALBANY   Stop your mouth, dame,
150   Or with this paper shall I stopple it.
      Thou worse than anything, read thine own evil.
      Nay, no tearing, lady. I perceive you know't.
GONERIL
153   Say if I do, the laws are mine, not thine.
154   Who shall arraign me for't?
ALBANY
      Most monstrous! Know'st thou this paper?
GONERIL
      Ask me not what I know.   *Exit.*
ALBANY
157   Go after her. She's desperate; govern her.
                                    [Exit an Officer.]
EDMUND
      What you have charged me with, that have I done,

---

139 *being* nature   **140** *disdain and spurn* i.e., ask what I am entitled to know
142 *hell-hated* hateful as hell   **143** *Which, for they* since those treasons   **144**
way access   **146** *Save him* i.e., don't kill him; *This is mere practice* i.e., you've
been tricked   **148** *opposite* opponent   **149** *cozened* cheated   **153** *the . . .
mine* (Goneril is queen; Albany is her consort)   **154** *arraign* try (the
monarch, having no peers, could not be prosecuted)   **157** *govern* take care
of

And more, much more. The time will bring it out.
'Tis past, and so am I. But what art thou   *160*
That hast this fortune on me? If thou beest noble,   161
I do forgive thee.
EDGAR   Let's exchange charity.
I am no less in blood than thou art, Edmund;
If more, the more thou hast wronged me.
    [Removing his helmet]
My name is Edgar, and thy father's son.
The gods are just, and of our pleasant virtues   166
Make instruments to scourge us.
The dark and vicious place where thee he got   168
Cost him his eyes.
EDMUND   Thou hast spoken truth.
The wheel is come full circled; I am here.   170
ALBANY
Methought thy very gait did prophesy
A royal nobleness. I must embrace thee.
Let sorrow split my heart if I did ever hate
Thee or thy father.
EDGAR   Worthy prince, I know't.
ALBANY
Where have you hid yourself?
How have you known the miseries of your father?
EDGAR
By nursing them, my lord. List a brief tale,   177
And when 'tis told, O that my heart would burst!
The bloody proclamation to escape   179
That followed me so near – O our lives' sweetness,   180
That with the pain of death would hourly die

---

161 *fortune on* victory over 162 *charity* forgiveness 166 *pleasant virtues*
e.g., sexual prowess: what we are good at in the realm of pleasure (F's "pleasant vices" is an obvious revision, clarifying the sense but muting the irony;
Q's "vertues" cannot have been a compositor's misreading of "vices.") 168
dark . . . place adulterous bed, illicit genitals; *got* begot 170 *I . . . here* i.e., at
the bottom of Fortune's wheel again 177 *List* hear 179 *bloody proclamation* (declaring him an outlaw) 180 *our . . . sweetness* how sweet life is to us

Rather than die at once! – taught me to shift
Into a madman's rags, to assume a semblance
That very dogs disdained; and in this habit
185 Met I my father with his bleeding rings,
The precious stones new lost; became his guide,
Led him, begged for him, saved him from despair,
Never – O father! – revealed myself unto him
Until some half hour past, when I was armed.
190 Not sure, though hoping of this good success,
I asked his blessing, and from first to last
Told him my pilgrimage; but his flawed heart,
Alack too weak the conflict to support,
'Twixt two extremes of passion, joy and grief,
Burst smilingly.
EDMUND   This speech of yours hath moved me,
And shall perchance do good. But speak you on;
You look as you had something more to say.
ALBANY
If there be more, more woeful, hold it in,
199 For I am almost ready to dissolve,
200 Hearing of this.
EDGAR   This would have seemed a period
201 To such as love not sorrow; but another
To amplify too much would make much more,
And top extremity.
204 Whilst I was big in clamor came there in a man
205 Who, having seen me in my worst estate,
Shunned my abhorred society; but then, finding
Who 'twas that so endured, with his strong arms
He fastened on my neck and bellowed out
As he'd burst heaven; threw him on my father,
209
210 Told the most piteous tale of Lear and him

---

185 *rings* sockets   199 *dissolve* (in tears)   200 *a period* the limit   201–3 *another . . . extremity* to describe another sorrow too fully would exceed the limit   204 *big in clamor* loudly lamenting   205 *in . . . estate* at my worst   209 *As* as if; *him* himself

That ever ear received, which in recounting
His grief grew puissant and the strings of life   212
Began to crack. Twice then the trumpets sounded,
And there I left him trancèd.

ALBANY   But who was this?

EDGAR
Kent, sir, the banished Kent, who in disguise
Followed his enemy king, and did him service
Improper for a slave.
        Enter [a Gentleman] with a bloody knife.

GENTLEMAN   Help, help!

ALBANY
What kind of help?
What means that bloody knife?   220

GENTLEMAN   It's hot, it smokes;
It came even from the heart of –

ALBANY   Who, man? speak!

GENTLEMAN
Your lady, sir, your lady; and her sister
By her is poisonèd – she hath confessed it.

EDMUND
I was contracted to them both; all three
Now marry in an instant.   225

ALBANY
Produce their bodies, be they alive or dead.
                                [Exit Attendant.]
This justice of the heavens that makes us tremble
Touches us not with pity.

EDGAR
Here comes Kent, sir.
        Enter Kent [as himself].

ALBANY
O, 'tis he. The time will not allow   230
The compliment that very manners urges.

---

212 *puissant* powerful   225 *marry* unite

KENT
    I am come
233   To bid my king and master aye good night.
    Is he not here?
  ALBANY   Great thing of us forgot!
    Speak, Edmund, where's the king, and where's Cordelia?
    The bodies of Goneril and Regan are brought in.
236   Seest thou this object, Kent?
  KENT   Alack, why thus?
  EDMUND
    Yet Edmund was beloved.
    The one the other poisoned for my sake,
    And after slew herself.
240 ALBANY   Even so. Cover their faces.
  EDMUND
    I pant for life. Some good I mean to do,
    Despite of my own nature. Quickly send –
243   Be brief in't – to th' castle, for my writ
    Is on the life of Lear and on Cordelia.
    Nay, send in time.
  ALBANY   Run, run, O run!
  EDGAR
247   To who, my lord? Who hath the office? Send
    Thy token of reprieve.
  EDMUND
    Well thought on. Take my sword. The captain,
250   Give it the captain.
  ALBANY   Haste thee for thy life.
                        [Exit Captain.]
  EDMUND
    He hath commission from thy wife and me
    To hang Cordelia in the prison, and
    To lay the blame upon her own despair,
254   That she fordid herself.

---

233 *aye* forever **236** *object* sight, spectacle **243** *brief* quick; *writ* order of execution **247** *office* commission **254** *fordid* destroyed

ALBANY
    The gods defend her! Bear him hence awhile.
                                    [Edmund is borne off.]
        Enter Lear with Cordelia in his arms [followed by
        Captain].
LEAR
    Howl, howl, howl, howl! O you are men of stones.
    Had I your tongues and eyes, I would use them so
    That heaven's vault should crack. She's gone forever.
    I know when one is dead and when one lives.
    She's dead as earth. Lend me a looking glass;   *260*
    If that her breath will mist or stain the stone,   *261*
    Why, then she lives.   *262*
KENT   Is this the promised end?
EDGAR
    Or image of that horror?   *263*
ALBANY   Fall and cease.
LEAR
    This feather stirs. She lives. If it be so,
    It is a chance which does redeem all sorrows
    That ever I have felt.
KENT   Ah, my good master –
LEAR
    Prithee, away.
EDGAR   'Tis noble Kent, your friend.
LEAR
    A plague upon you, murderous traitors all!
    I might have saved her; now she's gone forever.
    Cordelia, Cordelia, stay a little. Ha?   *270*
    What is't thou sayest? – Her voice was ever soft,
    Gentle and low, an excellent thing in women.
    I killed the slave that was a-hanging thee.
CAPTAIN
    'Tis true, my lords, he did.

---

261 *stone* mirror of polished stone   262 *promised end* Judgment Day   263
Fall . . . cease let the world end

LEAR   Did I not, fellow?
275   I have seen the day, with my good biting falchion
       I would have made them skip. I am old now,
277   And these same crosses spoil me.
          [To Kent]
                                          Who are you?
          Mine eyes are not o' the best, I'll tell you straight.
       KENT
279   If fortune bragged of two she loved or hated,
280   One of them we behold.
       LEAR   Are not you Kent?
       KENT
281   The same, your servant Kent. Where is your servant
          Caius?
       LEAR
          He's a good fellow, I can tell you that.
          He'll strike, and quickly too. He's dead and rotten.
       KENT
          No, my good lord, I am the very man –
       LEAR
285   I'll see that straight.
       KENT
286   That from your first of difference and decay
287   Have followed your sad steps.
       LEAR   You're welcome hither.
       KENT
288   Nor no man else. All's cheerless, dark, and deadly.
289   Your eldest daughters have fordone themselves,
290   And desperately are dead.

---

275 *falchion* small sword   277 *crosses spoil* vexations weaken   279 *loved or
hated* first loved, then hated (Lear and a hypothetical other? Lear and
Cordelia? Lear and Kent, who are looking at each other?)   281 *Caius* (obviously Kent's alias; but the name appears nowhere else in the play)   285
I'll . . . straight I'll attend to it shortly   286 *difference and decay* quarrel and
decline   287 *You're . . . hither* (Lear fails to make the connection)   288
Nor . . . else i.e., no one is welcome here   289 *fordone* killed   290 *desperately*
in despair

LEAR   So think I, too.

ALBANY
  He knows not what he sees, and vain it is
  That we present us to him.   292

EDGAR   Very bootless.
      Enter Captain.

CAPTAIN
  Edmund is dead, my lord.

ALBANY
  That's but a trifle here.
  You lords and noble friends, know our intent.
  What comfort to this decay may come   296
  Shall be applied; for us, we will resign
  During the life of this old majesty
  To him our absolute power. *[To Edgar and Kent]* You
    to your rights,
  With boot and such addition as your honors   300
  Have more than merited. All friends shall taste
  The wages of their virtue, and all foes
  The cup of their deservings. O see, see!

LEAR
  And my poor fool is hanged. No, no life?   304
  Why should a dog, a horse, a rat have life,
  And thou no breath at all? O, thou wilt come no more.
  Never, never, never. – Pray you, undo
  This button. Thank you, sir. O, O, O, O!

EDGAR
  He faints. My lord, my lord!

LEAR
  Break, heart, I prithee break.   310
      [He dies.]

EDGAR   Look up, my lord.

---

292 *bootless* pointless   **296** *decay* ruin, Lear   **300** *boot* reward; *addition* advancement in rank   **304** *fool* (A term of endearment; here, Cordelia. The fool disappears after III.6.)

KENT

311   Vex not his ghost. O, let him pass. He hates him
312   That would upon the rack of this tough world
       Stretch him out longer.

EDGAR   O, he is gone indeed.

KENT

       The wonder is he hath endured so long.
       He but usurped his life.

ALBANY

       Bear them from hence. Our present business
       Is to general woe. *[To Edgar and Kent]* Friends of my
           soul, you twain
318   Rule in this kingdom, and the gored state sustain.

KENT

       I have a journey, sir, shortly to go;
320   My master calls, and I must not say no.

ALBANY

321   The weight of this sad time we must obey,
       Speak what we feel, not what we ought to say.
       The oldest have borne most; we that are young
       Shall never see so much, nor live so long.

                                        [Exeunt.]

---

311 *ghost* spirit   **312** *rack* i.e., a torture instrument   **318** *gored* wounded
321 Albany speaks the final lines as the highest-ranking person left alive. In
the folio, Edgar speaks them as the inheritor of Lear's kingdom.

The Tragedy of King Lear

1623 Folio Text

[NAMES OF THE ACTORS

LEAR, *King of Britain*
KING OF FRANCE
GONERIL, *Lear's eldest daughter*
DUKE OF ALBANY, *Goneril's husband*
REGAN, *Lear's second daughter*
DUKE OF CORNWALL, *Regan's husband*
CORDELIA, *Lear's youngest daughter*
DUKE OF BURGUNDY
EARL OF KENT
EARL OF GLOUCESTER
EDGAR, *Gloucester's elder son, later disguised as*
    Tom o' Bedlam
EDMUND, *Gloucester's younger, bastard son*
OSWALD, *Goneril's steward*
OLD MAN, *Gloucester's tenant*
CURAN, *Gloucester's servant*
FOOL, *attending on Lear*
SERVANTS, CAPTAINS, HERALD, KNIGHT,
    MESSENGERS, GENTLEMEN, SOLDIERS, ETC.

SCENE: *Britain*]
*

The Tragedy of King Lear

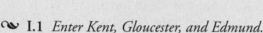

℘ I.1 *Enter Kent, Gloucester, and Edmund.*

KENT   I thought the king had more affected the Duke of 1
Albany than Cornwall. 2

GLOUCESTER   It did always seem so to us, but now in the
division of the kingdom, it appears not which of the
dukes he values most, for qualities are so weighed that 5
curiosity in neither can make choice of either's moiety. 6

KENT   Is not this your son, my lord?

GLOUCESTER   His breeding, sir, hath been at my charge.
I have so often blushed to acknowledge him that now I
am brazed to't. 10

KENT   I cannot conceive you. 11

GLOUCESTER   Sir, this young fellow's mother could,
whereupon she grew round-wombed and had indeed,
sir, a son for her cradle ere she had a husband for her
bed. Do you smell a fault?

KENT   I cannot wish the fault undone, the issue of it
being so proper. 17

GLOUCESTER   But I have a son, sir, by order of law, some 18
year elder than this, who yet is no dearer in my ac- 19
count. Though this knave came something saucily to 20
the world before he was sent for, yet was his mother

I.1 *Lear's palace* **s.d.** *Gloucester* (pronounced "Gloster") **1–2** *more affected . . . than* preferred . . . to **2** *Albany* i.e., Scotland **5** *qualities . . .
weighed* their qualities are so equal **6** *curiosity . . . moiety* thorough exami-
nation cannot find either's share preferable **10** *brazed* brazened **11** *conceive* understand **17** *proper* handsome **18** *by . . . law* legitimate **19–20**
account esteem **20** *something saucily* somewhat impertinently

fair; there was good sport at his making, and the
23   whoreson must be acknowledged. Do you know this
noble gentleman, Edmund?
EDMUND   No, my lord.
GLOUCESTER   My lord of Kent. Remember him hereafter
as my honorable friend.
EDMUND   My services to your lordship.
29   KENT   I must love you, and sue to know you better.
30   EDMUND   Sir, I shall study deserving.
31   GLOUCESTER   He hath been out nine years, and away he
32   shall again. The king is coming.
        Sennet.
        Enter King Lear, Cornwall, Albany, Goneril, Regan,
        Cordelia, and Attendants.
LEAR
Attend the lords of France and Burgundy, Gloucester.
GLOUCESTER
I shall, my lord.   *Exit.*
LEAR
35   Meantime we shall express our darker purpose.
Give me the map there. Know that we have divided
37   In three our kingdom, and 'tis our fast intent
To shake all cares and business from our age,
Conferring them on younger strengths, while we
40   Unburdened crawl toward death. Our son of Cornwall,
And you, our no less loving son of Albany,
42   We have this hour a constant will to publish
43   Our daughters' several dowers, that future strife
May be prevented now. The princes France and Burgundy,

---

23 *whoreson* (literally "bastard," but the word was also an affectionate term,
like "scamp")   **29** *sue* seek   **30** *study deserving* undertake to deserve it   **31**
out away   **32 s.d.** *Sennet* trumpet fanfare   **35** *darker purpose* secret plan   **37**
fast intent firm intention   **40** *son* son-in-law   **42** *constant . . . publish* deter-
mination to declare publicly   **43** *several dowers* individual dowries

Great rivals in our youngest daughter's love,
Long in our court have made their amorous sojourn,
And here are to be answered. Tell me, my daughters,
Since now we will divest us both of rule,
Interest of territory, cares of state,   49
Which of you shall we say doth love us most,   50
That we our largest bounty may extend
Where nature doth with merit challenge? Goneril,   52
Our eldest born, speak first.

GONERIL
Sir, I love you more than word can wield the matter,   54
Dearer than eyesight, space, and liberty,   55
Beyond what can be valued, rich or rare;
No less than life, with grace, health, beauty, honor;
As much as child e'er loved, or father found;
A love that makes breath poor and speech unable.   59
Beyond all manner of so much I love you.   60

CORDELIA   *[Aside]*
What shall Cordelia speak? Love and be silent.

LEAR
Of all these bounds, even from this line to this,
With shadowy forests and with champaigns riched,   63
With plenteous rivers and wide-skirted meads,   64
We make thee lady. To thine and Albany's issues   65
Be this perpetual. What says our second daughter?
Our dearest Regan, wife of Cornwall?

REGAN
I am made of that self mettle as my sister,   68
And prize me at her worth. In my true heart   69
I find she names my very deed of love;   70
Only she comes too short, that I profess   71

---

49 *Interest of* legal title to   52 *nature . . . challenge* the claims of natural affection are as strong as those of merit   54 *wield the matter* express the subject
55 *space* scope (to enjoy "liberty")   59 *breath* voice   63 *shadowy* shady;
champaigns riched cultivated plains   64 *wide-skirted meads* spreading meadows   65 *issues* heirs   68 *self* same   69 *prize me* value myself   71 *that* in that

Myself an enemy to all other joys
73 Which the most precious square of sense professes,
74 And find I am alone felicitate
In your dear highness' love.
CORDELIA   *[Aside]*   Then poor Cordelia,
And yet not so, since I am sure my love's
More ponderous than my tongue.
LEAR
To thee and thine hereditary ever
Remain this ample third of our fair kingdom,
80 No less in space, validity, and pleasure
Than that conferred on Goneril. Now our joy,
82 Although our last and least, to whose young love
The vines of France and milk of Burgundy
84 Strive to be interested, what can you say to draw
A third more opulent than your sisters? Speak.
CORDELIA   Nothing, my lord.
LEAR   Nothing?
CORDELIA   Nothing.
LEAR
89 Nothing will come of nothing; speak again.
CORDELIA
90 Unhappy that I am, I cannot heave
My heart into my mouth. I love your majesty
92 According to my bond, no more nor less.
LEAR
How, how, Cordelia? Mend your speech a little
Lest you may mar your fortunes.
CORDELIA   Good my lord,
You have begot me, bred me, loved me.
96 I return those duties back as are right fit,

---

73 *most . . . professes* measure of perception considers to be most precious (?)
74 *felicitate* made happy   80 *validity* value   82 *least* smallest   84 *interested*
entitled to a share   89 *Nothing . . . nothing* (quoting a famous scholastic
maxim derived from Aristotle, *nihil ex nihilo fit*)   92 *bond* duty   96 *I . . . fit*
I am properly dutiful in return

Obey you, love you, and most honor you.
Why have my sisters husbands, if they say
They love you all? Happily when I shall wed
That lord whose hand must take my plight shall carry   100
Half my love with him, half my care and duty.
Sure I shall never marry like my sisters.

LEAR
But goes thy heart with this?

CORDELIA   Ay, my good lord.

LEAR
So young and so untender?

CORDELIA
So young, my lord, and true.   105

LEAR
Let it be so. Thy truth then be thy dower;
For by the sacred radiance of the sun,
The mysteries of Hecate and the night,   108
By all the operation of the orbs   109
From whom we do exist and cease to be,   *110*
Here I disclaim all my paternal care,
Propinquity, and property of blood,   112
And as a stranger to my heart and me
Hold thee from this forever. The barbarous Scythian,   114
Or he that makes his generation messes   115
To gorge his appetite, shall to my bosom
Be as well neighbored, pitied, and relieved
As thou, my sometime daughter.

KENT   Good my liege –

LEAR
Peace, Kent!
Come not between the dragon and his wrath.   *120*

---

100 *plight* marriage vow   105 *true* honest   108 *Hecate* goddess of the underworld and patron of witchcraft   109 *operation . . . orbs* astrological influences   112 *Propinquity . . . blood* blood relationship   114 *this* this time;
Scythian Crimean tribesman, notorious for cruelty   115 *makes . . . messes*
devours his children

I loved her most, and thought to set my rest
122   On her kind nursery. *[To Cordelia]* Hence, and avoid
       my sight!
123   So be my grave my peace as here I give
       Her father's heart from her. Call France. Who stirs!
       Call Burgundy. Cornwall and Albany,
       With my two daughters' dowers digest the third.
       Let pride, which she calls plainness, marry her.
       I do invest you jointly with my power,
129   Preeminence, and all the large effects
130   That troop with majesty. Ourself by monthly course,
131   With reservation of an hundred knights
       By you to be sustained, shall our abode
       Make with you by due turn. Only we shall retain
134   The name, and all th' addition to a king. The sway,
       Revenue, execution of the rest,
       Belovèd sons, be yours; which to confirm,
137   This coronet part between you.
KENT   Royal Lear,
       Whom I have ever honored as my king,
       Loved as my father, as my master followed,
140   As my great patron thought on in my prayers –
LEAR
141   The bow is bent and drawn; make from the shaft.
KENT
142   Let it fall rather, though the fork invade
       The region of my heart. Be Kent unmannerly
       When Lear is mad. What wouldst thou do, old man?
       Think'st thou that duty shall have dread to speak
146   When power to flattery bows? To plainness honor's
       bound

---

122 *nursery* care   **123** *So . . . peace* let my only peace be in my grave   **129**
large effects rich trappings   **130** *troop with* accompany; *by . . . course* month
by month   **131** *With reservation of* legally retaining   **134** *all th' addition* i.e.,
the honors and prerogatives; *sway* authority   **137** *coronet* (which would have
crowned Cordelia)   **141** *make from* get out of the way of   **142** *fall* strike;
fork (two-pronged) arrowhead   **146** *plainness* straight talk

When majesty falls to folly. Reserve thy state,   147
And in thy best consideration check
This hideous rashness. Answer my life my judgment: 149
Thy youngest daughter does not love thee least,   *150*
Nor are those empty-hearted whose low sounds
Reverb no hollowness.   152

LEAR
Kent, on thy life, no more!

KENT
My life I never held but as a pawn   154
To wage against thine enemies; ne'er fear to lose it,   155
Thy safety being motive.   156

LEAR   Out of my sight!

KENT
See better, Lear, and let me still remain   157
The true blank of thine eye.   158

LEAR   Now by Apollo —

KENT
Now by Apollo, king, thou swear'st thy gods in vain.

LEAR
O vassal! Miscreant!   160

ALBANY AND CORNWALL   Dear sir, forbear.

KENT
Kill thy physician, and thy fee bestow
Upon the foul disease. Revoke thy gift,
Or whilst I can vent clamor from my throat,
I'll tell thee thou dost evil.

LEAR
Hear me, recreant; on thine allegiance hear me!   165
That thou hast sought to make us break our vows,   166

---

147 *Reserve . . . state* retain your authority   149 *Answer my life* I stake my
life on   152 *Reverb no hollowness* do not resonate hollowly   154 *pawn* (1)
stake, (2) the least valuable chess piece   155 *wage* wager, risk   156 *motive*
my motivation   157 *still* always   158 *true blank* exact bull's-eye; *Apollo* the
sun god   160 *Miscreant* (1) villain, (2) infidel; CORNWALL (or Cordelia: F's
speech heading is *Cor.*)   165 *recreant* (1) traitor, (2) infidel   166 *That* since

167 Which we durst never yet, and with strained pride
168 To come betwixt our sentences and our power,
169 Which nor our nature nor our place can bear,
170 Our potency made good, take thy reward:
Five days we do allot thee for provision
To shield thee from disasters of the world,
And on the sixth to turn thy hated back
Upon our kingdom. If on the tenth day following
175 Thy banished trunk be found in our dominions,
The moment is thy death. Away! By Jupiter,
This shall not be revoked.

KENT
178 Fare thee well, king. Sith thus thou wilt appear,
Freedom lives hence, and banishment is here.
[To Cordelia]
180 The gods to their dear shelter take thee, maid,
That justly think'st, and hast most rightly said.
[To Goneril and Regan]
182 And your large speeches may your deeds approve,
That good effects may spring from words of love.
Thus Kent, O princes, bids you all adieu;
185 He'll shape his old course in a country new.   *Exit.*
Flourish. Enter Gloucester with France and Burgundy,
Attendants.

CORDELIA
186 Here's France and Burgundy, my noble lord.

LEAR
My lord of Burgundy,
We first address toward you, who with this king
Hath rivaled for our daughter: what in the least

---

167 *strained* excessive 168 *our power* the power to execute them 169 *place*
royal office 170 *Our . . . good* hereby demonstrating my power 175 *trunk*
body 178 *Sith* since 182 *your . . . approve* i.e., may your actions justify
your words 185 s.d. *Flourish* fanfare 186 CORDELIA (Here again F reads
Cor.; Cordelia is a more likely speaker than Cornwall, but most editors follow Q and give the line to Gloucester.)

Will you require in present dower with her,   *190*
Or cease your quest of love?
BURGUNDY   Most royal majesty,
I crave no more than hath your highness offered,
Nor will you tender less.   193
LEAR   Right noble Burgundy,
When she was dear to us we did hold her so;
But now her price is fallen. Sir, there she stands.
If aught within that little seeming substance,   196
Or all of it, with our displeasure pieced   197
And nothing more, may fitly like your grace,   198
She's there, and she is yours.
BURGUNDY   I know no answer.
LEAR
Will you with those infirmities she owes,   200
Unfriended, new-adopted to our hate,
Dowered with our curse, and strangered with our oath,   202
Take her or leave her?
BURGUNDY   Pardon me, royal sir;
Election makes not up in such conditions.   204
LEAR
Then leave her, sir; for, by the power that made me,
I tell you all her wealth. *[To France]* For you, great king,
I would not from your love make such a stray   207
To match you where I hate; therefore beseech you
T' avert your liking a more worthier way   209
Than on a wretch whom nature is ashamed   210
Almost t' acknowledge hers.
FRANCE   This is most strange
That she whom even but now was your object,
The argument of your praise, balm of your age,   213

---

193 *tender* offer   196 *aught* anything; *little . . . substance* (1) mere shell of a
person, (2) person with few pretensions   197 *pieced* joined   198 *like* please
200 *owes* owns   202 *strangered with* made a stranger by   204 *Election . . .
conditions* choice is impossible on such terms   207 *make . . . stray* stray so far
as   209 *avert* turn   213 *argument* theme

The best, the dearest, should in this trice of time
215   Commit a thing so monstrous to dismantle
So many folds of favor. Sure her offense
Must be of such unnatural degree
218   That monsters it, or your fore-vouched affection
219   Fall into taint; which to believe of her
220   Must be a faith that reason without miracle
Should never plant in me.
CORDELIA   *[To Lear]*
I yet beseech your majesty,
223   If for I want that glib and oily art
To speak and purpose not, since what I well intend
I'll do't before I speak – that you make known
It is no vicious blot, murder, or foulness,
No unchaste action or dishonored step
That hath deprived me of your grace and favor,
But even for want of that for which I am richer –
230   A still-soliciting eye, and such a tongue
That I am glad I have not, though not to have it
Hath lost me in your liking.
LEAR   Better thou
Hadst not been born than not t' have pleased me better.
FRANCE
Is it but this? A tardiness in nature,
Which often leaves the history unspoke
That it intends to do? My lord of Burgundy,
What say you to the lady? Love's not love
238   When it is mingled with regards that stands
Aloof from th' entire point. Will you have her?
240   She is herself a dowry.
BURGUNDY   Royal king,
Give but that portion which yourself proposed,

---

215 *to dismantle* as to strip off **218** *monsters it* makes it monstrous
218–19 *fore-vouched . . . taint* the love you previously swore must now appear suspect **223** *for I want* because I lack **230** *still-soliciting* always begging **238–39** *regards . . . point* considerations irrelevant to love

And here I take Cordelia by the hand,
Duchess of Burgundy.

LEAR
Nothing. I have sworn. I am firm.

BURGUNDY   *[To Cordelia]*
I am sorry, then, you have so lost a father
That you must lose a husband.

CORDELIA
Peace be with Burgundy.
Since that respect and fortunes are his love,   248
I shall not be his wife.

FRANCE
Fairest Cordelia, that art most rich being poor,   250
Most choice forsaken, and most loved despised,
Thee and thy virtues here I seize upon.
Be it lawful I take up what's cast away.
Gods, gods! 'Tis strange that from their cold'st neglect
My love should kindle to inflamed respect.   255
Thy dowerless daughter, king, thrown to my chance,
Is queen of us, of ours, and our fair France.
Not all the dukes of wat'rish Burgundy   258
Can buy this unprized precious maid of me.   259
Bid them farewell, Cordelia, though unkind;   260
Thou losest here, a better where to find.   261

LEAR
Thou hast her, France. Let her be thine, for we
Have no such daughter, nor shall ever see
That face of hers again. Therefore be gone,
Without our grace, our love, our benison.   265
Come, noble Burgundy.
          Flourish. Exeunt [all except France and the sisters].

FRANCE
Bid farewell to your sisters.

---

248 *respect . . . fortunes* honor and wealth   **255** *inflamed respect* ardent admiration   **258** *wat'rish* (1) well-irrigated, (2) weak, wishy-washy   **259** *unprized* unappreciated   **261** *where* elsewhere   **265** *benison* blessing

CORDELIA

268 The jewels of our father, with washed eyes
Cordelia leaves you. I know you what you are,
270 And, like a sister, am most loath to call
271 Your faults as they are named. Love well our father.
272 To your professèd bosoms I commit him;
But yet, alas, stood I within his grace,
274 I would prefer him to a better place.
So, farewell to you both.

REGAN

Prescribe not us our duty.

GONERIL   Let your study
Be to content your lord, who hath received you
278 At fortune's alms. You have obedience scanted,
279 And well are worth the want that you have wanted.

CORDELIA

280 Time shall unfold what plighted cunning hides;
281 Who covers faults at last with shame derides.
Well may you prosper.

FRANCE   Come, my fair Cordelia.
                              Exeunt France and Cordelia.

GONERIL   Sister, it is not little I have to say of what most
nearly appertains to us both. I think our father will
hence tonight.

REGAN   That's most certain, and with you. Next month
with us.

GONERIL   You see how full of changes his age is. The observation we have made of it hath not been little. He al-
290 ways loved our sister most, and with what poor
291 judgment he hath now cast her off appears too grossly.

REGAN   'Tis the infirmity of his age; yet he hath ever but
slenderly known himself.

---

268 *washed* tearful **271** *as . . . named* by their real names **272** *professèd bosoms* proclaimed love **274** *prefer* promote **278** *At . . . alms* as charity from
Fortune **279** *well . . . wanted* are properly deprived of what you yourself
have lacked **281** *Who . . . derides* i.e., time finally exposes hidden faults to
shame **291** *grossly* obviously

GONERIL   The best and soundest of his time hath been   294
  but rash; then must we look from his age to receive not   295
  alone the imperfections of long-engraffed condition,   296
  but therewithal the unruly waywardness that infirm   297
  and choleric years bring with them.

REGAN   Such unconstant starts are we like to have from   299
  him as this of Kent's banishment.   *300*

GONERIL   There is further compliment of leave-taking   301
  between France and him. Pray you, let us hit together.   302
  If our father carry authority with such disposition as he
  bears, this last surrender of his will but offend us.   304

REGAN   We shall further think of it.

GONERIL   We must do something, and i' th' heat.   306

                                        Exeunt.

                          ✳

❧ **I.2**   *Enter Bastard [Edmund].*

EDMUND
  Thou, Nature, art my goddess. To thy law
  My services are bound. Wherefore should I
  Stand in the plague of custom and permit   3
  The curiosity of nations to deprive me   4
  For that I am some twelve or fourteen moonshines   5
  Lag of a brother? Why bastard? Wherefore base,   6
  When my dimensions are as well compact,   7
  My mind as generous, and my shape as true   8
  As honest madam's issue? Why brand they us   9

---

294 *The . . . been* even at his best he was   295 *then* therefore   296 *long-engraffed* deep-seated   297 *therewithal* along with that   299 *unconstant starts* fits of impulsiveness   301 *compliment* formality   302 *hit* consult   304 *last surrender* recent abdication   306 *i' th' heat* immediately ("while the iron is hot")
  I.2 1 Gloucester's house   **3** *Stand . . . custom* submit to the affliction of convention (whereby the eldest son inherits everything, and illegitimate sons have no claim on the estate)   **4** *curiosity* (legal) technicalities   **5** *For that* because; *moonshines* months   **6** *Lag of* younger than   **7** *compact* composed   **8** *My . . . generous* I am as well supplied with intelligence   **9** *honest* chaste (i.e., married)

10 With base, with baseness, bastardy? base, base?
11 Who in the lusty stealth of nature take
12 More composition and fierce quality
    Than doth within a dull, stale, tired bed
14 Go to th' creating a whole tribe of fops,
15 Got 'tween asleep and wake? Well then,
16 Legitimate Edgar, I must have your land.
    Our father's love is to the bastard Edmund
    As to th' legitimate. Fine word "legitimate."
19 Well, my legitimate, if this letter speed
20 And my invention thrive, Edmund the base
21 Shall to th' legitimate. I grow, I prosper.
    Now gods, stand up for bastards!
          Enter Gloucester. [Edmund reads a letter.]
    GLOUCESTER
23 Kent banished thus? and France in choler parted?
24 And the king gone tonight? prescribed his power
25 Confined to exhibition – all this done
26 Upon the gad? Edmund, how now? What news?
    EDMUND   So please your lordship, none.
    GLOUCESTER   Why so earnestly seek you to put up that
       letter?
30 EDMUND   I know no news, my lord.
    GLOUCESTER   What paper were you reading?
    EDMUND   Nothing, my lord.
33 GLOUCESTER   No? What needed then that terrible dis-
       patch of it into your pocket? The quality of nothing
       hath not such need to hide itself. Let's see. Come, if it
       be nothing I shall not need spectacles.

---

11 *the . . . nature* natural lust practiced in secret   12 *composition* physical excellence; *fierce* vigorous   14 *fops* fools, sissies   15 *Got* begotten   16 *land*
i.e., inheritance   19 *speed* succeed   20 *invention* scheme   21 *to* rise to,
equal   23 *in . . . parted* departed in anger   24 *tonight* i.e., last night; *prescribed . . . power* told how much power he is to have   25 *Confined . . . exhibition* limited to an allowance   26 *Upon . . . gad* suddenly, impulsively   33
terrible frightened

EDMUND I beseech you, sir, pardon me. It is a letter
from my brother that I have not all o'er-read; and for so
much as I have perused, I find it not fit for your o'er-
looking.   40

GLOUCESTER Give me the letter, sir.

EDMUND I shall offend either to detain or give it. The
contents, as in part I understand them, are to blame.   43

GLOUCESTER Let's see, let's see.

EDMUND I hope for my brother's justification he wrote
this but as an essay or taste of my virtue.   46

[He gives Gloucester the letter.]

GLOUCESTER *Reads.* "This policy and reverence of age   47
makes the world bitter to the best of our times, keeps   48
our fortunes from us till our oldness cannot relish
them. I begin to find an idle and fond bondage in the   50
oppression of aged tyranny, who sways not as it hath
power but as it is suffered. Come to me, that of this I   52
may speak more. If our father would sleep till I waked
him, you should enjoy half his revenue forever and live
the beloved of your brother Edgar." Hum, conspiracy!
"Sleep till I wake him, you should enjoy half his revenue"– my son Edgar! Had he a hand to write this, a
heart and brain to breed it in? When came you to this?
Who brought it?

EDMUND It was not brought me, my lord, there's the   60
cunning of it. I found it thrown in at the casement of   61
my closet.

GLOUCESTER You know the character to be your   63
brother's?

---

43 *to blame* blameworthy 46 *essay or taste* (both words mean "test")
47 *policy . . . of* policy of reverence for 48 *to . . . times* in the prime of
our lives 50 *idle . . . fond* worthless and foolish 52 *suffered* allowed to
do so 61–62 *casement . . . closet* window of my bedroom 63 *character*
handwriting

65 EDMUND   If the matter were good, my lord, I durst swear
66   it were his; but in respect of that, I would fain think it
  were not.

GLOUCESTER   It is his.

EDMUND   It is his hand, my lord, but I hope his heart is
70   not in the contents.

71 GLOUCESTER   Has he never before sounded you in this
  business?

EDMUND   Never, my lord; but I have heard him oft
74   maintain it to be fit that, sons at perfect age and fathers
75   declined, the father should be as ward to the son, and
  the son manage his revenue.

GLOUCESTER   O villain, villain – his very opinion in the
  letter. Abhorred villain, unnatural, detested, brutish vil-
79   lain – worse than brutish! Go, sirrah, seek him. I'll ap-
80   prehend him. Abominable villain! Where is he?

EDMUND   I do not well know, my lord. If it shall please
  you to suspend your indignation against my brother till
  you can derive from him better testimony of his intent,
84   you should run a certain course; where if you violently
  proceed against him, mistaking his purpose, it would
  make a great gap in your own honor and shake in
87   pieces the heart of his obedience. I dare pawn down my
88   life for him that he hath writ this to feel my affection to
89   your honor, and to no other pretense of danger.

90 GLOUCESTER   Think you so?

91 EDMUND   If your honor judge it meet, I will place you
92   where you shall hear us confer of this, and by an auric-
  ular assurance have your satisfaction, and that without
  any further delay than this very evening.

---

65 *matter* substance   66 *in . . . that* i.e., considering the content; *fain* prefer
to   71 *sounded you* sounded you out   74 *sons . . . age* when sons are mature
75 *as . . . to* placed under the guardianship of   79 *sirrah* (term of address
used to a child or social inferior)   84 *run . . . course* be sure of your course of
action; *where* whereas   87 *pawn down* stake   88 *feel* test   89 *pretense of
danger* intent to do harm   91 *meet* appropriate   92–93 *an . . . assurance* the
testimony of your own ears

GLOUCESTER   He cannot be such a monster. Edmund, seek him out, wind me into him. I pray you, frame the business after your own wisdom. I would unstate myself to be in a due resolution.   96 97

EDMUND   I will seek him, sir, presently, convey the business as I shall find means, and acquaint you withal.   99 100

GLOUCESTER   These late eclipses in the sun and moon portend no good to us. Though the wisdom of nature can reason it thus and thus, yet nature finds itself scourged by the sequent effects. Love cools, friendship falls off, brothers divide; in cities mutinies, in countries discord, in palaces treason, and the bond cracked 'twixt son and father. This villain of mine comes under the prediction: there's son against father; the king falls from bias of nature, there's father against child. We have seen the best of our time. Machinations, hollowness, treachery, and all ruinous disorders follow us disquietly to our graves. Find out this villain, Edmund. It shall lose thee nothing. Do it carefully. And the noble and true-hearted Kent banished, his offense honesty: 'tis strange.   101 102 103 105 108 109 110

Exit.

EDMUND   This is the excellent foppery of the world, that when we are sick in fortune – often the surfeits of our own behavior – we make guilty of our disasters the sun, the moon, and stars, as if we were villains on necessity, fools by heavenly compulsion, knaves, thieves, and treachers by spherical predominance, drunkards, liars, and adulterers by an enforced obedience of planetary   115 116 120 121

---

96 *wind . . . him* worm your way into his confidence for me; *frame* arrange **97–98** *unstate . . . resolution* give up everything to resolve my doubts **99** *presently* immediately; *convey* conduct **100** *withal* with the result **101** *late* recent **102–3** *wisdom . . . thus* natural science can supply various explanations **103–4** *nature . . . effects* humanity ("nature") suffers the consequences **105** *mutinies* rebellions **108** *prediction* ill omen **109** *bias of nature* his natural inclination **110** *hollowness* insincerity **115** *foppery* foolishness **116** *surfeits* overindulgences **120** *treachers* traitors; *spherical predominance* astrological influence **121** *of* to

122   influence; and all that we are evil in by a divine thrust-
       ing on. An admirable evasion of whoremaster man,
124   to lay his goatish disposition on the charge of a star!
125   My father compounded with my mother under the
126   Dragon's tail, and my nativity was under Ursa Major so
       that it follows I am rough and lecherous. I should have
       been that I am had the maidenliest star in the firma-
       ment twinkled on my bastardizing.
          Enter Edgar.
130   Pat – he comes like the catastrophe of the old comedy;
131   my cue is villainous melancholy, with a sigh like Tom
132   o' Bedlam. – O these eclipses do portend these divi-
       sions. Fa, sol, la, mi.
       EDGAR   How now, brother Edmund, what serious con-
          templation are you in?
       EDMUND   I am thinking, brother, of a prediction I read
          this other day, what should follow these eclipses.
       EDGAR   Do you busy yourself with that?
139   EDMUND   I promise you, the effects he writes of succeed
140   unhappily. When saw you my father last?
       EDGAR   The night gone by.
       EDMUND   Spake you with him?
       EDGAR   Ay, two hours together.
       EDMUND   Parted you in good terms? Found you no dis-
145   pleasure in him by word nor countenance?
       EDGAR   None at all.
       EDMUND   Bethink yourself wherein you may have of-
          fended him, and at my entreaty forbear his presence
149   until some little time hath qualified the heat of his dis-

---

122–23 *thrusting on* enforcement   123 *admirable* astonishing   124 *goatish*
lecherous   125 *compounded* had sex   126 *Dragon's tail, Ursa Major* the constellations of Draco and the Great Bear   130 *Pat* right on cue; *catastrophe . . . comedy* conclusion in early comedy (i.e., often arbitrary or
unmotivated, but at the appointed time)   131 *villainous* severe   131–32
Tom o' Bedlam a beggar from Bedlam (Bethlehem) Hospital, the London
madhouse   132–33 *divisions* (1) conflicts, (2) musical phrases   139 *succeed*
conclude   145 *countenance* look   149 *qualified* moderated

pleasure, which at this instant so rageth in him that   *150*
with the mischief of your person it would scarcely allay.   151

EDGAR   Some villain hath done me wrong.

EDMUND   That's my fear. I pray you have a continent   153
forbearance till the speed of his rage goes slower; and,
as I say, retire with me to my lodging, from whence I
will fitly bring you to hear my lord speak. Pray ye, go: 156
there's my key. If you do stir abroad, go armed.

EDGAR   Armed, brother?

EDMUND   Brother, I advise you to the best. I am no honest man if there be any good meaning toward you. I   *160*
have told you what I have seen and heard but faintly,
nothing like the image and horror of it. Pray you, away.   162

EDGAR   Shall I hear from you anon?

EDMUND   I do serve you in this business.   *Exit [Edgar].*
A credulous father, and a brother noble,
Whose nature is so far from doing harms
That he suspects none, on whose foolish honesty
My practices ride easy. I see the business.   168
Let me, if not by birth, have lands by wit.   169
All with me's meet that I can fashion fit.   *Exit.*   170

*

∾ **I.3** *Enter Goneril and Steward [Oswald].*

GONERIL
    Did my father strike my gentleman
    For chiding of his fool?

OSWALD   Ay, madam.

GONERIL
    By day and night he wrongs me. Every hour
    He flashes into one gross crime or other   4

---

151 *the mischief of* injury to; *allay* be allayed   153 *continent* patient   156
fitly when it is appropriate   162 *image . . . it* as horrible as it seemed   168
practices plots; *I . . . business* the plan is now clear   169 *wit* intelligence
170 *with . . . meet* suits me; *fashion fit* shape to serve my purpose   I.3 Albany's castle   4 *crime* offense

That sets us all at odds. I'll not endure it.
His knights grow riotous, and himself upbraids us
On every trifle. When he returns from hunting
I will not speak with him. Say I am sick.
9   If you come slack of former services
10   You shall do well; the fault of it I'll answer.
     [Horns within.]
OSWALD   He's coming, madam, I hear him.
GONERIL
Put on what weary negligence you please,
13   You and your fellows. I'd have it come to question.
14   If he distaste it, let him to my sister,
     Whose mind and mine I know in that are one.
     Remember what I have said.
OSWALD   Well, madam.
GONERIL
And let his knights have colder looks among you;
What grows of it, no matter. Advise your fellows so.
19   I'll write straight to my sister to hold my course.
20   Prepare for dinner.   *Exeunt.*

                    ✳

∽ **I.4** *Enter Kent [disguised].*

KENT
1   If but as well I other accents borrow
2   That can my speech defuse, my good intent
3   May carry through itself to that full issue
4   For which I razed my likeness. Now, banished Kent,
     If thou canst serve where thou dost stand condemned,

---

9 *come . . . services* serve him less well than usual   10 *answer* answer for   13
come . . . question made an issue   14 *distaste* dislike   19 *hold . . . course* pursue the same course I do
    I.4 1 *If . . . borrow* i.e., if I disguise my voice as effectively as I do my appearance   **2** *defuse* confuse, disguise   **3** *issue* outcome   **4** *razed . . . likeness*
erased my appearance (including "razoring" his beard)

So may it come thy master, whom thou lov'st,   6
Shall find thee full of labors.   7
    Horns within. Enter Lear and Attendants.
LEAR   Let me not stay a jot for dinner. Go get it ready.   8
    [Exit Attendant].
How now, what art thou?   9
KENT   A man, sir.   10
LEAR   What dost thou profess? What wouldst thou with   11
us?
KENT   I do profess to be no less than I seem, to serve him
truly that will put me in trust, to love him that is hon-
est, to converse with him that is wise and says little, to   15
fear judgment, to fight when I cannot choose, and to   16
eat no fish.   17
LEAR   What art thou?
KENT   A very honest-hearted fellow, and as poor as the
king.   20
LEAR   If thou be'st as poor for a subject as he's for a king,
thou art poor enough. What wouldst thou?
KENT   Service.
LEAR   Who wouldst thou serve?
KENT   You.
LEAR   Dost thou know me, fellow?
KENT   No, sir, but you have that in your countenance
which I would fain call master.   28
LEAR   What's that?
KENT   Authority.   30
LEAR   What services canst thou do?
KENT   I can keep honest counsel, ride, run, mar a curi-   32
ous tale in telling it, and deliver a plain message

---

6 *come* happen that   7 *full . . . labors* i.e., hard at work   7 **s.d.** *Horns within*
hunting horns offstage   8 *stay* wait   9 *what* who   11 *dost . . . profess* is your
trade   15 *converse* associate   16 *fear judgment* show respect for authority;
choose avoid it   17 *eat no fish* (A joke whose point has obviously been lost:
not to be Catholic, and thus forbidden to eat meat on Fridays? To be a meat-
eater only – i.e., manly?)   28 *fain* like to   32 *keep . . . counsel* respect confidences   32–33 *curious* complicated

bluntly. That which ordinary men are fit for I am qualified in, and the best of me is diligence.

LEAR How old art thou?

KENT Not so young, sir, to love a woman for singing,
nor so old to dote on her for anything. I have years on
my back forty-eight.

40 LEAR Follow me. Thou shalt serve me. If I like thee no
worse after dinner, I will not part from thee yet. Din-
42 ner, ho, dinner! Where's my knave, my fool? Go you
and call my fool hither.   *[Exit Knight.]*
    Enter Steward [Oswald].
You, you, sirrah, where's my daughter?

OSWALD So please you –   *Exit.*

46 LEAR What says the fellow there? Call the clotpoll back.
[Exit Knight.] Where's my fool, ho? I think the world's
asleep. *[Reenter Knight.]* How now, where's that mongrel?

50 KNIGHT He says, my lord, your daughter is not well.

LEAR Why came not the slave back to me when I called
him?

53 KNIGHT Sir, he answered me in the roundest manner he
would not.

LEAR He would not?

KNIGHT My lord, I know not what the matter is, but to
57 my judgment your highness is not entertained with
58 that ceremonious affection as you were wont. There's a
59 great abatement of kindness appears as well in the gen-
60 eral dependents as in the duke himself also, and your
daughter.

LEAR Ha, sayest thou so?

KNIGHT I beseech you pardon me, my lord, if I be mis-
taken, for my duty cannot be silent when I think your
highness wronged.

---

42 *knave* boy (the term could be affectionate) 46 *clotpoll* blockhead 53
roundest rudest 57 *entertained* treated 58 *wont* accustomed to 59–60
the . . . dependents all the servants

LEAR Thou but rememb'rest me of mine own concep- 66
tion. I have perceived a most faint neglect of late,
which I have rather blamed as mine own jealous curios- 68
ity than as a very pretense and purpose of unkindness. I 69
will look further into't. But where's my fool? I have not 70
seen him this two days.

KNIGHT Since my young lady's going into France, sir,
the fool hath much pined away.

LEAR No more of that, I have noted it well. Go you and
tell my daughter I would speak with her. *[Exit Knight.]*
Go you, call hither my fool.   *[Exit another Attendant.]*
  Enter Steward [Oswald].
O, you sir, you, come you hither, sir. Who am I, sir?

OSWALD My lady's father.

LEAR My lady's father? My lord's knave, you whoreson
dog, you slave, you cur!   80

OSWALD I am none of these, my lord; I beseech your
pardon.

LEAR Do you bandy looks with me, you rascal?
  [Lear strikes him.]

OSWALD I'll not be struck, my lord.

KENT *[Tripping him]* Nor tripped neither, you base
football player.   86

LEAR *[To Kent]* I thank thee, fellow; thou serv'st me, and
I'll love thee.

KENT *[To Oswald]* Come, sir, arise, away. I'll teach you
differences. Away, away. If you will measure your lub- 90
ber's length again, tarry; but away, go to. Have you wis- 91
dom? So.

                                    [Exit Oswald.]

LEAR Now, my friendly knave, I thank thee. There's
earnest of thy service.   94

---

66 *rememb'rest* remind **66–67** *conception* perception **68–69** *jealous curiosity* hypersensitiveness **69** *very pretense* real intention **86** *football player*
(football was a lower-class street game) **90** *differences* distinctions of rank
90–91 *measure . . . length* i.e., have me trip you up again; *lubber* oaf **91** *go
to* get out **94** *earnest of* a down payment on

[Lear gives Kent money.] Enter Fool.

FOOL   Let me hire him, too. Here's my coxcomb.

LEAR   How now, my pretty knave, how dost thou?

97 FOOL   Sirrah, you were best take my coxcomb.

LEAR   Why, my boy?

FOOL   Why, for taking one's part that's out of favor. Nay,
100   an thou canst not smile as the wind sits, thou'lt catch
cold shortly. There, take my coxcomb. Why, this fellow
102   has banished two on's daughters and did the third a
blessing against his will. If thou follow him, thou must
104   needs wear my coxcomb. How now, nuncle? Would I
had two coxcombs and two daughters.

LEAR   Why, my boy?

107 FOOL   If I gave them all my living I'd keep my coxcombs
myself. There's mine; beg another of thy daughters.

LEAR   Take heed, sirrah – the whip.

110 FOOL   Truth's a dog must to kennel. He must be
111   whipped out when the Lady Brach may stand by th' fire
and stink.

113 LEAR   A pestilent gall to me!

FOOL   Sirrah, I'll teach thee a speech.

LEAR   Do.

FOOL   Mark it, nuncle:
Have more than thou showest,
Speak less than thou knowest,
119   Lend less than thou owest,
120   Ride more than thou goest,
121   Learn more than thou trowest,

---

97 *coxcomb* fool's cap   100 *an* if   100–101 *an . . . shortly* if you can't please
those in power, you'll soon be out in the cold   102 *banished* (as Kent says,
"Freedom lives hence, and banishment is here," I.1.180.); *on's* of his   104
nuncle (mine) uncle   107 *living* possessions   107–8 *I'd . . . myself* I'd be a
double fool   111 *out* out of doors   111–12 *when . . . stink* i.e., as Goneril
and Regan are favored and the truthful Cordelia exiled   111 *brach* bitch
113 *gall* bitterness, sore   119 *owest* own   120 *goest* walk   121 *trowest* believe (i.e., don't believe everything you hear)

Set less than thou throwest,   122
Leave thy drink and thy whore,
And keep in-a-door;
And thou shalt have more
Than two tens to a score.   126

KENT   This is nothing, fool.

FOOL   Then 'tis like the breath of an unfeed lawyer: you   128
gave me nothing for't. Can you make no use of noth-
ing, nuncle?   130

LEAR   Why no, boy. Nothing can be made out of nothing.

FOOL   *[To Kent]* Prithee, tell him so much the rent of his 133
land comes to. He will not believe a fool.

LEAR   A bitter fool.

FOOL   Dost thou know the difference, my boy, between
a bitter fool and a sweet one?

LEAR   No, lad, teach me.

FOOL   Nuncle, give me an egg, and I'll give thee two
crowns.   140

LEAR   What two crowns shall they be?

FOOL   Why, after I have cut the egg i' th' middle and eat
up the meat, the two crowns of the egg. When thou   143
clovest thy crowns i' th' middle and gavest away both
parts, thou bor'st thine ass on thy back o'er the dirt.
Thou hadst little wit in thy bald crown when thou
gav'st thy golden one away. If I speak like myself in this,   147
let him be whipped that first finds it so.   148
     [Sings.]
          Fools had ne'er less grace in a year,   149
          For wise men are grown foppish,   150

---

122 *Set . . . throwest* bet less than you win (at dice)   126 *score* twenty (i.e.,
you'll do better than break even)   128 *breath* speech; *unfeed* unpaid (lawyers
proverbially will not plead without a fee)   133–34 *so . . . to* i.e., he no longer
has any land, and therefore no income from it   143 *two . . . egg* i.e., the
empty shell   147 *like myself* i.e., foolishly   148 *that . . . so* i.e., for being a
fool himself   149 *had . . . year* are now out of fashion   150 *foppish* foolish

151   And know not how their wits to wear,
152   Their manners are so apish.
153   LEAR When were you wont to be so full of songs, sirrah?
      FOOL I have used it, nuncle, e'er since thou mad'st thy
      daughters thy mothers; for when thou gav'st them the
      rod and putt'st down thine own breeches,
          [Sings.]
          Then they for sudden joy did weep,
              And I for sorrow sung,
159   That such a king should play bopeep
160   And go the fools among.
      Prithee, nuncle, keep a schoolmaster that can teach thy
162   fool to lie. I would fain learn to lie.
163   LEAR An you lie, sirrah, we'll have you whipped.
      FOOL I marvel what kin thou and thy daughters are.
      They'll have me whipped for speaking true, thou'lt
      have me whipped for lying, and sometimes I am
      whipped for holding my peace. I had rather be any
      kind o' thing than a fool; and yet I would not be thee,
      nuncle. Thou hast pared thy wit o' both sides, and left
170   nothing i' th' middle.
          Enter Goneril.
      Here comes one o' the parings.
172   LEAR How now, daughter, what makes that frontlet on?
      You are too much of late i' th' frown.
      FOOL Thou wast a pretty fellow when thou hadst no
175   need to care for her frowning. Now thou art an O with-
      out a figure. I am better than thou art now; I am a fool,
      thou art nothing. *[To Goneril]* Yes, forsooth, I will hold
      my tongue; so your face bids me, though you say noth-
      ing.

      _____

      151 *their . . . wear* to use their heads   **152** *apish* (1) stupid, (2) imitative
      153 *wont* accustomed   **159** *play bopeep* i.e., act like a child   **162** *fain* gladly
      163 *An* if   **172** *what . . . on* why are you wearing such a face; *frontlet* fore-
      head or a headband worn on it   **175–176** *an . . . figure* a zero with no num-
      ber in front of it (i.e., nothing)

[Sings.]
        Mum, mum.   *180*
        He that keeps nor crust nor crumb,
        Weary of all, shall want some.
That's a shelled peasecod.   *183*
GONERIL
    Not only, sir, this your all-licensed fool,   *184*
    But other of your insolent retinue
    Do hourly carp and quarrel, breaking forth
    In rank and not-to-be-endurèd riots. Sir,   *187*
    I had thought by making this well known unto you
    To have found a safe redress, but now grow fearful,   *189*
    By what yourself too late have spoke and done,   *190*
    That you protect this course, and put it on   *191*
    By your allowance; which if you should, the fault
    Would not scape censure nor the redresses sleep,   *193*
    Which in the tender of a wholesome weal   *194*
    Might in their working do you that offense   *195*
    Which else were shame, that then necessity   *196*
    Will call discreet proceeding.
FOOL   For you know, nuncle,
        [Sings.]
        The hedge-sparrow fed the cuckoo so long   *199*
        That it's had it head bit off by it young;   *200*
So out went the candle, and we were left darkling.   *201*
LEAR   Are you our daughter?
GONERIL
    I would you would make use of your good wisdom

---

183 *shelled peasecod* empty pea pod   **184** *all-licensed* allowed to do anything   **187** *rank* gross   **189** *safe redress* sure remedy   **190** *too late* lately   **191** *put . . . on* encourage it   **193** *redresses sleep* punishment lie dormant   **194** *tender . . . weal* government of a healthy commonwealth   **195–97** *Might . . . proceeding* might humiliate you, but, being necessary, would be merely prudent   **196** *necessity* what the situation demands   **199–200** *The . . . young* (the cuckoo lays its eggs in other birds' nests; the young cuckoos eventually destroy the sparrow that has been feeding them)   **200** *it . . . it* its . . . its   **201** *darkling* in darkness

204   Whereof I know you are fraught, and put away
205   These dispositions which of late transport you
       From what you rightly are.

FOOL   May not an ass know when the cart draws the
       horse?
          [Sings.]
209   Whoop, Jug, I love thee!

LEAR
210   Does any here know me? This is not Lear.
       Does Lear walk thus? Speak thus? Where are his eyes?
212   Either his notion weakens, his discernings
213   Are lethargied. – Ha, waking? 'Tis not so.
       Who is it that can tell me who I am?

FOOL   Lear's shadow.

LEAR   Your name, fair gentlewoman?

GONERIL
217   This admiration, sir, is much o' th' savor
       Of other your new pranks. I do beseech you
       To understand my purposes aright.
220   As you are old and reverend, should be wise.
       Here do you keep a hundred knights and squires,
222   Men so disordered, so debauched and bold
       That this our court, infected with their manners,
224   Shows like a riotous inn; epicurism and lust
       Makes it more like a tavern or a brothel
226   Than a graced palace. The shame itself doth speak
       For instant remedy. Be then desired
       By her that else will take the thing she begs,
229   A little to disquantity your train,
230   And the remainders that shall still depend

---

204 *fraught* full   205 *dispositions* moods   209 *Jug* Joan (generic name for a
whore)   212 *notion* mind; *discernings* perceptions   213 *waking* am I awake
217 *admiration* spectacle (something to be wondered at)   222 *bold* impudent   224 *Shows* looks; *epicurism* gluttony   226 *graced* dignified   229 *disquantity . . . train* reduce the size of your retinue   230 *depend* be your
dependents

To be such men as may besort your age,   231
Which know themselves and you.
LEAR   Darkness and devils!
Saddle my horses, call my train together!   233
Degenerate bastard, I'll not trouble thee.
Yet have I left a daughter.
GONERIL
You strike my people, and your disordered rabble
Make servants of their betters.
        Enter Albany.
LEAR
Woe that too late repents!
        [To Albany]
Is it your will? Speak, sir. – Prepare my horses!
Ingratitude, thou marble-hearted fiend,   240
More hideous when thou show'st thee in a child
Than the sea monster –
ALBANY   Pray, sir, be patient.
LEAR   *[To Goneril]*
Detested kite, thou liest.   244
My train are men of choice and rarest parts,   245
That all particulars of duty know,
And in the most exact regard support   247
The worships of their name. O most small fault,   248
How ugly didst thou in Cordelia show!
Which, like an engine, wrenched my frame of nature   250
From the fixed place, drew from my heart all love
And added to the gall! O Lear, Lear, Lear!
Beat at this gate that let thy folly in   253
And thy dear judgment out. Go, go, my people!

---

231 *besort* befit   **233** *Saddle . . . together* (most editors send some knights off
to do Lear's bidding, but it is more likely that everyone is immobilized with
astonishment: he has to order the horses saddled again at l. 239.)   **244** *Detested kite* detestable bird of prey   **245** *parts* qualities   **247** *in . . . regard*
with the most scrupulous attention   **248** *worships* honor   **250** *engine* machine   **250–51** *my . . . place* the structure of my being from its foundations
253 *this gate* i.e., his head

ALBANY
    My lord, I am guiltless, as I am ignorant,
    Of what hath moved you.
LEAR   It may be so, my lord.
    Hear, Nature, hear, dear goddess, hear:
    Suspend thy purpose if thou didst intend
    To make this creature fruitful.
260   Into her womb convey sterility;
    Dry up in her the organs of increase,
262   And from her derogate body never spring
263   A babe to honor her. If she must teem,
264   Create her child of spleen, that it may live
265   And be a thwart disnatured torment to her.
    Let it stamp wrinkles in her brow of youth,
267   With cadent tears fret channels in her cheeks,
268   Turn all her mother's pains and benefits
    To laughter and contempt, that she may feel
270   How sharper than a serpent's tooth it is
271   To have a thankless child. Away, away.
                [Exeunt Lear, Kent, and Attendants.]

ALBANY
    Now gods that we adore, whereof comes this?
GONERIL
    Never afflict yourself to know more of it,
274   But let his disposition have that scope
    As dotage gives it.
        Reenter Lear.
LEAR
    What! fifty of my followers at a clap?
    Within a fortnight?
ALBANY   What's the matter, sir?
LEAR
    I'll tell thee. *[To Goneril]* Life and death! I am ashamed

---

262 *derogate* debased   263 *teem* breed   264 *spleen* malice   265 *thwart disnatured* perverse unnatural   267 *cadent* falling; *fret* wear   268 *pains* care
271 s.d.   The Fool apparently remains onstage.   274 *disposition* mood

That thou hast power to shake my manhood thus,
That these hot tears which break from me perforce   280
Should make thee worth them. Blasts and fogs upon
    thee!
Th' untented woundings of a father's curse   282
Pierce every sense about thee! Old fond eyes,   283
Beweep this cause again I'll pluck ye out   284
And cast you with the waters that you loose   285
To temper clay. Ha! Let it be so.   286
I have another daughter,
Who, I am sure, is kind and comfortable.   288
When she shall hear this of thee, with her nails
She'll flay thy wolvish visage. Thou shalt find   290
That I'll resume the shape which thou dost think
I have cast off forever.   *Exit.*
GONERIL   Do you mark that?
ALBANY
I cannot be so partial, Goneril,   293
To the great love I bear you –
GONERIL
Pray you, content. What, Oswald, ho!
    [To Fool]
You, sir, more knave than fool, after your master!
FOOL   Nuncle Lear, nuncle Lear, tarry; take the fool with
    thee.
            A fox, when one has caught her,
            And such a daughter,
            Should sure to the slaughter,   300
            If my cap would buy a halter.   301
            So the fool follows after.   *Exit.*   302
GONERIL
    This man hath had good counsel. A hundred knights!

---

280 *perforce* i.e., against my will   **282** *untented woundings* wounds too deep
to be probed   **283** *fond* foolish   **284** *Beweep* if you weep over   **285** *loose* let
loose   **286** *temper* soften   **288** *comfortable* comforting   **293–94** *partial . . .*
To biased . . . by   **301** *sure* surely be sent   **302** *halter* noose

305 'Tis politic and safe to let him keep
306 At point a hundred knights! – yes, that on every dream,
307 Each buzz, each fancy, each complaint, dislike,
308 He may enguard his dotage with their powers,
309 And hold our lives in mercy. Oswald, I say!

ALBANY

310 Well, you may fear too far.

GONERIL

Safer than trust too far.

312 Let me still take away the harms I fear,
313 Not fear still to be taken. I know his heart.
What he hath uttered I have writ my sister;
If she sustain him and his hundred knights
When I have showed th' unfitness –
          Enter Steward [Oswald].
                              How now, Oswald?
What, have you writ that letter to my sister?

OSWALD   Ay, madam.

GONERIL

Take you some company, and away to horse.
320 Inform her full of my particular fear,
And thereto add such reasons of your own
322 As may compact it more. Get you gone,
And hasten your return.   *[Exit Oswald.]*
                    No, no, my lord,
324 This milky gentleness and course of yours,
325 Though I condemn not, yet under pardon,
326 You are much more ataskèd for want of wisdom
Than praised for harmful mildness.

ALBANY

How far your eyes may pierce I cannot tell;
Striving to better, oft we mar what's well.

---

305 *politic* prudent 306 *At point* armed 307 *buzz* murmur, whim 308
enguard safeguard 309 *in mercy* at his mercy 312 *still* always 313 *Not*
rather than 322 *compact* confirm 324 *milky ... course* mild and gentle
way 325 *under pardon* if you'll pardon me 326 *ataskèd* taken to task

GONERIL
Nay, then —   330
ALBANY   Well, well, th' event.   *Exeunt.*

                        *

∾ **I.5** *Enter Lear, Kent [disguised], and Fool.*

LEAR   *[To Kent]* Go you before to Gloucester with these   1
    letters. Acquaint my daughter no further with anything
    you know than comes from her demand out of the let-   3
    ter. If your diligence be not speedy, I shall be there afore
    you.
KENT   I will not sleep, my lord, till I have delivered your
    letter.   *Exit.*
FOOL   If a man's brains were in's heels, were't not in dan-
    ger of kibes?   9
LEAR   Ay, boy.   10
FOOL   Then I prithee be merry; thy wit shall not go slip- 11
    shod.
LEAR   Ha, ha, ha!
FOOL   Shalt see thy other daughter will use thee kindly,   14
    for though she's as like this as a crab's like an apple, yet 15
    I can tell what I can tell.
LEAR   What canst tell, boy?
FOOL   She will taste as like this as a crab does to a crab.
    Thou canst tell why one's nose stands i' th' middle on's 19
    face?   20
LEAR   No.

---

330 *th' event* let's await the outcome
    I.5 1 *before* ahead of me; *Gloucester* (apparently not the earl but the town,
which would therefore be the location of Regan and Cornwall's castle)   **1–2**
these letters this letter (i.e., the letters that constitute one message; cf. "these
words")   **3** *demand . . . of* questions prompted by   **9** *kibes* chilblains
11–12 *shall . . . slipshod* will not have to wear slippers because of chilblains
(the point is that feet with brains would not make this journey)   **14** *Shalt*
thou shalt; *kindly* (1) affectionately, (2) after her kind (i.e., in the same way)
15 *crab* crab apple (proverbially sour)   **19** *on's* of his

FOOL   Why, to keep one's eyes of either side's nose, that
what a man cannot smell out, he may spy into.

24 LEAR   I did her wrong.

FOOL   Canst tell how an oyster makes his shell?

LEAR   No.

FOOL   Nor I neither; but I can tell why a snail has a
house.

LEAR   Why?

30 FOOL   Why, to put's head in, not to give it away to his
31 daughters and leave his horns without a case.

32 LEAR   I will forget my nature. So kind a father! Be my
horses ready?

34 FOOL   Thy asses are gone about 'em. The reason why the
seven stars are no more than seven is a pretty reason.

LEAR   Because they are not eight.

FOOL   Yes indeed; thou wouldst make a good fool.

38 LEAR   To take't again perforce! Monster ingratitude!

FOOL   If thou wert my fool, nuncle, I'd have thee beaten
40 for being old before thy time.

LEAR   How's that?

FOOL   Thou shouldst not have been old till thou hadst
been wise.

LEAR
O, let me not be mad, not mad, sweet heaven!
45 Keep me in temper; I would not be mad.
     [Enter a Gentleman.]
How now, are the horses ready?

GENTLEMAN   Ready, my lord.

LEAR   *[To Fool]* Come, boy.

---

24 *her* Cordelia   31 *horns* (with a quibble on the cuckold's horns, implying
that Goneril and Regan are illegitimate)   32 *nature* paternal instincts
34–35 *the seven stars* the constellation the Pleiades   38 *To . . . perforce* to
take it back forcibly (Lear either rages at Goneril's revocation of his privileges
or contemplates reasserting his power)   45 *in temper* temperate, sane

FOOL
　　She that's a maid now, and laughs at my departure,　　49
　　Shall not be a maid long, unless things be cut shorter.　50
　　　　　　　　　　　　　　　　　　　Exeunt.

　　　　　　　　　　　✳

∾ **II.1** *Enter Bastard [Edmund] and Curan severally.*

EDMUND Save thee, Curan.　　　　　　　　　　　　1
CURAN And you, sir. I have been with your father, and
　　given him notice that the Duke of Cornwall and Regan
　　his duchess will be here with him this night.
EDMUND How comes that?
CURAN Nay, I know not. You have heard of the news
　　abroad? – I mean, the whispered ones, for they are yet
　　but ear-kissing arguments.　　　　　　　　　　　　8
EDMUND Not I. Pray you, what are they?
CURAN Have you heard of no likely wars toward 'twixt 10
　　the Dukes of Cornwall and Albany?
EDMUND Not a word.
CURAN You may do then in time. Fare you well, sir.
　　　　　　　　　　　　　　　　　　　Exit.
EDMUND
　　The duke be here tonight! The better best.　　　　14
　　This weaves itself perforce into my business.　　　15
　　My father hath set guard to take my brother,
　　And I have one thing of a queasy question　　　　17
　　Which I must act. Briefness and fortune work!　　18
　　Brother, a word, descend; brother, I say.　　　　　19

49–50 *She . . . shorter* i.e., the maid who laughed at my leaving would be a
fool, and would not remain a virgin unless men were castrated
　　II.1 Gloucester's house　**s.d.** *severally* separately　**1** *Save thee* God save
thee (a casual greeting like "good day")　**8** *ear-kissing arguments* whispered
matters　**10** *toward* impending　**14** *better best* very best　**15** *perforce* necessarily　**17** *queasy question* delicate problem　**18** *Briefness . . . work* may
speed and luck work for me　**19** *descend* (possibly Edgar has appeared on the
upper-stage gallery)

Enter Edgar.

20   My father watches. O, sir, fly this place;
21   Intelligence is given where you are hid.
      You have now the good advantage of the night.
      Have you not spoken 'gainst the Duke of Cornwall?
      He's coming hither now, i' th' night, i' th' haste,
      And Regan with him. Have you nothing said
26   Upon his party 'gainst the Duke of Albany?
27   Advise yourself.
EDGAR   I am sure on't, not a word.
EDMUND
      I hear my father coming. Pardon me:
      In cunning I must draw my sword upon you.
30   Draw, seem to defend yourself. Now quit you well. –
         [They fight.]
      Yield, come before my father! Light ho, here!
      (Fly, brother!) Torches, torches! (So, farewell.)
                                              Exit Edgar.
33   Some blood drawn on me would beget opinion
      Of my more fierce endeavor.
         [He wounds his arm.]
                              I have seen drunkards
      Do more than this in sport. – Father, father!
      Stop, stop! no help?
         Enter Gloucester and Servants with torches.
GLOUCESTER   Now, Edmund, where's the villain?
EDMUND
      Here stood he in the dark, his sharp sword out,
      Mumbling of wicked charms, conjuring the moon
39   To stand auspicious mistress.
GLOUCESTER   But where is he?

---

21 *Intelligence* information   26 *Upon . . . 'gainst* relating to his quarrel with
27 *Advise yourself* think about it; *on't* of it   30 *quit you* acquit yourself
33–34 *beget . . . endeavor* give the impression that I fought fiercely   39
stand act as his

EDMUND
　Look, sir, I bleed.   40
GLOUCESTER   Where is the villain, Edmund?
EDMUND
　Fled this way, sir, when by no means he could –
GLOUCESTER
　Pursue him, ho! Go after.   *[Exeunt Servants.]*
　　　　　　　　　　　　By no means what?
EDMUND
　Persuade me to the murder of your lordship,
　But that I told him the revenging gods   44
　'Gainst parricides did all the thunder bend,   45
　Spoke with how manifold and strong a bond
　The child was bound to th' father. Sir, in fine,   47
　Seeing how loathly opposite I stood   48
　To his unnatural purpose, in fell motion   49
　With his preparèd sword he charges home   50
　My unprovided body, latched mine arm;   51
　And when he saw my best alarumed spirits   52
　Bold in the quarrel's right roused to th' encounter,   53
　Or whether ghasted by the noise I made,   54
　Full suddenly he fled.
GLOUCESTER   Let him fly far.
　Not in this land shall he remain uncaught;
　And found, dispatch! The noble duke my master,   57
　My worthy arch and patron, comes tonight.   58
　By his authority I will proclaim it
　That he which finds him shall deserve our thanks,   60
　Bringing the murderous coward to the stake.
　He that conceals him, death.

---

44 *But that* however   45 *thunder bend* thunderbolts aim   47 *in fine* finally
48 *loathly opposite* loathingly opposed   49 *fell motion* deadly action   50
charges home thrusts directly at   51 *unprovided* unprotected; *latched* hit   52
best alarumed fully aroused   53 *quarrel's right* justice of the cause   54
ghasted frightened   57 *found, dispatch!* once found, death!   58 *arch . . . patron* chief patron

EDMUND
When I dissuaded him from his intent,
64 And found him pight to do it, with curst speech
65 I threatened to discover him. He replied,
66 "Thou unpossessing bastard, dost thou think
67 If I would stand against thee, would the reposal
Of any trust, virtue, or worth in thee
69 Make thy words faithed? No, what should I deny –
70 As this I would, though thou didst produce
71 My very character – I'd turn it all
72 To thy suggestion, plot, and damnèd practice;
73 And thou must make a dullard of the world
If they not thought the profits of my death
75 Were very pregnant and potential spirits
76 To make thee seek it."

GLOUCESTER   O strange and fastened villain!
77 Would he deny his letter, said he?
Tucket within.
Hark, the duke's trumpets. I know not why he comes.
79 All ports I'll bar; the villain shall not scape;
80 The duke must grant me that. Besides, his picture
I will send far and near that all the kingdom
May have due note of him; and of my land,
Loyal and natural boy, I'll work the means
84 To make thee capable.
Enter Cornwall, Regan, and Attendants.

CORNWALL
How now, my noble friend? Since I came hither,
86 Which I can call but now, I have heard strange news.

---

64 *pight* determined; *curst* angry 65 *discover* expose 66 *unpossessing* un-
propertied, landless 67 *reposal* placing 69 *faithed* believed; *what . . . I*
whatever I would 71 *character* handwriting (i.e., evidence in my own hand)
turn ascribe 72 *practice* evil schemes 73 *make . . . world* consider everyone
stupid 75 *pregnant . . . spirits* large and powerful motives 76 *strange . . .*
fastened unnatural and hardened 77 **s.d.** *Tucket* trumpet signal 79 *ports*
(1) seaports, (2) town gates 84 *capable* legally able to inherit 86 *call but*
say was only

REGAN
   If it be true, all vengeance comes too short
   Which can pursue th' offender. How dost, my lord?
GLOUCESTER
   O madam, my old heart is cracked, it's cracked.
REGAN
   What, did my father's godson seek your life?   90
   He whom my father named, your Edgar?
GLOUCESTER
   O, lady, lady, shame would have it hid.
REGAN
   Was he not companion with the riotous knights
   That tended upon my father?
GLOUCESTER
   I know not, madam. 'Tis too bad, too bad.
EDMUND
   Yes, madam, he was of that consort.   96
REGAN
   No marvel then though he were ill affected.   97
   'Tis they have put him on the old man's death,   98
   To have th' expense and waste of his revenues.   99
   I have this present evening from my sister   100
   Been well informed of them, and with such cautions
   That if they come to sojourn at my house
   I'll not be there.
CORNWALL   Nor I, assure thee, Regan.
   Edmund, I hear that you have shown your father
   A childlike office.
EDMUND   It was my duty, sir.
GLOUCESTER
   He did bewray his practice, and received   106
   This hurt you see, striving to apprehend him.
CORNWALL   Is he pursued?
GLOUCESTER   Ay, my good lord.

---

96 *consort* company   97 *though* that; *ill affected* disposed to evil   98 *put* set
99 *waste* plunder   106 *bewray . . . practice* expose Edgar's plot

CORNWALL
110 If he be taken, he shall never more
111 Be feared of doing harm. Make your own purpose
How in my strength you please. For you, Edmund,
Whose virtue and obedience doth this instant
So much commend itself, you shall be ours.
Natures of such deep trust we shall much need.
You we first seize on.

EDMUND   I shall serve you, sir,
117 Truly, however else.

GLOUCESTER
For him I thank your grace.

CORNWALL
You know not why we came to visit you?

REGAN
120 Thus out of season threading dark-eyed night:
121 Occasions, noble Gloucester, of some prize,
Wherein we must have use of your advice.
Our father he hath writ, so hath our sister,
124 Of differences which I best thought it fit
125 To answer from our home. The several messengers
126 From hence attend dispatch. Our good old friend,
Lay comforts to your bosom, and bestow
128 Your needful counsel to our businesses,
129 Which craves the instant use.

GLOUCESTER   I serve you, madam.
130 Your graces are right welcome.   *Exeunt. Flourish.*

*

111–12 *Make . . . please* carry out your intentions making what use you wish of my powers   **117** *however else* if nothing else   **120** *out of season* untimely (i.e., traveling at night)   **121** *prize* price, importance   **124** *differences* quarrels   **125** *answer . . . home* deal with away from home; *several* various   **126** *attend* await   **128** *needful* needed   **129** *the . . . use* immediate action

❧ **II.2** *Enter Kent [disguised] and Steward [Oswald]
severally.*

OSWALD   Good dawning to thee, friend. Art of this   1
house?

KENT   Ay.   3

OSWALD   Where may we set our horses?

KENT   I' th' mire.

OSWALD   Prithee, if thou lov'st me, tell me.   6

KENT   I love thee not.

OSWALD   Why then, I care not for thee.

KENT   If I had thee in Lipsbury Pinfold I would make   9
thee care for me.   10

OSWALD   Why dost thou use me thus? I know thee not.   11

KENT   Fellow, I know thee.

OSWALD   What dost thou know me for?

KENT   A knave, a rascal, an eater of broken meats, a base,   14
proud, shallow, beggarly, three-suited, hundred-pound,   15
filthy worsted-stocking knave; a lily-livered, action-   16
taking, whoreson, glass-gazing, super-serviceable, fini-   17
cal rogue; one-trunk-inheriting slave; one that wouldst   18
be a bawd in way of good service, and art nothing but   19
the composition of a knave, beggar, coward, pander,   20
and the son and heir of a mongrel bitch, one whom I
will beat into clamorous whining if thou deniest the
least syllable of thy addition.   23

II.2 1 *Art of* are you a servant in   3 *Ay* (since the house is Gloucester's, Kent
is lying, presumably as a way of picking a fight with Oswald)   6 *if . . . me* i.e.,
be kind enough to   9 *Lipsbury Pinfold* in the pen of my lips (i.e., between my
teeth)   11 *use* treat   14 *broken meats* leftover food, fit for menials   15 *three-
suited* (male household servants were furnished with three suits per year: Kent
attacks Oswald's pretensions to gentility); *hundred-pound* (the minimum annual income for a gentleman)   16 *worsted-stocking* coarse wool stocking (a
gentleman would wear silk); *lily-livered* cowardly   16–17 *action-taking* litigious (resorting to legal action instead of fighting)   17–18 *glass-gazing . . .
finical* vain, toadying, fussy   18 *one-trunk-inheriting* owning no more than
will fit in a single trunk   19 *a bawd . . . service* a pimp if asked   20 *composition* composite   23 *addition* title (i.e., the names I have just called you)

OSWALD   Why, what a monstrous fellow art thou, thus to
rail on one that is neither known of thee nor knows
thee!

27   KENT   What a brazen-faced varlet art thou, to deny thou
knowest me! Is it two days ago since I tripped up thy
heels and beat thee before the king? *[Kent draws his*
30   *sword.]* Draw, you rogue, for though it be night, yet the
31   moon shines. I'll make a sop o' th' moonshine of you,
32   you whoreson, cullionly barbermonger, draw!

OSWALD   Away, I have nothing to do with thee.

KENT   Draw, you rascal. You come with letters against
35   the king, and take Vanity the puppet's part against the
36   royalty of her father. Draw, you rogue, or I'll so car-
37   bonado your shanks – draw, you rascal, come your
ways!

OSWALD   Help, ho, murder, help!

40   KENT   Strike, you slave; stand, rogue, stand, you neat
slave, strike.

OSWALD   Help, ho, murder, murder!
Enter Bastard [Edmund, followed by] Cornwall,
Regan, Gloucester, Servants.

EDMUND   How now, what's the matter? Part!

44   KENT   With you, goodman boy. If you please come, I'll
45   flesh ye; come on, young master.

GLOUCESTER   Weapons? Arms? What's the matter here?

CORNWALL   Keep peace, upon your lives. He dies that
strikes again. What is the matter?

REGAN   The messengers from our sister and the king.

---

27 *varlet* rogue   31 *make . . . moonshine* fill you with holes so your body will
sop up moonshine   32 *cullionly* despicable (cullions are testicles; the insult is
analogous to calling someone a prick); *barbermonger* (a particularly inventive
insult: on the model of whoremonger, a pimp for barbers, one who supplies
them with clients, hence who caters to the needs of effeminate men)   35
take . . . part support the vain, overdressed Goneril   36–37 *carbonado* slash
37–38 *come . . . ways* come on, get to it   40 *neat* prissy   44 *goodman boy*
(both are deliberate insults to Edmund as a gentleman); *goodman* yeoman or
farmer   45 *flesh ye* give you your first taste of blood

CORNWALL　What is your difference? Speak.　　　50
OSWALD　I am scarce in breath, my lord.
KENT　No marvel, you have so bestirred your valor, you
cowardly rascal. Nature disclaims in thee; a tailor made　53
thee.
CORNWALL　Thou art a strange fellow: a tailor make a
man?
KENT　A tailor, sir. A stonecutter or a painter could not
have made him so ill though they had been but two　58
years o' th' trade.　　　59
CORNWALL　Speak yet; how grew your quarrel?　　　60
OSWALD　This ancient ruffian, sir, whose life I have
spared at suit of his gray beard –　　　62
KENT　Thou whoreson zed, thou unnecessary letter! My　63
lord, if you will give me leave, I will tread this unbolted　64
villain into mortar and daub the wall of a jakes with　65
him. *[To Oswald]* Spare my gray beard, you wagtail?　66
CORNWALL　Peace, sirrah. You beastly knave, know you
no reverence?
KENT　Yes, sir, but anger hath a privilege.
CORNWALL　Why art thou angry?　　　70
KENT
That such a slave as this should wear a sword,
Who wears no honesty. Such smiling rogues as these,
Like rats, oft bite the holy cords a-twain　　　73
Which are too intrince t' unloose; smooth every passion　74
That in the natures of their lords rebel,　　　75
Being oil to fire, snow to the colder moods,
Renege, affirm, and turn their halcyon beaks　　　77

---

50 *difference* quarrel　**53** *disclaims in* disowns　**58** *ill* badly　**59** *o' th* at the
62 *at suit* at the plea　**63** *zed* the letter *z* ("unnecessary" because its sound is
also represented by *s*, and because it is not used in Latin)　**64** *unbolted* unsifted (as flour or plaster)　**65** *jakes* toilet　**66** *wagtail* (a bird that constantly
wags its tail; hence a nervous or effeminate person)　**73** *holy cords* sacred
bonds　**74** *too intrince* too intertwined; *smooth* flatter　**75** *rebel* i.e., against
reason　**77** *Renege* deny; *halcyon* kingfisher (its beak was said to be usable as
a weather vane)

78   With every gall and vary of their masters,
      Knowing naught, like dogs, but following.
      [To Oswald]
80   A plague upon your epileptic visage!
81   Smile you my speeches as I were a fool?
82   Goose, if I had you upon Sarum Plain
83   I'd drive ye cackling home to Camelot.
      CORNWALL
      What, art thou mad, old fellow?
      GLOUCESTER   How fell you out?
      Say that.
      KENT
86   No contraries hold more antipathy
      Than I and such a knave.
      CORNWALL
      Why dost thou call him knave?
89   What is his fault?
      KENT   His countenance likes me not.
      CORNWALL
90   No more perchance does mine, nor his, nor hers.
      KENT
      Sir, 'tis my occupation to be plain:
      I have seen better faces in my time
      Than stands on any shoulder that I see
      Before me at this instant.
      CORNWALL   This is some fellow
95   Who, having been praised for bluntness, doth affect
96   A saucy roughness, and constrains the garb
97   Quite from his nature. He cannot flatter, he;

---

78 *gall ... vary* varying irritation   **80** *epileptic* grinning   **81** *Smile you* do you smile at; *as* as if   **82** *Sarum Plain* Salisbury Plain (near Winchester; Oswald is a goose because he is laughing, but it is not clear why Shakespeare associates geese with Salisbury Plain)   **83** *Camelot* (legendary capital of King Arthur, thought to have been on the site of Winchester)   **86** *contraries* opposites   **89** *His ... not* I don't like his face   **95** *affect* adopt   **96–97** *constrains ... nature* forces plain speaking away from its proper function   **96** *garb* style of speech   **97** *his* its

An honest mind and plain, he must speak truth,
An they will take it, so; if not, he's plain.   99
These kind of knaves I know, which in this plainness   100
Harbor more craft and more corrupter ends
Than twenty silly-ducking observants   102
That stretch their duties nicely.   103

KENT
  Sir, in good faith, in sincere verity,
  Under th' allowance of your great aspect,
  Whose influence, like the wreath of radiant fire
  On flick'ring Phoebus' front –   107
CORNWALL   What mean'st by this?
KENT   To go out of my dialect, which you discommend   108
  so much. I know, sir, I am no flatterer. He that beguiled 109
  you in a plain accent was a plain knave, which for my   110
  part I will not be, though I should win your displeasure
  to entreat me to't.   112
CORNWALL
  [To Oswald] What was th' offense you gave him?
OSWALD
  I never gave him any.
  It pleased the king his master very late   115
  To strike at me upon his misconstruction,   116
  When he, compact, and flattering his displeasure,   117
  Tripped me behind; being down, insulted, railed,
  And put upon him such a deal of man   119
  That worthied him, got praises of the king   120
  For him attempting who was self-subdued,   121

---

99 *An* if; *so* well and good; *he's plain* his excuse is his bluntness   102 *silly . . .*
observants bowing attendants   103 *nicely* excessively   107 *Phoebus' front* the
sun god's forehead   108 *go . . . dialect* depart from my usual way of speaking
109–10 *He . . . you* whoever deceived you   112 *to . . . to't* i.e., even if you
begged me to be a knave   115 *very late* recently   116 *misconstruction* misunderstanding me   117 *compact* in league (with the king)   119 *deal . . .*
man macho act   120 *worthied him* made him a hero   121 *For . . . subdued*
for attacking a man who refused to fight

122 And in the fleshment of this dread exploit,
    Drew on me here again.
KENT
124 None of these rogues and cowards
    But Ajax is their fool.
CORNWALL   Fetch forth the stocks!
    You stubborn, ancient knave, you reverend braggart,
    We'll teach you.
KENT   Sir, I am too old to learn.
    Call not your stocks for me; I serve the king,
    On whose employment I was sent to you.
130 You shall do small respects, show too bold malice
    Against the grace and person of my master,
    Stocking his messenger.
CORNWALL   Fetch forth the stocks!
    As I have life and honor, there shall he sit till noon.
REGAN
    Till noon? Till night, my lord, and all night too.
KENT
    Why, madam, if I were your father's dog
    You should not use me so.
REGAN
137 Sir, being his knave I will.
        Stocks brought out.
CORNWALL
138 This is a fellow of the selfsame color
139 Our sister speaks of. Come, bring away the stocks.
GLOUCESTER
140 Let me beseech your grace not to do so.
    The king his master needs must take it ill
    That he, so slightly valued in his messenger,
143 Should have him thus restrained.

---

122 *fleshment* excitement   124–25 *None . . . fool* (i.e., Oswald is making a
fool out of Cornwall, whom Kent identifies with the dull-witted and boastful Greek hero Ajax)   137 *being* as you are   138 *color* kind   139 *away* forward   143 *answer* answer for

CORNWALL   I'll answer that.

REGAN

My sister may receive it much more worse
To have her gentlemen abused, assaulted.
[Kent is put in the stocks.]

CORNWALL   *[To Gloucester]*
Come, my lord, away.
                    [Exeunt all but Kent and Gloucester.]

GLOUCESTER

I am sorry for thee, friend. 'Tis the duke's pleasure,
Whose disposition, all the world well knows,
Will not be rubbed nor stopped. I'll entreat for thee.   149

KENT

Pray do not, sir. I have watched and traveled hard.   150
Some time I shall sleep out; the rest I'll whistle.
A good man's fortune may grow out at heels.   152
Give you good morrow.

GLOUCESTER

The duke's to blame in this; 'twill be ill taken.   *Exit.*

KENT

Good king, that must approve the common saw: 155
Thou out of heaven's benediction com'st   156
To the warm sun.
Approach, thou beacon to this under globe,   158
That by thy comfortable beams I may   159
Peruse this letter. Nothing almost sees miracles   160
But misery. I know 'tis from Cordelia,
Who hath most fortunately been informed
Of my obscurèd course. "– And shall find time   163

---

149 *rubbed* deflected (term from the game of bowls)   150 *watched* stayed
awake   152 *grow . . . heels* wear thin   155 *approve . . . saw* prove the truth
of the old saying   156–57 *Thou . . . sun* you go from God's blessing into the
hot sun (i.e., you go from good to bad)   158 *beacon* (presumably the moon,
since it is night)   159 *comfortable* comforting   160–61 *Nothing . . . misery*
miracles are rarely seen by any but the miserable   163 *obscurèd* disguised
163–65 *And . . . remedies* (a famously incoherent crux: is Kent reading a bit
of Cordelia's letter?)

164 From this enormous state, seeking to give
165 Losses their remedies." All weary and o'erwatched,
166 Take vantage, heavy eyes, not to behold
    This shameful lodging. Fortune, good night;
168 Smile once more; turn thy wheel.
    [Sleeps.]

        *

～ **II.3** *Enter Edgar.*

EDGAR
1   I heard myself proclaimed,
2   And by the happy hollow of a tree
    Escaped the hunt. No port is free, no place
    That guard and most unusual vigilance
5   Does not attend my taking. Whiles I may scape
6   I will preserve myself, and am bethought
    To take the basest and most poorest shape
8   That ever penury in contempt of man
    Brought near to beast. My face I'll grime with filth,
10 Blanket my loins, elf all my hairs in knots,
11 And with presented nakedness outface
    The winds and persecutions of the sky.
13 The country gives me proof and precedent
14 Of Bedlam beggars who with roaring voices
15 Strike in their numbed and mortifièd arms
    Pins, wooden pricks, nails, sprigs of rosemary,

---

164 *enormous state* terrible situation   **165** *oe'rwatched* too long without sleep
166 *Take vantage* take advantage (by falling asleep)   **168** *turn . . . wheel*
change my luck (The goddess Fortuna is depicted with a large vertical wheel,
which she turns arbitrarily; Kent is now at the bottom.)
    II.3 1 s.d. Kent remains onstage in the stocks, asleep, but he and Edgar
are clearly not part of the same scene.   **1** *proclaimed* i.e., as an outlaw   **2**
happy hollow i.e., lucky hiding place   **5** *attend . . . taking* prepare to arrest me
6 *am bethought* have a plan   **8** *of* for   **10** *elf* tangle (into "elf locks")   **11** *pre-*
sented the show of   **13** *proof* experience   **14** *Bedlam beggars* (see I.2.132)
15 *Strike* stick; *mortifièd* dead to pain

And with this horrible object from low farms,   17
Poor pelting villages, sheepcotes, and mills   18
Sometimes with lunatic bans, sometime with prayers   19
Enforce their charity. "Poor Turlygod! poor Tom!"   20
That's something yet. Edgar I nothing am.   *Exit.* 21

*

∾ **II.4** *Enter Lear, Fool, and Gentleman. [Kent still in
the stocks.]*

LEAR
    'Tis strange that they should so depart from home
    And not send back my messenger.
GENTLEMAN   As I learned,
    The night before there was no purpose in them   3
    Of this remove.
KENT   Hail to thee, noble master.
LEAR
    Ha! Mak'st thou this shame thy pastime?
KENT   No, my lord.
FOOL   Ha, ha, he wears cruel garters. Horses are tied by   7
    the heads, dogs and bears by th' neck, monkeys by th'
    loins, and men by th' legs. When a man's overlusty at   9
    legs, then he wears wooden netherstocks.   10
LEAR
    What's he that hath so much thy place mistook
    To set thee here?
KENT   It is both he and she,
    Your son and daughter.   13
LEAR   No.
KENT   Yes.

---

17 *object* spectacle 18 *pelting* paltry 19 *bans* curses 20 *Turlygod* (unexplained, but evidently another name for a Bedlam beggar) 21 *Edgar* i.e., as
Edgar
    II.4 3–4 *there . . . remove* they had no intention of making this trip
7 *cruel* (punning on "crewel," worsted cloth) 9–10 *overlusty . . . legs* too
eager to run 10 *netherstocks* stockings 13 *son* i.e., son-in-law

LEAR   No, I say.

KENT
   I say yea.

LEAR   By Jupiter, I swear no!

KENT
15   By Juno, I swear ay.

LEAR   They durst not do't,
   They could not, would not do't. 'Tis worse than murder
17   To do upon respect such violent outrage.
18   Resolve me with all modest haste which way
   Thou mightst deserve or they impose this usage,
20   Coming from us.

KENT   My lord, when at their home
21   I did commend your highness' letters to them,
   Ere I was risen from the place that showed
23   My duty kneeling, came there a reeking post
   Stewed in his haste, half breathless, panting forth
   From Goneril his mistress salutations;
26   Delivered letters spite of intermission,
27   Which presently they read; on those contents
28   They summoned up their meiny, straight took horse,
   Commanded me to follow and attend
30   The leisure of their answer, gave me cold looks;
   And meeting here the other messenger,
   Whose welcome I perceived had poisoned mine,
   Being the very fellow which of late
34   Displayed so saucily against your highness,
35   Having more man than wit about me, drew.
   He raised the house with loud and coward cries.
   Your son and daughter found this trespass worth
   The shame which here it suffers.

---

15 *Juno* queen of the gods, wife of Jupiter 17 *upon respect* to one who should be respected (as the king's messenger) 18 *Resolve* explain to; *modest* decent 21 *commend* deliver 23–24 *reeking . . . Stewed* hot and sweaty messenger 26 *spite . . . intermission* though he was interrupting me 27 *presently* immediately 28 *meiny* retinue 34 *Displayed* behaved 35 *wit* sense; *drew* drew my sword

FOOL   Winter's not gone yet if the wild geese fly that way.   39
    Fathers that wear rags   40
     Do make their children blind,   41
    But fathers that bear bags   42
     Shall see their children kind.
    Fortune, that arrant whore,
    Ne'er turns the key to th' poor.   45
But for all this thou shalt have as many dolors for thy   46
daughters as thou canst tell in a year.   47

LEAR
 O, how this mother swells up toward my heart!   48
 Hysterica passio, down, thou climbing sorrow,   49
 Thy element's below. Where is this daughter?   50

KENT   With the earl, sir, here within.

LEAR   Follow me not; stay here.   *Exit.*

GENTLEMAN
 Made you no more offense but what you speak of?

KENT   None.
 How chance the king comes with so small a number?

FOOL   An thou hadst been set i' th' stocks for that ques-   56
tion, thou'dst well deserved it.

KENT   Why, fool?

FOOL   We'll set thee to school to an ant, to teach thee   59
there's no laboring i' th' winter. All that follow their   60
noses are led by their eyes but blind men, and there's
not a nose among twenty but can smell him that's
stinking. Let go thy hold when a great wheel runs down
a hill, lest it break thy neck with following; but the

---

39 *Winter's . . . way* if the geese are flying south (*that way,* the way they fly in winter), winter's not over yet (i.e., things will get worse)   **41** *blind* (to their father's needs)   **42** *bags* moneybags   **45** *turns the key* opens the door   **46** *dolors* sorrows (punning on "dollars," a term used for various European coins)   **47** *tell* count   **48** *mother* hysteria   **49** *Hysterica passio* (the medical term for hysteria)   **50** *Thy . . . below* (hysteria's natural place, "element," was said to be the abdomen or, in women, the womb)   **56** *An* if   **59–60** *We'll . . . winter* (ants proverbially do not work in winter – implying that working for Lear is now unprofitable)

great one that goes upward, let him draw thee after.
When a wise man gives thee better counsel, give me
67   mine again. I would have none but knaves follow it,
since a fool gives it.
            That sir which serves and seeks for gain
70   And follows but for form,
71   Will pack when it begins to rain,
                 And leave thee in the storm.
             But I will tarry, the fool will stay,
             And let the wise man fly.
75   The knave turns fool that runs away,
76   The fool no knave, perdy.
KENT   Where learned you this, fool?
FOOL   Not i' th' stocks, fool.
       Enter Lear and Gloucester.
LEAR
    Deny to speak with me? They are sick, they are weary,
80   They have traveled all the night? Mere fetches,
81   The images of revolt and flying off.
    Fetch me a better answer.
GLOUCESTER   My dear lord,
83   You know the fiery quality of the duke,
    How unremovable and fixed he is
    In his own course.
LEAR
    Vengeance, plague, death, confusion!
    Fiery? What quality? Why, Gloucester, Gloucester,
    I'd speak with the Duke of Cornwall and his wife.
GLOUCESTER
    Well, my good lord, I have informed them so.
LEAR
90   Informed them? Dost thou understand me, man?
GLOUCESTER   Ay, my good lord.

---

67 *again* back   70 *form* show   71 *pack* leave   75 *knave . . . away* i.e., dis-
loyalty is the real folly   76 *perdy* by God (*par Dieu*)   80 *fetches* pretenses
81 *images* signs; *flying off* insurrection   83 *quality* disposition

LEAR
   The king would speak with Cornwall; the dear father
   Would with his daughter speak, commands, tends   93
      service.
   Are they informed of this? My breath and blood –
   Fiery? The fiery duke? Tell the hot duke that –
   No, but not yet; maybe he is not well.
   Infirmity doth still neglect all office   97
   Whereto our health is bound. We are not ourselves   98
   When nature, being oppressed, commands the mind
   To suffer with the body. I'll forbear,   100
   And am fallen out with my more headier will   101
   To take the indisposed and sickly fit   102
   For the sound man. – Death on my state! wherefore   103
   Should he sit here? This act persuades me   104
   That this remotion of the duke and her   105
   Is practice only. Give me my servant forth.   106
   Go tell the duke and's wife I'd speak with them,
   Now, presently. Bid them come forth and hear me,   108
   Or at their chamber door I'll beat the drum
   Till it cry sleep to death.   110
GLOUCESTER   I would have all well betwixt you.   *Exit.*
LEAR
   O me, my heart! My rising heart! But down!
FOOL   Cry to it, nuncle, as the cockney did to the eels   113
   when she put 'em i' th' paste alive. She knapped 'em o' 114
   th' coxcombs with a stick, and cried "Down, wantons,   115

---

93 *tends service* awaits their obedience   97 *still . . . office* always neglects duty
98 *Whereto . . . bound* which in health we are bound to obey   101 *fallen out*
angry; *headier* headstrong   102 *To take* that mistook   103 *Death . . . state*
(the expletive is ironic: "Let my royal power die")   104 *he* Kent   105 *remo-*
tion (1) removal (from their home), (2) aloofness (from Lear)   106 *practice*
trickery; *Give . . . forth* release my servant   108 *presently* instantly   110
Till . . . death till it kills sleep with the noise   113 *cockney* Londoner (i.e., a
city dweller)   114 *paste* pastry   114–15 *knapped 'em o' th' coxcombs* knocked
them on the head   115 *wantons* rascals (with a quibble on lechers, and on
deflating erections)

down!" 'Twas her brother that, in pure kindness to his
117   horse, buttered his hay.
       Enter Cornwall, Regan, Gloucester, Servants.

LEAR
    Good morrow to you both.
CORNWALL   .   Hail to your grace.
REGAN
    I am glad to see your highness.
       Kent here set at liberty.
LEAR
120   Regan, I think you are. I know what reason
       I have to think so. If thou shouldst not be glad
       I would divorce me from thy mother's tomb,
123   Sepulch'ring an adult'ress. *[To Kent]* O, are you free?
       Some other time for that. – Belovèd Regan,
125   Thy sister's naught. O, Regan, she hath tied
       Sharp-toothed unkindness like a vulture here.
       I can scarce speak to thee. Thou'lt not believe
       With how depraved a quality – O Regan!
REGAN
    I pray you, sir, take patience. I have hope
130   You less know how to value her desert
       Than she to scant her duty.
LEAR   Say? How is that?
REGAN
    I cannot think my sister in the least
    Would fail her obligation. If, sir, perchance
    She have restrained the riots of your followers,
    'Tis on such ground and to such wholesome end
    As clears her from all blame.
LEAR   My curses on her.

---

117 *buttered* . . . *hay* (misguided kindness: horses will not eat grease)   123
Sepulch'ring . . . *adult'ress* i.e., it would prove you were not my daughter   125
naught wicked (cf. "naughty")   130–31 *You* . . . *duty* the problem is that you
are unable to evaluate her merit rather than that she has failed in her duty

REGAN
  O, sir, you are old;
  Nature in you stands on the very verge   138
  Of his confine. You should be ruled and led
  By some discretion that discerns your state   140
  Better than you yourself. Therefore I pray you
  That to our sister you do make return;
  Say you have wronged her.
LEAR   Ask her forgiveness?
  Do you but mark how this becomes the house?   144
    [Kneels.]
  "Dear daughter, I confess that I am old;
  Age is unnecessary. On my knees I beg   146
  That you'll vouchsafe me raiment, bed, and food."
REGAN
  Good sir, no more. These are unsightly tricks.
  Return you to my sister.
LEAR *[Rising]*   Never, Regan.
  She hath abated me of half my train,   150
  Looked black upon me, struck me with her tongue
  Most serpentlike upon the very heart.
  All the stored vengeances of heaven fall
  On her ingrateful top! Strike her young bones,   154
  You taking airs, with lameness.   155
CORNWALL   Fie, sir, fie.
LEAR
  You nimble lightnings, dart your blinding flames
  Into her scornful eyes. Infect her beauty,
  You fen-sucked fogs drawn by the pow'rful sun   158
  To fall and blister.   159

138–39 *Nature . . . confine* your life stands at the very edge of its allotted space
140 *discretion . . . state* discerning person who understands your condition
144 *house* family   **146** *Age is* old people are   **150** *abated* deprived   **154** *top*
head   **155** *taking airs* infectious vapors   **158** *fen-sucked . . . sun* (the sun was
believed to draw infectious vapors from swamps)   **159** *fall . . . blister* strike
and blister her

REGAN

160   O the blest gods!
    So will you wish on me when the rash mood is on.

LEAR

    No, Regan, thou shalt never have my curse.

163   Thy tender-hefted nature shall not give
    Thee o'er to harshness. Her eyes are fierce, but thine
    Do comfort and not burn. 'Tis not in thee
    To grudge my pleasures, to cut off my train,

167   To bandy hasty words, to scant my sizes,

168   And, in conclusion, to oppose the bolt
    Against my coming in. Thou better know'st

170   The offices of nature, bond of childhood,

171   Effects of courtesy, dues of gratitude;
    Thy half o' th' kingdom hast thou not forgot,

173   Wherein I thee endowed.

REGAN   Good sir, to th' purpose.

    Tucket within.

LEAR

    Who put my man i' th' stocks?

CORNWALL   What trumpet's that?

    Enter Steward [Oswald].

REGAN

175   I know't, my sister's. This approves her letter
    That she would soon be here. *[To Oswald]* Is your lady
      come?

LEAR

177   This is a slave whose easy, borrowed pride
    Dwells in the sickly grace of her he follows.
    [To Oswald]

179   Out, varlet, from my sight!

CORNWALL   What means your grace?

---

163 *tender-hefted* gently disposed   167 *sizes* allowance   168 *oppose the bolt* bolt the door   170 *offices* duties   171 *Effects* obligations   173 *to . . . purpose* get to the point   175 *approves* confirms   177 *easy* impudent; *borrowed* assumed   179 *varlet* scoundrel

LEAR
  Who stocked my servant? Regan, I have good hope   *180*
  Thou didst not know on't.   181
    Enter Goneril.
                        Who comes here? O heavens,
  If you do love old men, if your sweet sway
  Allow obedience, if you yourselves are old,   *183*
  Make it your cause; send down and take my part.
    [To Goneril]
  Art not ashamed to look upon this beard?
  O Regan, will you take her by the hand?
GONERIL
  Why not by th' hand, sir? How have I offended?
  All's not offense that indiscretion finds   *188*
  And dotage terms so.   189
LEAR   O sides, you are too tough!
  Will you yet hold? How came my man i' th' stocks?   *190*
CORNWALL
  I set him there, sir, but his own disorders
  Deserved much less advancement.   192
LEAR   You? Did you?
REGAN
  I pray you, father, being weak, seem so.
  If till the expiration of your month
  You will return and sojourn with my sister,
  Dismissing half your train, come then to me.
  I am now from home, and out of that provision   *197*
  Which shall be needful for your entertainment.   198
LEAR
  Return to her, and fifty men dismissed?
  No, rather I abjure all roofs, and choose   *200*
  To wage against the enmity o' th' air,   201

---

181 *on't* of it   **183** *Allow* approve of   **188** *indiscretion* poor judgment   **189** *sides* breast (which should burst with grief)   **192** *less advancement* less of a promotion (i.e., a worse punishment)   **197** *from* away from   **198** *entertainment* reception   **201** *wage* fight

To be a comrade with the wolf and owl –
Necessity's sharp pinch. Return with her?
Why, the hot-blooded France that dowerless took
Our youngest born – I could as well be brought
206 To knee his throne and, squirelike, pension beg
To keep base life afoot. Return with her?
208 Persuade me rather to be slave and sumpter
To this detested groom. *[Points at Oswald.]*

GONERIL   At your choice, sir.

LEAR
210 I prithee, daughter, do not make me mad.
I will not trouble thee, my child. Farewell.
We'll no more meet, no more see one another.
But yet thou art my flesh, my blood, my daughter –
Or rather a disease that's in my flesh,
Which I must needs call mine. Thou art a boil,
216 A plague-sore, or embossèd carbuncle
In my corrupted blood. But I'll not chide thee.
Let shame come when it will, I do not call it.
219 I do not bid the thunder-bearer shoot,
220 Nor tell tales of thee to high-judging Jove.
Mend when thou canst; be better at thy leisure.
I can be patient, I can stay with Regan,
I and my hundred knights.

REGAN
. Not altogether so;
I looked not for you yet, nor am provided
For your fit welcome. Give ear, sir, to my sister;
227 For those that mingle reason with your passion
Must be content to think you old, and so –
But she knows what she does.

LEAR   Is this well spoken?

---

206 *knee* kneel to   208 *sumpter* packhorse   216 *embossèd carbuncle* swollen
tumor   219 *the thunder-bearer* Jove   227 *mingle . . . passion* deal rationally
with your intemperate behavior

REGAN
I dare avouch it, sir. What, fifty followers?   230
Is it not well? What should you need of more,
Yea, or so many, sith that both charge and danger   232
Speak 'gainst so great a number? How in one house
Should many people under two commands
Hold amity? 'Tis hard, almost impossible.

GONERIL
Why might not you, my lord, receive attendance
From those that she calls servants, or from mine?

REGAN
Why not, my lord? If then they chanced to slack ye,   238
We could control them. If you will come to me –
For now I spy a danger – I entreat you   240
To bring but five-and-twenty; to no more
Will I give place or notice.   242

LEAR
I gave you all.

REGAN   And in good time you gave it.

LEAR
Made you my guardians, my depositaries,   244
But kept a reservation to be followed   245
With such a number. What, must I come to you
With five-and-twenty, Regan? Said you so?

REGAN
And speak't again, my lord. No more with me.

LEAR
Those wicked creatures yet do look well favored   249
When others are more wicked. Not being the worst   250
Stands in some rank of praise. *[To Goneril]* I'll go with   251
  thee.

---

230 *avouch* swear   **232** *sith that* since; *charge* expense   **238** *slack* neglect
242 *notice* recognition   **244** *depositaries* trustees   **245** *kept . . . be* stipulated
that I be   **249** *well favored* attractive   **251** *Stands . . . of* deserves at least
some

Thy fifty yet doth double five-and-twenty,
253   And thou art twice her love.
GONERIL   Hear me, my lord:
What need you five-and-twenty, ten, or five,
To follow in a house where twice so many
Have a command to tend you?
REGAN   What need one?
LEAR
257   O reason not the need! Our basest beggars
258   Are in the poorest thing superfluous.
259   Allow not nature more than nature needs,
260   Man's life is cheap as beast's. Thou art a lady;
261   If only to go warm were gorgeous,
Why, nature needs not what thou gorgeous wear'st,
Which scarcely keeps thee warm. But for true need –
You heavens, give me that patience, patience I need:
You see me here, you gods, a poor old man,
As full of grief as age, wretched in both.
If it be you that stirs these daughters' hearts
268   Against their father, fool me not so much
To bear it tamely. Touch me with noble anger.
270   And let not women's weapons, waterdrops,
Stain my man's cheeks! No, you unnatural hags,
I will have such revenges on you both
That all the world shall – I will do such things –
What they are, yet I know not; but they shall be
The terrors of the earth. You think I'll weep:
No, I'll not weep.
I have full cause of weeping, but this heart
                              Storm and tempest.
278   Shall break into a hundred thousand flaws
279   Or ere I'll weep. – O fool, I shall go mad!

---

253 *twice . . . love* twice as loving as she   257 *reason* calculate   258 *Are . . .
superfluous* have something more than is absolutely necessary   259 *Allow not*
if you do not grant   261 *If . . . gorgeous* if warmth were the measure of fashionable dress   268–69 *fool . . . To* don't make me such a fool as to   278
flaws fragments   279 *Or ere* before

   Exeunt [Lear, Gloucester, Kent, Gentleman, and Fool].

CORNWALL
 Let us withdraw; 'twill be a storm.   *280*

REGAN
 This house is little. The old man and's people
 Cannot be well bestowed.

GONERIL
 'Tis his own blame hath put himself from rest,
 And must needs taste his folly.

REGAN
 For his particular I'll receive him gladly, *285*
 But not one follower.

GONERIL   So am I purposed.
 Where is my lord of Gloucester?

CORNWALL
 Followed the old man forth.

  Enter Gloucester.

       He is returned.

GLOUCESTER
 The king is in high rage.

CORNWALL   Whither is he going?

GLOUCESTER
 He calls to horse, but will I know not whither. *290*

CORNWALL
 'Tis best to give him way. He leads himself.

GONERIL *[To Gloucester]*
 My lord, entreat him by no means to stay.

GLOUCESTER
 Alack, the night comes on, and the high winds
 Do sorely ruffle. For many miles about *294*
 There's scarce a bush.

REGAN   O sir, to willful men
 The injuries that they themselves procure
 Must be their schoolmasters. Shut up your doors.

---

285 *his particular* himself alone 294 *ruffle* rage

298   He is attended with a desperate train,
299   And what they may incense him to, being apt
300   To have his ear abused, wisdom bids fear.
        CORNWALL
        Shut up your doors, my lord; 'tis a wild night.
        My Regan counsels well. Come out o' th' storm.

                                                    Exeunt.

                        *

∾ **III.1** *Storm still. Enter Kent [disguised] and a*
        Gentleman severally.

        KENT
        Who's there besides foul weather?
        GENTLEMAN
        One minded like the weather, most unquietly.
        KENT
        I know you. Where's the king?
        GENTLEMAN
        Contending with the fretful elements;
        Bids the wind blow the earth into the sea
6   Or swell the curlèd waters 'bove the main,
        That things might change or cease.
        KENT   But who is with him?
        GENTLEMAN
8   None but the fool, who labors to outjest
        His heart-struck injuries.
        KENT   Sir, I do know you,
10   And dare upon the warrant of my note
11   Commend a dear thing to you. There is division,
        Although as yet the face of it is covered
        With mutual cunning, 'twixt Albany and Cornwall;

_____

298 *desperate train* violent troop   299–300 *apt . . . abused* i.e., likely to be
misled
    III.1 A heath   6 *main* mainland   8 *outjest* overcome with jesting   10
my note what I have observed about you   11 *Commend . . . thing* entrust a
precious matter; *division* dissension

Who have – as who have not that their great stars   14
Throned and set high? – servants who seem no less,   15
Which are to France the spies and speculations   16
Intelligent of our state. What hath been seen,
Either in snuffs and packings of the dukes,   18
Or the hard rein which both of them hath borne   19
Against the old kind king; or something deeper,   20
Whereof perchance these are but furnishings –   21
GENTLEMAN
I will talk further with you.
KENT   No, do not.
For confirmation that I am much more
Than my outwall, open this purse and take   24
What it contains. If you shall see Cordelia,
As fear not but you shall, show her this ring,
And she will tell you who that fellow is   27
That yet you do not know. Fie on this storm!
I will go seek the king.
GENTLEMAN
Give me your hand. Have you no more to say?   30
KENT
Few words, but to effect more than all yet: 31
That when we have found the king – in which your   32
  pain
That way, I'll this – he that first lights on him
Holla the other.   *Exeunt [in different directions].*
                              ✳

---

14 *that . . . stars* whom destiny has   15 *who . . . less* i.e., who appear really to
be servants   16–17 *speculations Intelligent* observant informers   18 *snuffs
and packings* quarrels and intrigues   19 *hard rein* harsh treatment; *borne*
used   21 *furnishings* pretexts   24 *outwall* outward appearance   27 *who . . .
is* i.e., who I am   31 *to effect* in importance   32–33 *your . . . way* in your efforts, go that way

∾ **III.2** *Storm still. Enter Lear and Fool.*

LEAR

1 Blow, winds, and crack your cheeks! Rage, blow,
2 You cataracts and hurricanoes, spout
3 Till you have drenched our steeples, drown the cocks!
4 You sulphurous and thought-executing fires,
5 Vaunt-couriers of oak-cleaving thunderbolts,
  Singe my white head; and thou all-shaking thunder,
  Strike flat the thick rotundity o' th' world,
8 Crack nature's molds, all germens spill at once
  That makes ingrateful man.
10 FOOL   O nuncle, court holy water in a dry house is better than this rainwater out o' door. Good nuncle, in;
  ask thy daughters' blessing. Here's a night pities neither
  wise men nor fools.

LEAR

  Rumble thy bellyful! Spit, fire; spout, rain!
  Nor rain, wind, thunder, fire are my daughters.
16 I tax not you, you elements, with unkindness.
  I never gave you kingdom, called you children.
18 You owe me no subscription. Then let fall
  Your horrible pleasure. Here I stand your slave,
20 A poor, infirm, weak, and despised old man,
21 But yet I call you servile ministers,
  That will with two pernicious daughters join
23 Your high-engendered battles 'gainst a head
  So old and white as this. O, ho, 'tis foul!

III.2 Elsewhere on the heath   **1** *crack . . . cheeks* (as winds are represented on old maps, heads with cheeks puffed out)   **2** *cataracts . . . hurricanoes* torrential rains and hurricanes   **3** *cocks* weather vanes   **4** *thought-executing* (1) annihilating thought, (2) acting as fast as thought   **5** *Vaunt-couriers* heralds   **8** *nature's molds* (in which life is given form); *germens* seeds   **10** *court holy water* flattery   **16** *tax* charge   **18** *subscription* deference   **21** *ministers* agents   **23** *high-engendered battles* heavenly battalions

FOOL   He that has a house to put's head in has a good
headpiece.   26
             The codpiece that will house   27
             Before the head has any,
             The head and he shall louse,   29
             So beggars marry many.   *30*
             The man that makes his toe   31
             What he his heart should make
             Shall of a corn cry woe
             And turn his sleep to wake.
For there was never yet fair woman but she made   35
mouths in a glass.
    Enter Kent [disguised].

LEAR
No, I will be the pattern of all patience.
I will say nothing.

KENT   Who's there?

FOOL   Marry, here's grace and a codpiece, that's a wise   40
man and a fool.

KENT   *[To Lear]*
Alas, sir, are you here? Things that love night
Love not such nights as these. The wrathful skies
Gallow the very wanderers of the dark   44
And make them keep their caves. Since I was man   45
Such sheets of fire, such bursts of horrid thunder,
Such groans of roaring wind and rain I never
Remember to have heard. Man's nature cannot carry   48
Th' affliction nor the fear.

---

26 *headpiece* (1) helmet, (2) brain   **27** *codpiece* the pouch for the genitals on
men's breeches (here used for the penis); *house* lodge (in copulation)   **29–30**
The . . . many will infest both the head and the codpiece with lice, and end
in married poverty   **31–32** *The . . . make* (a parallel instance of preferring
the lower part to the higher)   **35–36** *made . . . glass* practiced smiling in a
mirror (i.e., was afflicted with vanity)   **40** *Marry* (a mild exclamation, originally an oath on the name of the Virgin)   **44** *Gallow* frighten   **45** *keep* stay
inside   **48** *carry* endure

LEAR   Let the great gods,
50 That keep this dreadful pudder o'er our heads,
    Find out their enemies now. Tremble, thou wretch,
    That hast within thee undivulgèd crimes
53 Unwhipped of justice; hide thee, thou bloody hand,
54 Thou perjured and thou simular of virtue
55 That art incestuous; caitiff, to pieces shake,
56 That under covert and convenient seeming
57 Hast practiced on man's life; close pent-up guilts,
58 Rive your concealing continents, and cry
    These dreadful summoners grace. I am a man
60 More sinned against than sinning.
    KENT   Alack, bareheaded?
61 Gracious my lord, hard by here is a hovel.
    Some friendship will it lend you 'gainst the tempest.
    Repose you there while I to this hard house –
    More harder than the stones whereof 'tis raised,
65 Which even but now, demanding after you,
    Denied me to come in – return and force
67 Their scanted courtesy.
    LEAR
    My wits begin to turn.
      [To Fool]
    Come on, my boy. How dost, my boy? Art cold?
70 I am cold myself. Where is this straw, my fellow?
    The art of our necessities is strange,
    And can make vile things precious. Come, your hovel.
    Poor fool and knave, I have one part in my heart
    That's sorry yet for thee.

---

50 *pudder* tumult   53 *of* by   54 *simular of* pretender to   55 *caitiff* wretch
56 *seeming* hypocrisy   57 *practiced on* plotted against; *close* secret   58 *Rive*
split open; *continents* coverings   58–59 *cry . . . grace* beg for mercy from
these terrible agents of justice (summoners are officers of church courts)   61
hard close   65 *demanding* as I was asking   67 *scanted* deficient

FOOL
> He that has and a little tiny wit,   75
>   With heigh-ho, the wind and the rain,
> Must make content with his fortunes fit,   77
> Though the rain it raineth every day.   78

LEAR   True, boy. Come, bring us to this hovel.
>   *[Exeunt Lear and Kent.]*

FOOL   This is a brave night to cool a courtesan. I'll speak   80
a prophecy ere I go:
> When priests are more in word than matter,   82
> When brewers mar their malt with water,   83
> When nobles are their tailors' tutors,   84
> No heretics burned but wenches' suitors,   85
> When every case in law is right,
> No squire in debt, nor no poor knight,
> When slanders do not live in tongues,
> Nor cutpurses come not to throngs,   89
> When usurers tell their gold i' th' field,   90
> And bawds and whores do churches build,
> Then shall the realm of Albion   92
> Come to great confusion;
> Then comes the time, who lives to see't,
> That going shall be used with feet.   95

This prophecy Merlin shall make, for I live before his
time.   *Exit.*

                        ✳

---

75 *and* only, even   **77** *make . . . fit* be content with his lot   **78** (the song re-figures Feste's song at the end of *Twelfth Night*)   **80** *a . . . courtesan* a fine night to cool off the lust of a prostitute   **82** *more . . . matter* preach better than they practice   **83** *mar* dilute   **84** *are . . . tutors* teach tailors about fashion (i.e., know what they want)   **85** *No . . . suitors* (1) the only people who burn are lovers (who burn with passion), (2) the only heretics who burn are faithless lovers (who burn with venereal disease)   **89** *cutpurses* pickpockets   **90** *tell . . . field* count their money openly (because they have nothing to hide)   **92** *Albion* England   **95** *going . . . feet* walking will be done on foot (i.e., things will be just as they are now)

ᦿ **III.3** *Enter Gloucester and Edmund.*

GLOUCESTER   Alack, alack, Edmund, I like not this unnatural dealing. When I desired their leave that I might
3   pity him, they took from me the use of mine own
house, charged me on pain of perpetual displeasure neither to speak of him, entreat for him, or any way sustain him.
EDMUND   Most savage and unnatural!
8   GLOUCESTER   Go to, say you nothing. There is division
between the dukes, and a worse matter than that. I
10   have received a letter this night; 'tis dangerous to be
11   spoken. I have locked the letter in my closet. These in-
12   juries the king now bears will be revenged home. There
13   is part of a power already footed. We must incline to
14   the king. I will look him and privily relieve him. Go
you and maintain talk with the duke, that my charity
16   be not of him perceived. If he ask for me, I am ill and
gone to bed. If I die for it – as no less is threatened
me – the king my old master must be relieved. There is
19   strange things toward, Edmund. Pray you, be careful.
                                                        Exit.

EDMUND
20   This courtesy forbid thee shall the duke
Instantly know, and of that letter too.
22   This seems a fair deserving, and must draw me
That which my father loses: no less than all.
The younger rises when the old doth fall.   *Exit.*
                              ✳

III.3 Gloucester's house   **3** *pity* take pity on   **8** *Go to* be quiet   **11** *closet*
(any private room: study, bedroom)   **12** *home* thoroughly   **13** *power* army;
footed landed; *incline to* side with   **14** *look* search for; *privily* secretly   **16** *of*
by   **19** *toward* impending   **20** *courtesy . . . thee* kindness you have been forbidden to show   **22** *fair deserving* action that would deserve a fair reward

❧ **III.4** *Enter Lear, Kent [disguised], and Fool.*

KENT
    Here is the place, my lord; good my lord, enter.
    The tyranny of the open night's too rough
    For nature to endure.   3
        Storm still.
LEAR   Let me alone.
KENT
    Good my lord, enter here.
LEAR   Wilt break my heart?
KENT
    I had rather break mine own. Good my lord, enter.
LEAR
    Thou think'st 'tis much that this contentious storm
    Invades us to the skin so – 'tis to thee;
    But where the greater malady is fixed,   8
    The lesser is scarce felt. Thou'dst shun a bear,
    But if thy flight lay toward the roaring sea   10
    Thou'dst meet the bear i' th' mouth. When the mind's   11
      free,
    The body's delicate. The tempest in my mind   12
    Doth from my senses take all feeling else
    Save what beats there: filial ingratitude.
    Is it not as this mouth should tear this hand   15
    For lifting food to't? But I will punish home.   16
    No, I will weep no more. In such a night
    To shut me out? Pour on, I will endure.
    In such a night as this! O Regan, Goneril,
    Your old kind father, whose frank heart gave all –   20
    O, that way madness lies. Let me shun that;
    No more of that.

───────

III.4 Before a hovel on the heath   3 *nature* humanity, human frailty   8
fixed lodged   11 *i' th' mouth* head-on; *When . . . free* only when the mind is
untroubled   12 *delicate* sensitive to pain   15 *as* as if   16 *home* thoroughly

KENT   Good my lord, enter here.

LEAR

Prithee, go in thyself; seek thine own ease.

This tempest will not give me leave to ponder

25   On things would hurt me more – but I'll go in.

[To Fool]

In, boy, go first. You houseless poverty –

Nay, get thee in. I'll pray, and then I'll sleep.

                                        Exit [Fool].

Poor naked wretches, wheresoe'er you are,

29   That bide the pelting of this pitiless storm,

30   How shall your houseless heads and unfed sides,

31   Your looped and windowed raggedness defend you

32   From seasons such as these? O, I have ta'en

33   Too little care of this. Take physic, pomp,

Expose thyself to feel what wretches feel,

35   That thou may'st shake the superflux to them

And show the heavens more just.

37 EDGAR   *[Within]* Fathom and half, fathom and half!

Poor Tom!

FOOL   *[Within]* Come not in here, nuncle; here's a spirit.

40   Help me, help me!

KENT   Give me thy hand. Who's there?

FOOL   *[Within]* A spirit, a spirit. He says his name's Poor

Tom.

KENT   What art thou that dost grumble there i' th' straw?

Come forth.

        Enter Edgar [disguised as a madman].

46 EDGAR   Away, the foul fiend follows me. "Through the

sharp hawthorn blow the winds" – Hum! Go to thy

bed and warm thee.

---

25 *would* that would   29 *bide* endure, wait out   31 *looped, windowed* (both mean "full of holes")   32 *seasons* weather   33 *Take . . . pomp* grandeur, purge yourself   35 *shake . . . superflux* pour out your surplus   37 *Fathom . . . half* nine feet of water (the call of a sailor taking soundings)   46–47 *Through . . . winds* (apparently a fragment of a ballad, quoted again at l. 98)

LEAR
   Didst thou give all to thy daughters,
   And art thou come to this?   50
EDGAR   Who gives anything to Poor Tom, whom the
   foul fiend hath led through fire and through flame,
   through ford and whirlpool, o'er bog and quagmire;
   that hath laid knives under his pillow and halters in his   54
   pew, set ratsbane by his porridge, made him proud of   55
   heart to ride on a bay trotting-horse over four-inched
   bridges, to course his own shadow for a traitor. Bless   57
   thy five wits, Tom's acold. O do, de, do, de, do, de.   58
   Bless thee from whirlwinds, star-blasting, and taking.   59
   Do Poor Tom some charity, whom the foul fiend vexes.   60
   There could I have him, now – and there – and there
   again – and there –
      Storm still.
LEAR
   Has his daughters brought him to this pass?
      [To Edgar]
   Couldst thou save nothing? Wouldst thou give 'em all?
FOOL   Nay, he reserved a blanket, else we had been all
   shamed.
LEAR   *[To Edgar]*
   Now all the plagues that in the pendulous air   67
   Hang fated o'er men's faults light on thy daughters!   68
KENT   He hath no daughters, sir.
LEAR
   Death, traitor! Nothing could have subdued nature   70
   To such a lowness but his unkind daughters.

54–55 *halters . . . pew* nooses on his balcony; *knives, halters, ratsbane* (all
temptations to suicide)   55–57 *made . . . bridges* i.e., made him take mad
risks   57 *course . . . traitor* hunt his own shadow as if it were an enemy   58
five wits (the constituent parts of intelligence in Renaissance theories of cognition: common wit, imagination, fantasy, estimation, memory)   59 *star-
blasting, taking* malignant stars, infection   67 *pendulous* overhanging   68
fated ominously

Is it the fashion that discarded fathers
Should have thus little mercy on their flesh?
Judicious punishment: 'twas this flesh begot
75   Those pelican daughters.
76 EDGAR   Pillicock sat on pillicock hill, alow, alow, loo, loo.
FOOL   This cold night will turn us all to fools and mad-men.
80 EDGAR   Take heed o' th' foul fiend; obey thy parents;
81   keep thy word's justice; swear not; commit not with
82   man's sworn spouse; set not thy sweet heart on proud array. Tom's acold.
LEAR   What hast thou been?
EDGAR   A servingman, proud in heart and mind, that
86   curled my hair, wore gloves in my cap, served the lust of my mistress' heart, and did the act of darkness with her; swore as many oaths as I spake words, and broke
89   them in the sweet face of heaven; one that slept in the
90   contriving of lust, and waked to do it. Wine loved I
91   dearly, dice dearly, and in woman out-paramoured the
92   Turk. False of heart, light of ear, bloody of hand; hog in sloth, fox in stealth, wolf in greediness, dog in madness,
94   lion in prey. Let not the creaking of shoes nor the rustling of silks betray thy poor heart to woman. Keep
96   thy foot out of brothels, thy hand out of plackets, thy
97   pen from lenders' books, and defy the foul fiend. "Still

---

75 *pelican* cannibalistic (young pelicans were said to feed on their mother's blood)   **76–77** *Pillicock . . . loo* (a fragment of a nursery rhyme)   **76** *Pillicock* (1) an endearment, (2) baby talk for penis   **80** *Take heed* beware; *obey . . . parents* (this and the following injunctions are from the Ten Commandments)   **81** *keep . . . justice* i.e., do not lie; *commit not* i.e., do not commit adultery   **82–83** *proud array* luxurious clothing   **86** *wore . . . cap* (as courtly lovers did with tokens from their mistresses)   **89–90** *slept . . . lust* went to sleep planning acts of lechery   **91–92** *out-paramoured . . . Turk* had more lovers than the sultan has in his harem   **92** *light of ear* attentive to gossip and slander   **94–95** *creaking . . . silks* (both fashionable in women)   **96** *plackets* slits in women's skirts (hence, vaginas)   **97** *pen . . . books* i.e., stay out of debt

through the hawthorn blows the cold wind," says
suum, mun, nonny. Dolphin my boy, boy, sessa, let him   99
trot by.   *100*
   Storm still.
LEAR   Thou wert better in a grave than to answer with   101
thy uncovered body this extremity of the skies. Is man
no more than this? Consider him well. Thou owest the
worm no silk, the beast no hide, the sheep no wool, the
cat no perfume. Ha! here's three on's are sophisticated.   105
Thou art the thing itself. Unaccommodated man is no   106
more but such a poor, bare, forked animal as thou art.
Off, off, you lendings! *[Removes his clothing.]* Come,   108
unbutton here.
FOOL   Prithee, nuncle, be contented. 'Tis a naughty   110
night to swim in. Now a little fire in a wild field were
like an old lecher's heart, a small spark, all the rest on's
body cold. Look, here comes a walking fire.
   Enter Gloucester with a torch.
EDGAR   This is the foul Flibbertigibbet. He begins at   114
curfew and walks till the first cock. He gives the web   115
and the pin, squints the eye, and makes the harelip;   116
mildews the white wheat, and hurts the poor creature   117
of earth.

---

99 *Dolphin . . . sessa* (Unexplained; possibly a bit of a ballad, possibly a hunting call: Dolphin is usually taken to refer to the French crown prince the
dauphin, but it sounds more like a hunting dog's name; *sessa* (French *cessez*)
stop.)   **101** *answer* experience   **105** *cat* civet cat (from whose secretions perfume was made); *on's* of us; *sophisticated* artificial   **106** *Unaccommodated* unadorned, unfurnished   **108** *lendings* borrowed articles (because not part of
his body)   **110** *naughty* evil   **114** *Flibbertigibbet* (in Elizabethan folklore, a
dancing devil)   **115** *curfew* 9 P.M.; *first cock* midnight   **115–16** *the web . . .
pin* eye cataracts   **116** *squints* makes squint   **117** *white* almost ripe

> *[Sings.]*
119　　　　　Swithold footed thrice the wold,
120　　　　　He met the night mare and her ninefold;
121　　　　　　Bid her alight
122　　　　　　And her troth plight,
123　　　　　And aroint thee, witch, aroint thee!

KENT　How fares your grace?

LEAR　What's he?

KENT　*[To Gloucester]* Who's there? What is't you seek?

GLOUCESTER　What are you there? Your names?

EDGAR　Poor Tom, that eats the swimming frog, the
129　toad, the tadpole, the wall newt and the water; that in
130　the fury of his heart, when the foul fiend rages, eats cow
131　dung for sallets, swallows the old rat and the ditch dog,
132　drinks the green mantle of the standing pool; who is
133　whipped from tithing to tithing, and stocked, pun-
　　　ished, and imprisoned; who hath had three suits to his
　　　back, six shirts to his body,
　　　　　Horse to ride, and weapon to wear;
137　　　　　But mice and rats and such small deer
　　　　　Have been Tom's food for seven long year.
139　Beware my follower. Peace, Smulkin; peace, thou fiend!

GLOUCESTER　*[To Lear]*
140　What, hath your grace no better company?

EDGAR　The Prince of Darkness is a gentleman; Modo
　　　he's called, and Mahu.

---

119 *Swithold* Saint Withold (invoked as a general protector against harm);
footed . . . wold walked the plain three times　120 *night mare* incubus, female demon; *ninefold* nine offspring　121 *Bid . . . alight* ordered her to get
off (the sleeper's chest)　122 *her troth plight* give her promise (not to do it
again)　123 *aroint thee* begone　129 *wall newt* lizard; *water* i.e., water newt
131 *sallets* delicacies; *ditch dog* dead dog thrown in a ditch　132 *green mantle* scum; *standing* stagnant　133 *tithing* parish; *stocked* put in the stocks
137 *deer* game (the jingle is adapted from the popular romance *Bevis of
Hampton*)　139 *Smulkin* (like Modo and Mahu below, devils identified in
Samuel Harsnett's *Declaration of Egregious Popish Impostures,* 1603)

GLOUCESTER *[To Lear]*
　Our flesh and blood, my lord, is grown so vile
　That it doth hate what gets it.   144
EDGAR Poor Tom's acold.
GLOUCESTER *[To Lear]*
　Go in with me. My duty cannot suffer   146
　T' obey in all your daughters' hard commands.
　Though their injunction be to bar my doors
　And let this tyrannous night take hold upon you,
　Yet have I ventured to come seek you out   *150*
　And bring you where both fire and food is ready.
LEAR
　First let me talk with this philosopher.
　What is the cause of thunder?
KENT
　　　　　　　　　　Good my lord,
　Take his offer; go into th' house.
LEAR
　I'll talk a word with this same learnèd Theban.   155
　What is your study?   156
EDGAR How to prevent the fiend, and to kill vermin.   157
LEAR Let me ask you one word in private.
　　　　　　　　　　　[They talk apart.]
KENT
　Importune him once more to go, my lord;
　His wits begin t' unsettle.   *160*
GLOUCESTER   Canst thou blame him?
　　Storm still.
　His daughters seek his death. Ah, that good Kent,
　He said it would be thus, poor banished man!
　Thou sayest the king grows mad; I'll tell thee, friend,
　I am almost mad myself. I had a son,
　Now outlawed from my blood; he sought my life   165

---

144 *gets* begets 146 *suffer* allow me 155 *learnèd Theban* Greek scholar
156 *study* field of study 157 *prevent* thwart 165 *outlawed ... blood* disowned, disinherited

166 But lately, very late. I loved him, friend;
     No father his son dearer. True to tell thee,
     The grief hath crazed my wits. What a night's this!
        [To Lear]
     I do beseech your grace –
170 LEAR   O, cry you mercy, sir! *[To Edgar]*
     Noble philosopher, your company.
     EDGAR   Tom's acold.
     GLOUCESTER
        In, fellow, there, into th' hovel; keep thee warm.
     LEAR
        Come, let's in all.
     KENT   This way, my lord.
     LEAR   With him;
        I will keep still with my philosopher.
176 KENT   Good my lord, soothe him; let him take the fel-
        low.
178 GLOUCESTER   Take him you on.
     KENT   Sirrah, come on. Go along with us.
     LEAR
180 Come, good Athenian.
     GLOUCESTER   No words, no words, hush!
     EDGAR
181   Child Roland to the dark tower came,
182   His word was still "Fie, fo, and fum;
        I smell the blood of a British man."   *Exeunt.*

                        *

---

166 *late* recently   **170** *cry . . . mercy* I beg your pardon   **176** *soothe* humor
178 *you on* along with you   **180** *Athenian* philosopher   **181** *Child . . . came*
(presumably a line from a ballad about the hero of *La Chanson de Roland*);
Child a knight in training   **182** *word* motto, *still* always.)   **182–83** *His . . .
man* (Edgar switches to a ballad about Jack the Giant Killer)   **182** *word*
motto; *still* always

∾ **III.5** *Enter Cornwall and Edmund.*

CORNWALL   I will have my revenge ere I depart his
house.

EDMUND   How, my lord, I may be censured that nature   3
thus gives way to loyalty, something fears me to think   4
of.

CORNWALL   I now perceive it was not altogether your
brother's evil disposition made him seek his death, but   7
a provoking merit set awork by a reprovable badness in   8
himself.   9

EDMUND   How malicious is my fortune that I must re-   10
pent to be just! This is the letter which he spoke of,
which approves him an intelligent party to the advan-   12
tages of France. O heavens, that this treason were not,
or not I the detector!

CORNWALL   Go with me to the duchess.

EDMUND   If the matter of this paper be certain, you have
mighty business in hand.

CORNWALL   True or false, it hath made thee Earl of
Gloucester. Seek out where thy father is, that he may be
ready for our apprehension.   20

EDMUND   *[Aside]* If I find him comforting the king, it   21
will stuff his suspicion more fully. *[To Cornwall]* I will
persever in my course of loyalty, though the conflict be
sore between that and my blood.   24

CORNWALL   I will lay trust upon thee, and thou shalt
find a dear father in my love.   *Exeunt.*

✳

III.5 Gloucester's house **3** *censured* criticized **3–4** *nature . . . loyalty* (the
contrast is between familial and political bonds) **4** *something . . . me* I am
almost afraid **7** *his* Gloucester's **8** *a . . . awork* a virtue incited to work
9 *himself* Gloucester (i.e., however wicked parricide is, Gloucester got what
he deserved) **12** *approves* proves **12–13** *intelligent . . . advantages* spy on
behalf of **20** *apprehension* arrest **21** *comforting* abetting **24** *blood* family
ties

∾ **III.6** *Enter Kent [disguised] and Gloucester.*

GLOUCESTER   Here is better than the open air; take it
2   thankfully. I will piece out the comfort with what addition I can. I will not be long from you.
4 KENT   All the power of his wits have given way to his impatience; the gods reward your kindness!
Exit [Gloucester].
Enter Lear, Edgar [as Poor Tom], and Fool.
6 EDGAR   Frateretto calls me, and tells me Nero is an an-
gler in the Lake of Darkness. Pray, innocent, and beware the foul fiend.
FOOL   Prithee, nuncle, tell me whether a madman be a
10   gentleman or a yeoman.
LEAR   A king, a king!
12 FOOL   No, he's a yeoman that has a gentleman to his son,
13   for he's a mad yeoman that sees his son a gentleman be-
fore him.
LEAR
To have a thousand with red burning spits
Come hissing in upon 'em!
EDGAR   Bless thy five wits.
KENT
O pity! Sir, where is the patience now
That you so oft have boasted to retain?
EDGAR   *[Aside]*
20   My tears begin to take his part so much
They mar my counterfeiting.
LEAR
22   The little dogs and all,
Trey, Blanch, and Sweetheart, see, they bark at me.

III.6 *Within the hovel* 2 *piece out* augment 4–5 *impatience* passion, rage
6 *Frateretto* (another devil from Harsnett's *Declaration;* see III.4.139); *Nero*
(the diabolical Roman emperor, here condemned, following Chaucer's
Monk's Tale, to fish in the lake of Hell) 10 *yeoman* a landowner, but not a
gentleman 12 *to* as 13–14 *before him* i.e., before he himself has been
raised to the gentry 22 *The . . . all* even the lapdogs

EDGAR   Tom will throw his head at them. Avaunt, you   24
curs!

> Be thy mouth or black or white,   .   26
> Tooth that poisons if it bite,
> Mastiff, greyhound, mongrel grim,
> Hound or spaniel, brach or him,   29
> Or bobtail tyke or trundle-tail,   30
> Tom will make him weep and wail;
> For with throwing thus my head,
> Dogs leaped the hatch, and all are fled.   33

Do de, de, de. Sessa! Come, march to wakes and fairs   34
And market towns. Poor Tom, thy horn is dry.   35

LEAR   Then let them anatomize Regan, see what breeds   36
about her heart. Is there any cause in nature that make
these hard hearts? *[To Edgar]* You, sir, I entertain for   38
one of my hundred, only I do not like the fashion of
your garments. You will say they are Persian; but let   40
them be changed.

KENT
Now, good my lord, lie here and rest awhile.

LEAR   Make no noise, make no noise; draw the curtains.   43
So, so. We'll go to supper i' th' morning.

FOOL   And I'll go to bed at noon.
    Enter Gloucester.

GLOUCESTER   *[To Kent]*
Come hither, friend. Where is the king my master?

KENT
Here, sir, but trouble him not; his wits are gone.

GLOUCESTER
Good friend, I prithee take him in thy arms.

---

24 *throw* shake; *Avaunt* get away   26 *or* either   29 *brach . . . him* bitch or male   30 *bobtail . . . trundle-tail* short- or long-tailed mongrel   33 *hatch* lower half of a Dutch door   34 *Sessa!* stop (French *cessez*); *wakes* festivals 35 *horn is dry* drinking horn is empty (i.e., "I've run out of steam")   36 *anatomize* dissect   38 **s.d.** or perhaps addressed to Kent, who has, ironically, been in Lear's service; *entertain* employ   40 *Persian* luxurious   43 *curtains* i.e., about an imaginary four-poster bed

49 I have o'erheard a plot of death upon him.
50 There is a litter ready. Lay him in't
And drive toward Dover, friend, where thou shalt meet
Both welcome and protection. Take up thy master.
If thou shouldst dally half an hour, his life,
With thine and all that offer to defend him,
55 Stand in assurèd loss. Take up, take up,
56 And follow me, that will to some provision
Give thee quick conduct. Come, come away.
Exeunt [bearing Lear].

*

∾ **III.7** *Enter Cornwall, Regan, Goneril, Bastard
[Edmund], and Servants.*

1 CORNWALL *[To Goneril]* Post speedily to my lord your
husband; show him this letter. The army of France is
landed. *[To servants]* Seek out the traitor Gloucester.
[Exeunt some Servants.]
REGAN Hang him instantly.
GONERIL Pluck out his eyes.
CORNWALL Leave him to my displeasure. Edmund, keep
7 you our sister company. The revenges we are bound to
take upon your traitorous father are not fit for your be-
9 holding. Advise the duke where you are going to a most
10 festinate preparation; we are bound to the like. Our
11 posts shall be swift and intelligent betwixt us. Farewell,
12 dear sister. Farewell, my lord of Gloucester.
Enter Steward [Oswald].
How now, where's the king?
OSWALD
My lord of Gloucester hath conveyed him hence.

---

49 *upon* against 55 *Stand . . . loss* will surely be lost 56–57 *to . . . conduct*
quickly lead you to provisions for the journey
   III.7 Gloucester's house 1 *Post* ride 7 *sister* i.e., Goneril 9–10 *a . . . preparation* prepare quickly 10 *are . . . to* must do 11 *posts* messengers; *intelligent*
informative 12 *my . . . Gloucester* (Edmund has been given his father's title)

Some five or six and thirty of his knights,
Hot questrists after him, met him at gate,   16
Who, with some other of the lord's dependents,
Are gone with him toward Dover, where they boast
To have well-armèd friends.

CORNWALL
Get horses for your mistress.   *Exit [Oswald].* 20

GONERIL
Farewell, sweet lord, and sister.

CORNWALL
Edmund, farewell.   *[Exeunt Goneril and Edmund.]*
     [To Servants]   Go, seek the traitor Gloucester.
Pinion him like a thief; bring him before us.   23
     [Exeunt Servants.]
Though well we may not pass upon his life   24
Without the form of justice, yet our power
Shall do a curtsy to our wrath, which men   26
May blame but not control.
     Enter Gloucester and Servants.
                         Who's there? The traitor?

REGAN
Ingrateful fox, 'tis he.

CORNWALL   *[To Servants]*
Bind fast his corky arms.   29

GLOUCESTER
What means your graces? Good my friends, consider   30
You are my guests. Do me no foul play, friends.

CORNWALL   *[To Servants]*
Bind him, I say!

REGAN   Hard, hard! O filthy traitor!

GLOUCESTER
Unmerciful lady as you are, I'm none.

CORNWALL
To this chair bind him. Villain, thou shalt find –

---

16 *questrists* searchers   **23** *Pinion him* tie him up   **24** *pass* pass sentence   **26**
do . . . to defer to   **29** *corky* dry, withered

[Regan plucks Gloucester's beard.]

GLOUCESTER
By the kind gods, 'tis most ignobly done
36   To pluck me by the beard.

REGAN
37   So white, and such a traitor!

GLOUCESTER   Naughty lady,
These hairs which thou dost ravish from my chin
39   Will quicken and accuse thee. I am your host.
40   With robbers' hands my hospitable favors
41   You should not ruffle thus. What will you do?

CORNWALL
42   Come, sir, what letters had you late from France?

REGAN
43   Be simple-answered, for we know the truth.

CORNWALL
And what confederacy have you with the traitors
45   Late footed in the kingdom?

REGAN   To whose hands
You have sent the lunatic king – speak!

GLOUCESTER
47   I have a letter guessingly set down,
Which came from one that's of a neutral heart,
And not from one opposed.

CORNWALL   Cunning.

REGAN   And false.

CORNWALL
50   Where hast thou sent the king?

GLOUCESTER   To Dover.

REGAN
51   Wherefore to Dover? Wast thou not charged at peril –

---

36 *To . . . beard* (considered an extreme insult) **37** *Naughty* evil **39** *quicken* come to life **40** *hospitable favors* welcoming face **41** *ruffle* tear at **42** *late* lately **43** *Be simple-answered* answer plainly **45** *Late footed* lately landed **47** *guessingly* speculatively **51** *charged at peril* ordered at peril of your life

CORNWALL
Wherefore to Dover? Let him answer that.
GLOUCESTER
I am tied to th' stake, and I must stand the course.   53
REGAN
Wherefore to Dover?
GLOUCESTER
Because I would not see thy cruel nails
Pluck out his poor old eyes, nor thy fierce sister
In his anointed flesh stick boarish fangs.   57
The sea, with such a storm as his bare head
In hell-black night endured, would have buoyed up   59
And quenched the stellèd fires.   60
Yet, poor old heart, he holp the heavens to rain.   61
If wolves had at thy gate howled that stern time,
Thou shouldst have said "Good porter, turn the key" –   63
All cruels else subscribe. But I shall see   64
The wingèd vengeance overtake such children.   65
CORNWALL
See't shalt thou never. Fellows, hold the chair.
Upon these eyes of thine I'll set my foot.
GLOUCESTER
He that will think to live till he be old
Give me some help. O, cruel! O you gods!
    [Cornwall puts out one of Gloucester's eyes.]
REGAN   One side will mock another; th' other too.   70
CORNWALL
If you see vengeance –
SERVANT   Hold your hand, my lord.
I have served you ever since I was a child,

---

53 *I . . . course* (the image is from bearbaiting, in which the animal is tied to a stake and attacked by dogs)   57 *anointed* consecrated   59 *buoyed* swelled   60 *stellèd* stellar   61 *holp* helped   63 *turn the key* open the door   64 *All . . . subscribe* all other cruel creatures submit (to feelings of compassion) (?)   65 *wingèd vengeance* avenging Furies

But better service have I never done you
Than now to bid you hold.

REGAN   How now, you dog!

SERVANT
If you did wear a beard upon your chin
76 I'd shake it on this quarrel. What do you mean?

CORNWALL
77 My villain!

SERVANT
78 Nay then, come on, and take the chance of anger.
      [They draw and fight. Cornwall is wounded.]

REGAN   *[To another servant]*
Give me thy sword. A peasant stand up thus!
      [She] kills him.

SERVANT
80 O, I am slain. My lord, you have one eye left
To see some mischief on him. O!   *[He dies.]*

CORNWALL
Lest it see more, prevent it. Out, vile jelly!
      [He puts out Gloucester's other eye.]
Where is thy luster now?

GLOUCESTER
All dark and comfortless. Where's my son Edmund?
Edmund, enkindle all the sparks of nature
86 To quit this horrid act.

REGAN   Out, treacherous villain!
Thou call'st on him that hates thee. It was he
88 That made the overture of thy treasons to us,
Who is too good to pity thee.

GLOUCESTER
90 O my follies! Then Edgar was abused.
Kind gods, forgive me that and prosper him!

---

76 *shake . . . quarrel* pluck it in this cause; *What . . . mean?* i.e., how dare you
77 *villain* (the word retained some of its original meaning of "serf" or "servant") 78 *chance . . . anger* risk of an angry fight 86 *quit* avenge 88
made . . . of revealed 90 *abused* wronged

REGAN
   Go thrust him out at gates, and let him smell
   His way to Dover.   *Exit [a servant] with Gloucester.* 93
   [To Cornwall] How is't, my lord, how look you?
CORNWALL
   I have received a hurt. Follow me, lady.
   Turn out that eyeless villain. Throw this slave
   Upon the dunghill. Regan, I bleed apace.
   Untimely comes this hurt. Give me your arm. *Exeunt.*

✴

∾ **IV.1** *Enter Edgar [as Poor Tom].*

EDGAR
   Yet better thus and known to be contemned   1
   Than still contemned and flattered. To be worst,   2
   The lowest and most dejected thing of fortune,
   Stands still in esperance, lives not in fear.   4
   The lamentable change is from the best,
   The worst returns to laughter. Welcome then,   6
   Thou unsubstantial air that I embrace:
   The wretch that thou hast blown unto the worst
   Owes nothing to thy blasts.   9
     Enter Gloucester and an Old Man.
                       But who comes here?
   My father poorly led? World, world, O world! *10*
   But that thy strange mutations make us hate thee, 11
   Life would not yield to age.   12
OLD MAN   *[To Gloucester]*   O my good lord,
   I have been your tenant and your father's tenant
   These fourscore years.

---

93 *How . . . you* how do you feel
   IV.1 Open country   1 *contemned* despised   2 *still* always   4 *Stands . . .*
esperance always has hope (because he has no fear of falling lower)   6 *returns*
to laughter i.e., can only get better   9 *Owes nothing to* does not need to pay
for   11 *But* except   12 *yield to age* be reconciled to growing old

GLOUCESTER
Away, get thee away, good friend, begone.
Thy comforts can do me no good at all,
Thee they may hurt.

OLD MAN   You cannot see your way.

GLOUCESTER
I have no way, and therefore want no eyes.
I stumbled when I saw. Full oft 'tis seen
20   Our means secure us, and our mere defects
21   Prove our commodities. O dear son Edgar,
22   The food of thy abusèd father's wrath,
Might I but live to see thee in my touch,
I'd say I had eyes again.

OLD MAN   How now, who's there?

EDGAR   *[Aside]*
O gods! Who is't can say "I am at the worst"?
I am worse than e'er I was.

OLD MAN   'Tis poor mad Tom.

EDGAR   *[Aside]*
And worse I may be yet. The worst is not
So long as we can say "This is the worst."

OLD MAN   *[To Edgar]*
Fellow, where goest?

GLOUCESTER   Is it a beggarman?

OLD MAN
30   Madman and beggar too.

GLOUCESTER
31   He has some reason, else he could not beg.
I' th' last night's storm I such a fellow saw,
Which made me think a man a worm. My son
Came then into my mind, and yet my mind
Was then scarce friends with him. I have heard more
    since.

───────

20 *Our . . . us* our prosperity makes us overconfident; *mere defects* utter deprivation   21 *commodities* advantages   22 *food* prey   31 *reason* sanity

As flies to wanton boys are we to th' gods: 36
They kill us for their sport.
EDGAR   *[Aside]*   How should this be?
Bad is the trade that must play fool to sorrow,   38
Ang'ring itself and others. – Bless thee, master.
GLOUCESTER
Is that the naked fellow?   40
OLD MAN   Ay, my lord.
GLOUCESTER
Get thee away. If for my sake
Thou wilt o'ertake us hence a mile or twain,
I' th' way toward Dover, do it for ancient love,   43
And bring some covering for this naked soul,
Which I'll entreat to lead me.
OLD MAN
Alack, sir, he is mad.
GLOUCESTER
'Tis the times' plague when madmen lead the blind.   47
Do as I bid thee, or rather do thy pleasure.
Above the rest, begone.   49
OLD MAN
I'll bring him the best 'parel that I have,   50
Come on't what will.   *Exit.* 51
GLOUCESTER   Sirrah, naked fellow!
EDGAR
Poor Tom's acold. *[Aside]* I cannot daub it further.   52
GLOUCESTER
Come hither, fellow.
EDGAR   *[Aside]*
And yet I must. – Bless thy sweet eyes, they bleed.

---

36 *wanton* playful, irresponsible   **38** *Bad . . . sorrow* playing the fool in the presence of grief is a bad business   **43** *ancient love* our long relationship (as lord and tenant)   **47** *times' plague* sickness of the times   **49** *Above . . . rest* above all   **50** *'parel* apparel   **51** *Come . . . will* whatever may come of it   **52** *daub it* lay it on (i.e., act the part)

GLOUCESTER
 Know'st thou the way to Dover?
EDGAR   Both stile and gate, horseway and footpath. Poor
  Tom hath been scared out of his good wits. Bless thee,
  goodman's son, from the foul fiend.
GLOUCESTER
 Here, take this purse, thou whom the heavens' plagues
60 Have humbled to all strokes. That I am wretched
  Makes thee the happier. Heavens deal so still.
62 Let the superfluous and lust-dieted man
63 That slaves your ordinance, that will not see
  Because he does not feel, feel your power quickly.
  So distribution should undo excess,
  And each man have enough. Dost thou know Dover?
EDGAR   Ay, master.
GLOUCESTER
68 There is a cliff whose high and bending head
69 Looks fearfully in the confinèd deep.
70 Bring me but to the very brim of it
  And I'll repair the misery thou dost bear
  With something rich about me. From that place
  I shall no leading need.
EDGAR   Give me thy arm;
  Poor Tom shall lead thee.   *Exeunt.*

                          *

∾ **IV.2** *Enter Goneril with Bastard [Edmund], and*
  [separately] Steward [Oswald].

GONERIL
 Welcome, my lord. I marvel our mild husband
2 Not met us on the way.

---

60 *humbled to* reduced to bearing meekly **62** *superfluous . . . man* man who
has too much and feeds his desires **63** *slaves . . . ordinance* makes a slave of
heaven's injunction (to give to the poor) **68** *bending* overhanging **69**
in . . . deep over the straits (of the English Channel) below
  IV.2 Before Albany's castle **2** *Not* has not

     [To Oswald]   Now, where's your master?
OSWALD
  Madam, within; but never man so changed.
  I told him of the army that was landed;
  He smiled at it. I told him you were coming;
  His answer was "The worse." Of Gloucester's treachery
  And of the loyal service of his son
  When I informed him, then he called me sot,   8
  And told me I had turned the wrong side out.
  What most he should dislike seems pleasant to him;   *10*
  What like, offensive.
GONERIL   *[To Edmund]* Then shall you go no further.
  It is the cowish terror of his spirit   *12*
  That dares not undertake. He'll not feel wrongs   *13*
  Which tie him to an answer. Our wishes on the way
  May prove effects. Back, Edmund, to my brother.   *15*
  Hasten his musters and conduct his powers.   *16*
  I must change names at home, and give the distaff   *17*
  Into my husband's hands. This trusty servant
  Shall pass between us. Ere long you are like to hear,   *19*
  If you dare venture in your own behalf,   *20*
  A mistress's command. Wear this. Spare speech.   *21*
  Decline your head. This kiss, if it durst speak,
  Would stretch thy spirits up into the air.
  Conceive, and fare thee well.   *24*
EDMUND
  Yours in the ranks of death.   *Exit.* *25*
GONERIL   My most dear Gloucester!
  O, the difference of man and man.

---

8 *sot* fool 12 *cowish* cowardly 13 *undertake* commit himself to action
13–14 *He'll . . . answer* he'll ignore injuries that require him to retaliate 15
prove effects be fulfilled; *brother* brother-in-law, Cornwall 16 *musters* the
muster of his troops; *conduct . . . powers* guide his forces 17 *names* roles
17–18 *give . . . hands* give my husband the housewife's spinning staff 19
like likely 21 *Wear this* (Goneril gives Edmund a lover's token, such as a
handkerchief or a glove) 24 *Conceive* understand me 25 *in the ranks of*
even up to

To thee a woman's services are due;
28   My fool usurps my body.
OSWALD   Madam, here comes my lord.

[Exit Oswald.]

Enter Albany.

GONERIL
30   I have been worth the whistle.
ALBANY   O Goneril,
You are not worth the dust which the rude wind
32   Blows in your face.
GONERIL   Milk-livered man,
33   That bear'st a cheek for blows, a head for wrongs;
34   Who hast not in thy brows an eye discerning
Thine honor from thy suffering –
ALBANY   See thyself, devil.
36   Proper deformity seems not in the fiend
37   So horrid as in woman.
GONERIL   O vain fool!

Enter a Messenger.

MESSENGER
O my good lord, the Duke of Cornwall's dead,
Slain by his servant, going to put out
40   The other eye of Gloucester.
ALBANY   Gloucester's eyes?
MESSENGER
41   A servant that he bred, thrilled with remorse,
Opposed against the act, bending his sword
To his great master, who thereat enraged
Flew on him, and amongst them felled him dead,

---

28 *My . . . body* my idiot husband wrongfully possesses me   30 *I . . . whistle*
I used to be worth welcoming home (alluding to the proverbial poor dog
who is "not worth the whistle")   32 *Milk-livered* cowardly   33 *for* fit for
34–35 *discerning . . . suffering* that can distinguish what affects your honor
(and thus must be resisted) from what must be endured   36 *Proper . . . not* a
deformed nature does not appear   37 *vain* silly, worthless   41 *thrilled . . .
remorse* overwhelmed with pity

But not without that harmful stroke which since
Hath plucked him after.
ALBANY   This shows you are above,
You justices, that these our nether crimes   47
So speedily can venge. But O, poor Gloucester,
Lost he his other eye?
MESSENGER   Both, both, my lord.
This letter, madam, craves a speedy answer.   50
'Tis from your sister.
GONERIL   *[Aside]*   One way I like this well;
But being widow, and my Gloucester with her,   52
May all the building in my fancy pluck   53
Upon my hateful life. Another way   54
The news is not so tart. – I'll read and answer.   *[Exit.]* 55
ALBANY
Where was his son when they did take his eyes?
MESSENGER
Come with my lady hither.
ALBANY   He is not here.
MESSENGER
No, my good lord, I met him back again.   58
ALBANY
Knows he the wickedness?
MESSENGER
Ay, my good lord; 'twas he informed against him,   60
And quit the house on purpose that their punishment
Might have the freer course.
ALBANY   Gloucester, I live
To thank thee for the love thou show'dst the king,
And to revenge thine eyes. – Come hither, friend,
Tell me what more thou knowest.   *Exeunt.*
                          *

---

47 *justices* (heavenly) judges   52 *being* she being   53 *all . . . pluck* pull down
my dream castles   54 *Another way* (i.e., returning to the *One way* of l. 51)
55 *tart* distasteful   58 *back* returning

～ IV.3 *Enter, with drum and colors, Cordelia, Gentleman, and Soldiers.*

CORDELIA
Alack, 'tis he. Why, he was met even now,
As mad as the vexed sea, singing aloud,
3   Crowned with rank fumiter and furrow weeds,
With hardocks, hemlock, nettles, cuckooflowers,
5   Darnel, and all the idle weeds that grow
6   In our sustaining corn. A century send forth,
Search every acre in the high-grown field,
8   And bring him to our eye. What can man's wisdom
In the restoring his bereavèd sense,
10 He that helps him, take all my outward worth.

GENTLEMAN
There is means, madam.
12 Our foster nurse of nature is repose,
13 The which he lacks; that to provoke in him
14 Are many simples operative, whose power
Will close the eye of anguish.

CORDELIA   All blest secrets,
16 All you unpublished virtues of the earth,
17 Spring with my tears, be aidant and remediate
In the good man's distress! Seek, seek for him,
Lest his ungoverned rage dissolve the life
20 That wants the means to lead it.
        Enter Messenger.

MESSENGER   News, madam.
The British powers are marching hitherward.

IV.3 The French camp   **3** *fumiter* fumitory (this and the following are all field weeds)   **5** *idle* useless, uncultivated   **6** *sustaining corn* life-sustaining wheat; *century* troop of one hundred soldiers   **8** *What . . . wisdom* whatever man's wisdom can do   **10** *outward worth* material possessions   **12** *Our . . . nature* what naturally cares for us   **13** *provoke* induce   **14** *simples operative* herbal remedies   **16** *unpublished virtues* secret powers   **17** *be . . . remediate* aid and heal   **20** *wants* lacks

CORDELIA
  'Tis known before; our preparation stands
  In expectation of them. – O dear father,
  It is thy business that I go about;
  Therefore great France   25
  My mourning and importuned tears hath pitied.   26
  No blown ambition doth our arms incite,   27
  But love, dear love, and our agèd father's right.
  Soon may I hear and see him!   *Exeunt.*

✳

❧ **IV.4** *Enter Regan and Steward [Oswald].*

REGAN
  But are my brother's powers set forth?   1
OSWALD   Ay, madam.
REGAN
  Himself in person there?
OSWALD
  Madam, with much ado.   3
  Your sister is the better soldier.
REGAN
  Lord Edmund spake not with your lord at home?
OSWALD   No, madam.
REGAN
  What might import my sister's letter to him?
OSWALD   I know not, lady.
REGAN
  Faith, he is posted hence on serious matter.   9
  It was great ignorance, Gloucester's eyes being out, 10
  To let him live; where he arrives he moves
  All hearts against us. Edmund, I think, is gone,

---

25 *France* the King of France   26 *importuned* importuning   27 *blown* presumptuous
    IV.4 Gloucester's house   1 *brother's powers* Albany's forces   3 *ado* difficulty
9 *is posted hence* rushed away from here

In pity of his misery, to dispatch
14   His nighted life; moreover to descry
The strength o' th' enemy.
OSWALD
I must needs after him, madam, with my letter.
REGAN
Our troops set forth tomorrow. Stay with us.
The ways are dangerous.
OSWALD   I may not, madam;
19   My lady charged my duty in this business.
REGAN
20   Why should she write to Edmund? Might not you
21   Transport her purposes by word? Belike –
Some things, I know not what. I'll love thee much;
Let me unseal the letter.
OSWALD   Madam, I had rather –
REGAN
I know your lady does not love her husband;
26   I am sure of that, and at her late being here
27   She gave strange oeillades and most speaking looks
28   To noble Edmund. I know you are of her bosom.
OSWALD   I, madam?
REGAN
30   I speak in understanding; yare, I know't,
31   Therefore I do advise you take this note.
My lord is dead. Edmund and I have talked
33   And more convenient is he for my hand
34   Than for your lady's – you may gather more.
35   If you do find him, pray you give him this;

---

14 *nighted* (1) benighted, (2) blind; *descry* spy out   19 *charged* strictly commanded   21 *Belike* perhaps   26 *late* recently   27 *oeillades* amorous glances
28 *of . . . bosom* in her confidence (with a sexual overtone)   30 *understanding* certain knowledge   31 *take . . . note* take note of this   33 *convenient* appropriate   34 *gather more* infer more (from what I say)   35 *this* (Perhaps a
token; perhaps a letter: Edgar finds only Goneril's letter in Oswald's pockets
in IV.5.256 ff., but Oswald, dying, speaks of "letters," so perhaps Edgar
misses one. "Letters," on the other hand, could be singular.)

And when your mistress hears thus much from you,
I pray desire her call her wisdom to her.   37
So, fare you well.
If you do chance to hear of that blind traitor,
Preferment falls on him that cuts him off.   40
OSWALD
Would I could meet him, madam. I should show
What party I do follow.
REGAN   Fare thee well.   *Exeunt.*

*

∾ **IV.5** *Enter Gloucester and Edgar [disguised as a
peasant].*

GLOUCESTER
When shall I come to th' top of that same hill?
EDGAR
You do climb up it now; look how we labor.
GLOUCESTER
Methinks the ground is even.
EDGAR   Horrible steep.
Hark, do you hear the sea?
GLOUCESTER   No, truly.
EDGAR
Why then your other senses grow imperfect
By your eyes' anguish.
GLOUCESTER   So may it be indeed.
Methinks thy voice is altered, and thou speak'st
In better phrase and matter than thou didst.
EDGAR
You're much deceived: in nothing am I changed
But in my garments.   10
GLOUCESTER   Methinks you're better spoken.

---

37 *wisdom to her* back to reason   40 *cuts him off* cuts short his life
IV.5 Open country near Dover

EDGAR
    Come on, sir, here's the place. Stand still. How fearful
    And dizzy 'tis to cast one's eyes so low!
13   The crows and choughs that wing the midway air
14   Show scarce so gross as beetles. Halfway down
15   Hangs one that gathers samphire, dreadful trade!
    Methinks he seems no bigger than his head.
    The fishermen that walk upon the beach
18   Appear like mice, and yon tall anchoring bark
19   Diminished to her cock, her cock a buoy
20   Almost too small for sight. The murmuring surge
21   That on th' unnumbered idle pebble chafes
    Cannot be heard so high. I'll look no more,
    Lest my brain turn and the deficient sight
24   Topple down headlong.
GLOUCESTER   Set me where you stand.
EDGAR
    Give me your hand. You are now within a foot
    Of th' extreme verge. For all beneath the moon
27   Would I not leap upright.
GLOUCESTER   Let go my hand.
    Here, friend, 's another purse; in it a jewel
    Well worth a poor man's taking. Fairies and gods
30   Prosper it with thee! Go thou further off;
    Bid me farewell, and let me hear thee going.
EDGAR
    Now fare ye well, good sir.
GLOUCESTER   With all my heart.
EDGAR   *[Aside]*
    Why I do trifle thus with his despair
    Is done to cure it.

---

13 *choughs* jackdaws (pronounced "chuffs")   14 *Show* appear; *gross* large
15 *samphire* Saint Peter's herb (used in pickling; it grows on steep cliffs,
hence the danger in gathering it)   18 *bark* ship   19 *cock* dinghy   21 *unnumbered . . . pebble* barren reach of innumerable pebbles   24 *Topple* topple
me   27 *leap upright* jump upward (to jump forward would reveal to
Gloucester that he is not on the edge of a cliff)   30 *Prosper* increase

GLOUCESTER   *[kneeling]* O you mighty gods,
    This world I do renounce, and in your sights
    Shake patiently my great affliction off.
    If I could bear it longer, and not fall
    To quarrel with your great opposeless wills,
    My snuff and loathèd part of nature should   39
    Burn itself out. If Edgar live, O bless him!   40
    Now, fellow, fare thee well.
EDGAR   Gone, sir, farewell.
    [Gloucester falls forward.]
    [Aside]
    And yet I know not how conceit may rob   42
    The treasury of life, when life itself
    Yields to the theft. Had he been where he thought, 44
    By this had thought been past. – Alive or dead?   45
    Ho you, sir! Friend! Hear you, sir? Speak.
    [Aside]
    Thus might he pass indeed. Yet he revives.   47
    – What are you, sir?
GLOUCESTER   Away, and let me die.
EDGAR
    Hadst thou been aught but gossamer, feathers, air, 49
    So many fathom down precipitating   50
    Thou'dst shivered like an egg; but thou dost breathe, 51
    Hast heavy substance, bleed'st not, speak'st, art sound.
    Ten masts at each make not the altitude   53
    Which thou hast perpendicularly fell.
    Thy life's a miracle. Speak yet again.
GLOUCESTER
    But have I fall'n or no?
EDGAR
    From the dread summit of this chalky bourn.   57

---

39 *snuff* burnt-out candle end; *loathèd . . . nature* despised remnant of life
42 *conceit* illusion, imagination   **44** *Yields to* accedes to, welcomes   **45** *this*
this time   **47** *pass indeed* really die   **49** *aught* anything   **51** *shivered* shat-
tered   **53** *at each* placed end to end   **57** *chalky bourn* chalk cliff, the White
Cliffs of Dover

58 Look up a-height. The shrill-gorged lark so far
Cannot be seen or heard. Do but look up.

GLOUCESTER

60 Alack, I have no eyes.

61 Is wretchedness deprived that benefit
To end itself by death? 'Twas yet some comfort

63 When misery could beguile the tyrant's rage
And frustrate his proud will.

EDGAR   Give me your arm.
Up, so. How is't? Feel you your legs? You stand.

GLOUCESTER
Too well, too well.

EDGAR   This is above all strangeness.
Upon the crown o' th' cliff what thing was that
Which parted from you?

GLOUCESTER   A poor unfortunate beggar.

EDGAR
As I stood here below, methought his eyes

70 Were two full moons. He had a thousand noses,

71 Horns whelked and waved like the enragèd sea.

72 It was some fiend. Therefore, thou happy father,

73 Think that the clearest gods, who make them honors
Of men's impossibilities, have preserved thee.

GLOUCESTER
I do remember now. Henceforth I'll bear
Affliction till it do cry out itself
"Enough, enough," and die. That thing you speak of,
I took it for a man. Often 'twould say
"The fiend, the fiend." He led me to that place.

EDGAR

80 Bear free and patient thoughts.

---

58 *shrill-gorged* shrill-voiced 61 *deprived* denied 63 *beguile* cheat 71
whelked twisted 72 *happy father* lucky old man 73 *clearest* wisest, most
glorious 73–74 *who . . . impossibilities* whose glory consists in performing
miracles

Enter Lear [mad, crowned with weeds].
                              But who comes here?
The safer sense will ne'er accommodate   81
His master thus.

LEAR   No, they cannot touch me for crying; I am the   83
king himself.

EDGAR
O thou side-piercing sight!

LEAR   Nature's above art in that respect. There's your   86
press money. That fellow handles his bow like a crow-   87
keeper. Draw me a clothier's yard. Look, look, a mouse!   88
Peace, peace, this piece of toasted cheese will do't.   89
There's my gauntlet. I'll prove it on a giant. Bring up   90
the brown bills. O, well flown, bird; i' th' clout, i' th'   91
clout – whew! Give the word.   92

EDGAR   Sweet marjoram.

LEAR   Pass.

GLOUCESTER
I know that voice.

LEAR   Ha, Goneril with a white beard? They flattered me
like a dog, and told me I had the white hairs in my   97
beard ere the black ones were there. To say "ay" and
"no" to everything that I said "ay" and "no" to was no   99
good divinity. When the rain came to wet me once, and   100
the wind to make me chatter, when the thunder would
not peace at my bidding, there I found 'em, there I   102
smelt 'em out. Go to, they are not men o' their words.

---

81 *The . . . sense* a sane mind; *accommodate* array   83 *touch* arrest   86 *Nature's . . . respect* i.e., kings are born, not made   87 *press money* payment for volunteering or being drafted to fight (Lear is conscripting an imaginary army)   87–88 *crowkeeper* scarecrow   88 *Draw . . . yard* draw the bow out fully (a clothier's yard, 37 inches, was the length of an arrow)   89 *do't* catch the mouse   90 *prove it on* uphold my cause against   91 *brown bills* pike carriers (Lear continues to assemble his army); *bird* arrow; *clout* bull's-eye   92 *word* password   97 *like a dog* as a dog does (i.e., they fawned on me)   97–98 *the . . . beard* i.e., the wisdom of age   99–100 *no . . . divinity* bad theology   102 *found 'em* found them out

104 They told me I was everything; 'tis a lie, I am not ague-
proof.
GLOUCESTER
106 The trick of that voice I do well remember.
Is't not the king?
LEAR   Ay, every inch a king.
When I do stare, see how the subject quakes.
109 I pardon that man's life. What was thy cause?
110 Adultery?
Thou shalt not die; die for adultery? No,
The wren goes to't, and the small gilded fly
Does lecher in my sight.
Let copulation thrive, for Gloucester's bastard son
Was kinder to his father than my daughters
116 Got 'tween the lawful sheets. To't, luxury, pell-mell,
For I lack soldiers. Behold yon simp'ring dame
118 Whose face between her forks presages snow,
119 That minces virtue, and does shake the head
120 To hear of pleasure's name:
121 The fitchew nor the soilèd horse goes to't
With a more riotous appetite. Down from the waist
123 They are centaurs, though women all above;
124 But to the girdle do the gods inherit,
Beneath is all the fiend's – there's hell, there's darkness,
there's the sulphurous pit, burning, scalding, stench,
consumption. Fie, fie, fie; pah, pah! Give me an ounce
128 of civet, good apothecary, sweeten my imagination.
There's money for thee.

104–5 *ague-proof* immune to fever   106 *trick* special quality   109 *cause* offense   116 *Got* begotten; *luxury* lechery   118 *face . . . forks* (1) her face between the combs that hold her hair in place, (2) her genitals between her
forked legs; *snow* sexual coldness, frigidity   119 *minces* affects   121 *fitchew*
(1) polecat, (2) prostitute; *soilèd* pastured, well fed   123 *centaurs* (the classical centaurs were men to the waist and horses below, and were notoriously
lustful)   124 *But . . . girdle* only down to the waist; *inherit* possess   128
civet perfume

GLOUCESTER
O, let me kiss that hand!   *130*

LEAR   Let me wipe it first; it smells of mortality.

GLOUCESTER
O ruined piece of nature! This great world   *132*
Shall so wear out to naught. Dost thou know me?   *133*

LEAR   I remember thine eyes well enough. Dost thou
squiny at me? No, do thy worst, blind Cupid, I'll not   *135*
love. Read thou this challenge. Mark but the penning
of it.

GLOUCESTER
Were all thy letters suns, I could not see.

EDGAR
I would not take this from report. It is,   *139*
And my heart breaks at it.   *140*

LEAR   Read.

GLOUCESTER
What, with the case of eyes?   *142*

LEAR   O, ho, are you there with me? No eyes in your   *143*
head, nor no money in your purse? Your eyes are in a
heavy case, your purse in a light; yet you see how this   *145*
world goes.

GLOUCESTER
I see it feelingly.

LEAR   What, art mad? A man may see how this world
goes with no eyes. Look with thine ears. See how yon
justice rails upon yon simple thief. Hark in thine ear: *150*
change places, and handy-dandy, which is the justice,   *151*
which is the thief? Thou hast seen a farmer's dog bark at
a beggar?

GLOUCESTER   Ay, sir.

---

132 *piece* masterpiece   133 *so . . . naught* decay to nothing in the same way
135 *squiny* squint   139 *take* believe; *is* is actually happening   142 *case* sockets   143 *are . . . me* is that what you mean (with an overtone of "Are we both
blind?")   145 *heavy case* sad situation   150 *simple* mere   151 *handy-dandy*
the child's game "choose a hand"

155 LEAR   And the creature run from the cur? There thou
mightst behold the great image of authority: a dog's
157 obeyed in office.
158 Thou rascal beadle, hold thy bloody hand.
Why dost thou lash that whore? Strip thy own back.
160 Thou hotly lusts to use her in that kind
161 For which thou whipp'st her. The usurer hangs the
cozener.
Through tattered clothes great vices do appear;
163 Robes and furred gowns hide all. Plate sins with gold,
And the strong lance of justice hurtless breaks;
Arm it in rags, a pigmy's straw does pierce it.
166 None does offend, none, I say none. I'll able 'em.
167 Take that of me, my friend, who have the power
168 To seal th' accusers' lips. Get thee glass eyes,
169 And like a scurvy politician seem
170 To see the things thou dost not. Now, now, now, now.
[Sits.]
Pull off my boots; harder, harder! So.

EDGAR   *[Aside]*
172 O matter and impertinency mixed,
Reason in madness.

LEAR
If thou wilt weep my fortunes, take my eyes.
I know thee well enough; thy name is Gloucester.
Thou must be patient; we came crying hither.
Thou know'st the first time that we smell the air,
We waul and cry. I will preach to thee: mark.

GLOUCESTER
Alack, alack, the day!

---

155 *creature* man   157 *in office* in a position of power   158 *beadle* church
constable   160 *kind* way   161 *usurer . . . cozener* i.e., the big thief hangs the
little one; *usurer* moneylender; *cozener* cheat   163 *Plate . . . gold* cover sin in
golden armor   166 *able 'em* vouch for their innocence   167 *Take . . . me*
i.e., I pardon you too   168 *glass eyes* eyeglasses   169 *scurvy politician* vile
Machiavel   172 *matter . . . impertinency* sense and nonsense

LEAR

  When we are born, we cry that we are come   *180*

  To this great stage of fools. This' a good block.   181

  It were a delicate stratagem to shoe   182

  A troop of horse with felt; I'll put't in proof,   183

  And when I have stol'n upon these son-in-laws,

  Then kill, kill, kill, kill, kill, kill!

    Enter a Gentleman [with Attendants].

GENTLEMAN

  O, here he is. Lay hand upon him. – Sir,

  Your most dear daughter –

LEAR

  No rescue? What, a prisoner? I am even

  The natural fool of fortune. Use me well,   189

  You shall have ransom. Let me have surgeons;   *190*

  I am cut to th' brains.

GENTLEMAN   You shall have anything.

LEAR

  No seconds? All myself?   192

  Why, this would make a man a man of salt,   193

  To use his eyes for garden waterpots.   194

  I will die bravely, like a smug bridegroom.   195

  What, I will be jovial. Come, come,

  I am a king, masters, know you that?

GENTLEMAN

  You are a royal one, and we obey you.

LEAR   Then there's life in't. Come, an you get it, you shall   199

  get it by running. Sa, sa, sa, sa!   *200*

    Exit [Lear, followed by Attendants].

---

181 *This'* this is; *block* felt hat (either the hat decked with weeds, which he removes to begin his sermon, or an imaginary hat suggested by the crown of weeds)   **182** *delicate* subtle   **182–183** *shoe . . . felt* (and thus enable them to approach silently)   **183** *put't in proof* try it   **189** *natural fool* born plaything; *Use* treat   **192** *seconds* supporters   **193** *salt* tears   **194** *waterpots* watering cans   **195** *die* (with a quibble on the sexual sense, have an orgasm); *bravely* (1) courageously, (2) handsomely; *smug* neat, satisfied   **199** *there's . . . in't* i.e., there's still hope; *an* if   **200** *Sa* (a hunting cry)

GENTLEMAN
A sight most pitiful in the meanest wretch,
Past speaking of in a king. Thou hast a daughter
203   Who redeems nature from the general curse
204   Which twain have brought her to.
EDGAR   Hail, gentle sir.
GENTLEMAN
205   Sir, speed you; what's your will?
EDGAR
206   Do you hear aught, sir, of a battle toward?
GENTLEMAN
207   Most sure and vulgar; everyone hears that
208   Which can distinguish sound.
EDGAR   But, by your favor,
How near's the other army?
GENTLEMAN
210   Near and on speedy foot; the main descry
Stands on the hourly thought.
EDGAR
I thank you, sir; that's all.
GENTLEMAN
213   Though that the queen on special cause is here.
Her army is moved on.
EDGAR   I thank you, sir.
Exit [Gentleman].

GLOUCESTER
You ever gentle gods, take my breath from me.
216   Let not my worser spirit tempt me again
217   To die before you please.
EDGAR   Well pray you, father.

203–4 *general . . . to* the universal disruption caused by your other two
daughters (but also, the original sin caused by the filial ingratitude of the
original pair, Adam and Eve) **204** *gentle* noble **205** *speed* God prosper
206 *toward* impending **207** *vulgar* common knowledge **208** *Which* who
210–11 *the . . . thought* the sight of the main body is expected hourly **213**
Though that however; *on . . . cause* for a particular reason **216** *worser spirit*
"bad side" **217** *father* old man

GLOUCESTER
  Now, good sir, what are you?

EDGAR
  A most poor man made tame to fortune's blows,   219
  Who, by the art of known and feeling sorrows,   220
  Am pregnant to good pity. Give me your hand,   221
  I'll lead you to some biding.   222

GLOUCESTER   Hearty thanks.
  The bounty and the benison of heaven   223
  To boot, and boot.   224
    Enter Steward [Oswald].

OSWALD   A proclaimed prize! Most happy!
  That eyeless head of thine was first framed flesh   225
  To raise my fortunes. Thou old unhappy traitor,
  Briefly thyself remember. The sword is out   227
  That must destroy thee.

GLOUCESTER   Now let thy friendly hand
  Put strength enough to't.
    [Edgar interposes.]

OSWALD   Wherefore, bold peasant,
  Dar'st thou support a published traitor? Hence,   230
  Lest that th' infection of his fortune take
  Like hold on thee. Let go his arm.

EDGAR
  'Chill not let go, zir, without vurther 'casion.   233

OSWALD
  Let go, slave, or thou diest.

EDGAR   Good gentleman, go your gate, and let poor volk   235
  pass. An 'chud ha' been zwaggered out of my life,   236

---

219 *tame* submissive   **220** *art . . . sorrows* lesson of sorrows experienced and
deeply felt   **221** *pregnant* prone   **222** *biding* dwelling   **223–24** *bounty . . .
boot* may it bring you the bounty and blessing of heaven, and a reward in addition   **224** *proclaimed prize* criminal with a price on his head; *happy* lucky
225 *framed flesh* made human   **227** *thyself remember* i.e., remember your
sins and pray   **230** *published* proclaimed   **233** *'Chill* I'll (Edgar adopts a
west country dialect); *'casion* occasion, cause   **235** *go your gate* be on your
way   **236** *An . . . zwaggered* if I could have been bullied

'twould not ha' been zo long as 'tis by a vortnight. Nay,
238   come not near th' old man. Keep out, che vor' ye, or Ise
239   try whither your costard or my ballow be the harder.
240   'Chill be plain with you.
       OSWALD   Out, dunghill!
242   EDGAR   'Chill pick your teeth, zir. Come, no matter vor
243   your foins.
              [Oswald falls.]
       OSWALD
       Slave, thou hast slain me. Villain, take my purse.
       If ever thou wilt thrive, bury my body
246   And give the letters which thou find'st about me
       To Edmund, Earl of Gloucester. Seek him out
248   Upon the English party. O untimely death! Death –
              [He dies.]
       EDGAR
       I know thee well: a serviceable villain,
250   As duteous to the vices of thy mistress
       As badness would desire.
       GLOUCESTER   What, is he dead?
       EDGAR
       Sit you down, father, rest you.
       Let's see these pockets. The letters that he speaks of
       May be my friends. He's dead; I am only sorry
       He had no other deathsman. Let us see.
256   Leave, gentle wax, and manners blame us not.
       To know our enemies' minds we rip their hearts;
258   Their papers is more lawful.
              Reads the letter.

---

238 *che vor' ye* I warn you **239** *your . . . ballow* your head or my cudgel
242 *pick . . . teeth* i.e., with my club **243** *foins* sword thrusts **246** *letters*
(Oswald has a letter for Edmund from Goneril; if he has indeed been given
one by Regan too, as is implied at IV.4.35, Edgar fails to find it. But *letters*
may be singular – the letters that together compose one letter – as at I.5.1.)
248 *Upon* among **256** *Leave . . . wax* by your leave, kind seal **258** *Their* to
rip their

"Let our reciprocal vows be remembered. You have
many opportunities to cut him off. If your will want   260
not, time and place will be fruitfully offered. There is   261
nothing done if he return the conqueror; then am I the   262
prisoner, and his bed my jail, from the loathed warmth
whereof deliver me, and supply the place for your labor.   264
Your – wife, so I would say – affectionate servant,
                                                    Goneril."
O indistinguished space of woman's will.   267
A plot upon her virtuous husband's life,
And the exchange my brother. Here in the sands
Thee I'll rake up, the post unsanctified   270
Of murderous lechers; and in the mature time   271
With this ungracious paper strike the sight
Of the death-practiced duke. For him 'tis well   273
That of thy death and business I can tell.   274
                     [Exit with Oswald's body.]
GLOUCESTER
    The king is mad. How stiff is my vile sense,   275
    That I stand up and have ingenious feeling   276
    Of my huge sorrows. Better I were distract,   277
    So should my thoughts be severed from my griefs,
    And woes by wrong imaginations lose   279
    The knowledge of themselves.   280
        [Enter Edgar.] Drum afar off.

---

260 *him* Albany   260–61 *If . . . not* if you do not lack the will   261 *fruitfully* i.e., promising success   262 *done* accomplished   264 *supply* fill   267
indistinguished unlimited   270 *rake up* cover over; *post unsanctified* unholy
messenger   271 *in . . . time* when the time is ripe   273 *death-practiced*
whose death is plotted   274 **s.d.** None of the original texts makes any provision for the removal of Oswald's body. Editors since the eighteenth century
have had Edgar exit here dragging it offstage, and then return six lines later.
The very awkward alternative is for him to remove it while he is leading
Gloucester offstage.   275 *How . . . sense* how obstinate is my hateful consciousness   276 *ingenious* rational, intelligent   277 *distract* mad   279
wrong imaginations delusions

EDGAR   Give me your hand.
Far off, methinks, I hear the beaten drum.
Come, father, I'll bestow you with a friend.   *Exeunt.*

                                    *

∾ **IV.6** *Enter Cordelia, Kent [disguised], Gentleman.*

CORDELIA
O thou good Kent, how shall I live and work
To match thy goodness? My life will be too short,
And every measure fail me.
KENT
4   To be acknowledged, madam, is o'erpaid.
5   All my reports go with the modest truth,
6   Nor more, nor clipped, but so.
CORDELIA   Be better suited.
7   These weeds are memories of those worser hours;
I prithee put them off.
KENT   Pardon, dear madam.
9   Yet to be known shortens my made intent.
10 My boon I make it that you know me not
11 Till time and I think meet.
CORDELIA
Then be't so, my good lord. – How does the king?
GENTLEMAN
Madam, sleeps still.
CORDELIA
O you kind gods,
Cure this great breach in his abusèd nature;
16 Th' untuned and jarring senses O wind up
17 Of this child-changèd father.

IV.6 The French camp   **4** *o'erpaid* more than sufficient   **5** *go* accord
6 *clipped* less; *suited* dressed   **7** *weeds* clothes; *memories* reminders   **9** *Yet . . .*
intent to reveal myself now would spoil my plan (for Lear to recognize him as
Kent)   **10** *My . . . it* I ask as my reward   **11** *meet* suitable   **16** *jarring* discordant; *wind up* put in tune   **17** *child-changèd* (1) changed by his children,
(2) changed into a child

GENTLEMAN
So please your majesty
That we may wake the king? He hath slept long.

CORDELIA
Be governed by your knowledge, and proceed   20
I' th' sway of your own will. Is he arrayed?   21

GENTLEMAN
Ay, madam. In the heaviness of sleep
We put fresh garments on him.
    Enter Lear [sleeping] in a chair carried by Servants.
Be by, good madam, when we do awake him.
I doubt not of his temperance.   25

CORDELIA
O my dear father, restoration hang
Thy medicine on my lips, and let this kiss
Repair those violent harms that my two sisters
Have in thy reverence made.   29

KENT   Kind and dear princess!

CORDELIA
Had you not been their father, these white flakes   30
Did challenge pity of them. Was this a face   31
To be opposed against the jarring winds?
Mine enemy's dog, though he had bit me,
Should have stood that night against my fire;   34
And wast thou fain, poor father,   35
To hovel thee with swine and rogues forlorn
In short and musty straw? Alack, alack,   37
'Tis wonder that thy life and wits at once
Had not concluded all. – He wakes. Speak to him.

GENTLEMAN
Madam, do you; 'tis fittest.   40

CORDELIA
How does my royal lord? How fares your majesty?

---

21 *I' th' sway . . . will* as you see fit; *arrayed* properly dressed   25 *temperance*
self-control   29 *in . . . reverence* on the dignity of your age   30 *flakes* hairs
31 *challenge* demand   34 *against* beside   35 *fain* obliged   37 *short* broken

LEAR
You do me wrong to take me out o' th' grave.
Thou art a soul in bliss, but I am bound
44 Upon a wheel of fire, that mine own tears
Do scald like molten lead.
CORDELIA   Sir, do you know me?
LEAR
You are a spirit, I know. Where did you die?
CORDELIA
47 Still, still far wide.
GENTLEMAN
He's scarce awake. Let him alone awhile.
LEAR
Where have I been? Where am I? Fair daylight?
50 I am mightily abused. I should ev'n die with pity
To see another thus. I know not what to say.
I will not swear these are my hands. Let's see:
I feel this pin prick. Would I were assured
Of my condition.
CORDELIA   O look upon me, sir,
And hold your hand in benediction o'er me.
You must not kneel.
LEAR   Pray do not mock me.
57 I am a very foolish fond old man,
Fourscore and upward,
Not an hour more, nor less; and, to deal plainly,
60 I fear I am not in my perfect mind.
Methinks I should know you, and know this man;
62 Yet I am doubtful, for I am mainly ignorant
What place this is; and all the skill I have
Remembers not these garments; nor I know not
Where I did lodge last night. Do not laugh at me,

---

44 *wheel of fire* (the image combines the wheel on which prisoners were bound for beatings with the burning of heretics or of souls in hell) **47** *wide* wide of the mark **50** *abused* ill-used, deceived **57** *fond* (the word also means "foolish") **62** *mainly* entirely

For, as I am a man, I think this lady
To be my child Cordelia.
CORDELIA   And so I am, I am.
LEAR
Be your tears wet? Yes, faith, I pray, weep not.
If you have poison for me, I will drink it.
I know you do not love me, for your sisters   70
Have, as I do remember, done me wrong.
You have some cause, they have not.
CORDELIA
No cause, no cause.
LEAR
Am I in France?
KENT   In your own kingdom, sir.
LEAR
Do not abuse me.   75
GENTLEMAN
Be comforted, good madam. The great rage,
You see, is killed in him. Desire him to go in;
Trouble him no more till further settling.   78
CORDELIA
Will't please your highness walk?
LEAR   You must bear with me.
Pray you now, forget and forgive. I am old and foolish. 80
                                        Exeunt.

                          *

∾ **V.1** *Enter with drum and colors, Edmund, Regan,*
   Gentlemen, and Soldiers.

EDMUND
Know of the duke if his last purpose hold,   1
Or whether since he is advised by aught   2

---

75 *abuse* deceive   78 *settling* calm sets in
   V.1 The British camp   **1** *Know . . . hold* find out from Albany if his most
recent intention (to join in the fight against Cordelia's forces) still holds good
2 *since* since then

To change the course. He's full of alteration
4   And self-reproving. Bring his constant pleasure.
                                    [Exit Gentleman.]

REGAN
5   Our sister's man is certainly miscarried.

EDMUND
6   'Tis to be doubted, madam.

REGAN   Now, sweet lord,
     You know the goodness I intend upon you.
     Tell me but truly, but then speak the truth,
9   Do you not love my sister?

EDMUND   In honored love.

REGAN
10   But have you never found my brother's way
11   To the forfended place?

EDMUND   No, by mine honor, madam.

REGAN
     I never shall endure her. Dear my lord,
13   Be not familiar with her.

EDMUND   Fear me not.
     She and the duke her husband –
          Enter, with drum and colors, Albany, Goneril,
          Soldiers.

ALBANY
     Our very loving sister, well bemet.
     Sir, this I heard: the king is come to his daughter,
17   With others whom the rigor of our state
18   Forced to cry out.

REGAN   Why is this reasoned?

GONERIL
19   Combine together 'gainst the enemy,

————

4 *constant pleasure* firm decision   5 *sister's man* Oswald; *is . . . miscarried* has
certainly met with an accident   6 *doubted* feared   9 *honored* honorable   10
brother's Albany's   11 *forfended* forbidden   13 *familiar* intimate; *fear* doubt
17 *rigor . . . state* harshness of our rule   18 *Why . . . reasoned* i.e., why are
you telling us this   19 *Combine together* let us join our forces

For these domestic and particular broils   20
Are not the question here.
ALBANY   Let's then determine
With th' ensign of war on our proceeding.   22
REGAN
Sister, you'll go with us?
GONERIL   No.
REGAN
'Tis most convenient; pray, go with us.   25
GONERIL   *[Aside]*
O, ho, I know the riddle. – I will go.   26
     Enter Edgar [disguised].
EDGAR   *[To Albany]*
If e'er your grace had speech with man so poor,
Hear me one word.
                              Exeunt both the armies.
ALBANY   *[To the departing Soldiers]*
I'll overtake you. *[To Edgar]* Speak.
EDGAR
Before you fight the battle, ope this letter.   30
If you have victory, let the trumpet sound
For him that brought it. Wretched though I seem,
I can produce a champion that will prove   33
What is avouchèd there. If you miscarry,   34
Your business of the world hath so an end,
And machination ceases. Fortune love you.   36
ALBANY
Stay till I have read the letter.
EDGAR   I was forbid it.
When time shall serve, let but the herald cry,
And I'll appear again.   *Exit.*

---

20 *particular broils* private quarrels 22 *ensign of war* experienced senior officers 25 *convenient* proper that you do 26 *I . . . riddle* I get the point
(which is not to leave her alone with Edmund) 33 *prove* establish as true (in
a trial by single combat) 34 *avouchèd* asserted; *miscarry* lose the battle 36
machination plotting

ALBANY
40   Why, fare thee well. I will o'erlook thy paper.
      Enter Edmund.
EDMUND
      The enemy's in view; draw up your powers.
42   Here is the guess of their true strength and forces
43   By diligent discovery; but your haste
44   Is now urged on you.
      ALBANY   We will greet the time.   *Exit.*
EDMUND
      To both these sisters have I sworn my love,
46   Each jealous of the other as the stung
      Are of the adder. Which of them shall I take?
      Both, one, or neither? Neither can be enjoyed
      If both remain alive. To take the widow
50   Exasperates, makes mad, her sister Goneril,
51   And hardly shall I carry out my side,
      Her husband being alive. Now then, we'll use
53   His countenance for the battle, which being done,
      Let her who would be rid of him devise
55   His speedy taking off. As for the mercy
      Which he intends to Lear and to Cordelia,
      The battle done, and they within our power,
58   Shall never see his pardon; for my state
      Stands on me to defend, not to debate.   *Exit.*
                              *

---

40 s.d. presumably Albany has no time to read Oswald's letter before Edmund's entrance   **42** *guess* estimate   **43** *discovery* spying   **44** *greet the time*
be ready when the time comes   **46** *jealous* suspicious; *stung* those who have
been bitten   **51** *carry . . . side* accomplish my plan   **53** *countenance* authority, backing   **55** *taking off* murder   **58** *Shall* they shall   **58–59** *state . . . me*
situation requires me

❧ **V.2** *Alarum within. Enter, with Drum and Colors,*
Lear, Cordelia, and Soldiers over the stage, and exeunt.

Enter Edgar [disguised] and Gloucester.

EDGAR
Here, father, take the shadow of this tree   1
For your good host; pray that the right may thrive.   2
If ever I return to you again
I'll bring you comfort.
GLOUCESTER   Grace go with you, sir.
                                            Exit [Edgar].
Alarum and [sound of] retreat within. Enter Edgar.

EDGAR
Away, old man – give me thy hand, away!
King Lear hath lost, he and his daughter ta'en.
Give me thy hand. Come on.
GLOUCESTER
No further, sir; a man may rot even here.
EDGAR
What, in ill thoughts again? Men must endure
Their going hence even as their coming hither.   *10*
Ripeness is all. Come on.   *11*
GLOUCESTER   And that's true too.   *Exeunt.*
                          *

❧ **V.3** *Enter in conquest, with drum and colors, Edmund,*
Lear and Cordelia as prisoners, Soldiers, Captain.

EDMUND
Some officers take them away. Good guard,

V.2 A field   s.d. *Alarum within* trumpets offstage   **1** *father* old man (Edgar
still has not revealed his identity to Gloucester)   **2** *host* shelter   **11** *Ripeness
is all* i.e., the gods decree when fruit is ripe and falls; coming to that ripeness
is all that matters
    V.3 The British camp

2   Until their greater pleasures first be known
3   That are to censure them.
    CORDELIA   We are not the first
4   Who with best meaning have incurred the worst.
    For thee, oppressèd king, I am cast down,
6   Myself could else outfrown false fortune's frown.
    Shall we not see these daughters and these sisters?
    LEAR
    No, no, no, no. Come, let's away to prison.
    We two alone will sing like birds i' th' cage.
10   When thou dost ask me blessing, I'll kneel down
    And ask of thee forgiveness; so we'll live,
    And pray, and sing, and tell old tales, and laugh
    At gilded butterflies, and hear poor rogues
    Talk of court news, and we'll talk with them too,
    Who loses and who wins, who's in, who's out,
    And take upon's the mystery of things
17   As if we were God's spies; and we'll wear out
18   In a walled prison packs and sects of great ones
19   That ebb and flow by th' moon.
    EDMUND   Take them away.
    LEAR
20   Upon such sacrifices, my Cordelia,
21   The gods themselves throw incense. Have I caught thee?
22   He that parts us shall bring a brand from heaven
    And fire us hence like foxes. Wipe thine eyes.
24   The good years shall devour them, flesh and fell,
    Ere they shall make us weep. We'll see 'em starved
    first. Come.
                  Exeunt [Lear and Cordelia with Soldiers].

---

2 *their . . . pleasures* the wishes of those in command   3 *censure* pass judgment on   4 *meaning* intentions   6 *else* otherwise   17 *wear out* outlast   18 *packs and sects* parties and factions   19 *That . . . moon* whose power changes monthly   21 *throw incense* are celebrants; *Have . . . thee* i.e., do I really have you again   22 *brand* torch (i.e., it will take divine powers to separate us now)   24 *good years* passage of time, old age; *flesh . . . fell* meat and skin, entirely

EDMUND

    Come hither, captain, hark.

    Take thou this note; go follow them to prison.

    One step I have advanced thee; if thou dost   28

    As this instructs thee, thou dost make thy way

    To noble fortunes. Know thou this, that men   *30*

    Are as the time is; to be tender-minded   31

    Does not become a sword. Thy great employment   32

    Will not bear question. Either say thou'lt do't,   33

    Or thrive by other means.

CAPTAIN   I'll do't, my lord.

EDMUND

    About it; and write happy when th' hast done.   35

    Mark, I say instantly, and carry it so   36

    As I have set it down.   *Exit Captain.*

      Flourish. Enter Albany, Goneril, Regan, Soldiers.

ALBANY

    Sir, you have showed today your valiant strain,   38

    And fortune led you well. You have the captives

    Who were the opposites of this day's strife.   40

    I do require them of you so to use them   41

    As we shall find their merits and our safety

    May equally determine.

EDMUND

    Sir, I thought it fit

    To send the old and miserable king

    To some retention,   46

    Whose age had charms in it, whose title more,

    To pluck the common bosom on his side   48

    And turn our impressed lances in our eyes   49

    Which do command them. With him I sent the queen, *50*

---

28 *advanced* promoted **31** *Are . . . is* i.e., must seize their opportunities **32** *sword* i.e., soldier **33** *question* discussion **35** *write happy* call yourself fortunate **36** *carry it* carry it out **38** *strain* (1) qualities, (2) lineage **40** *opposites of* opponents in **41** *use* treat **46** *retention* detention **48** *pluck . . . on* draw popular sympathy to **49** *turn . . . eyes* i.e., turn our soldiers against us; *impressed lances* drafted pikemen

My reason all the same; and they are ready
52 Tomorrow, or at further space, t' appear
53 Where you shall hold your session.
ALBANY   Sir, by your patience,
54 I hold you but a subject of this war,
55 Not as a brother.
REGAN   That's as we list to grace him.
56 Methinks our pleasure might have been demanded
    Ere you had spoke so far. He led our powers,
58 Bore the commission of my place and person,
59 The which immediacy may well stand up
60 And call itself your brother.
GONERIL   Not so hot!
61 In his own grace he doth exalt himself
62 More than in your addition.
REGAN   In my rights
63 By me invested, he compeers the best.
ALBANY
64 That were the most if he should husband you.
REGAN
    Jesters do oft prove prophets.
GONERIL   Holla, holla –
66 That eye that told you so looked but asquint.
REGAN
    Lady, I am not well, else I should answer
68 From a full-flowing stomach. *[To Edmund]* General,
69 Take thou my soldiers, prisoners, patrimony.
70 Dispose of them, of me. The walls is thine.

---

52 *further space* a later time   53 *session* court hearing   54 *subject of* subordinate in   55 *we list* I please   56 *pleasure . . . demanded* wishes might have
been consulted   58 *Bore . . . person* i.e., acted with my authority   59 *immediacy* present status (as my deputy)   60 *hot* fast   61 *grace* merit   62 *your
addition* the honors conferred by you   63 *compeers* equals   64 *the most* i.e.,
the most complete investiture with your rights   66 *asquint* cross-eyed (i.e.,
jealously)   68 *stomach* anger   69 *patrimony* inheritance   70 *The . . . thine*
i.e., you have captured my castle

Witness the world that I create thee here
My lord and master.
GONERIL   Mean you to enjoy him?
ALBANY
The let-alone lies not in your good will.   73
EDMUND
Nor in thine, lord.   74
ALBANY   Half-blooded fellow, yes.
REGAN   *[To Edmund]*
Let the drum strike and prove my title thine.   75
ALBANY
Stay yet, hear reason. Edmund, I arrest thee
On capital treason, and in thy arrest *[indicating Goneril]*
This gilded serpent. *[To Regan]* For your claim, fair
    sister,
I bar it in the interest of my wife.
'Tis she is subcontracted to this lord,   80
And I, her husband, contradict your banns.   81
If you will marry, make your loves to me.   82
My lady is bespoke.   83
GONERIL   An interlude!
ALBANY
Thou art armed, Gloucester; let the trumpet sound.
If none appear to prove upon thy person
Thy heinous, manifest, and many treasons,
There is my pledge.   87
[Throws down a glove.] I'll make it on thy heart,
Ere I taste bread, thou art in nothing less   88
Than I have here proclaimed thee.
REGAN   Sick, O sick!

---

73 *let-alone* (1) permission, (2) veto **74** *Half-blooded* illegitimate (and only half noble) **75** *drum strike* (as a signal to prepare for battle) **80** *subcontracted* (because she is already contracted, by marriage, to Albany) **81** *banns* declaration of an intention to marry **82** *make . . . to* woo **83** *bespoke* already spoken for; *interlude* farce **87** *make* prove **88** *nothing less* no way less guilty

GONERIL   *[Aside]*
90   If not, I'll ne'er trust medicine.
EDMUND   *[Throws his glove.]*
91   There's my exchange. What in the world he is
That names me traitor, villainlike he lies.
Call by the trumpet. He that dares approach,
On him, on you – who not? – I will maintain
My truth and honor firmly.
ALBANY   A herald, ho!
     Enter a Herald.
96   Trust to thy single virtue, for thy soldiers,
All levied in my name, have in my name
Took their discharge.
REGAN   My sickness grows upon me.
ALBANY
She is not well. Convey her to my tent.
                 [Exit Regan, attended.]
100   Come hither, herald, let the trumpet sound,
And read out this.
     A trumpet sounds.
HERALD   *[Reads]* "If any man of quality or degree within
the lists of the army will maintain upon Edmund, sup-
posed Earl of Gloucester, that he is a manifold traitor,
let him appear by the third sound of the trumpet. He is
bold in his defense."
     First trumpet.
Again.
     Second trumpet.
108   Again.
     Third trumpet.
     Trumpet answers within.
     Enter Edgar armed.

---

90 *medicine* i.e., poison   91 *What . . . world* whoever   96 *single virtue* unaided strength   108 s.d. *armed* (Edgar wears a helmet with the beaver down,
covering his face)

ALBANY
    Ask him his purposes why he appears
    Upon this call o' th' trumpet.   *110*

HERALD   What are you,
    Your name, your quality, and why you answer   111
    This present summons?

EDGAR   Know my name is lost,
    By treason's tooth bare-gnawn and canker-bit.   113
    Yet am I noble as the adversary
    I come to cope.   115

ALBANY   Which is that adversary?

EDGAR
    What's he that speaks for Edmund, Earl of Gloucester?

EDMUND
    Himself. What say'st thou to him?

EDGAR   Draw thy sword,
    That if my speech offend a noble heart
    Thy arm may do thee justice. Here is mine.
      [Draws his sword.]
    Behold, it is my privilege,   *120*
    The privilege of mine honors,
    My oath, and my profession. I protest,   122
    Maugre thy strength, place, youth, and eminence,   123
    Despite thy victor sword and fire-new fortune,   124
    Thy valor and thy heart, thou art a traitor,   125
    False to thy gods, thy brother, and thy father,
    Conspirant 'gainst this high illustrious prince,   127
    And from th' extremest upward of thy head   128
    To the descent and dust below thy foot   129
    A most toad-spotted traitor. Say thou no,   130
    This sword, this arm, and my best spirits are bent

---

111 *quality* rank   **113** *treason's* treachery's; *canker-bit* eaten away by worms   **115** *cope* encounter   **122** *profession* i.e., as a knight   **123** *Maugre* despite   **124** *fire-new* newly forged   **125** *heart* courage   **127** *Conspirant* conspirator   **128** *upward* top   **129** *descent* lowest part   **130** *toad-spotted* venomous, reptilian

To prove upon thy heart, whereto I speak,
133 Thou liest.
    EDMUND   In wisdom I should ask thy name,
    But since thy outside looks so fair and warlike,
135 And that thy tongue some say of breeding breathes,
136 What safe and nicely I might well delay
    By rule of knighthood, I disdain and spurn.
    Back do I toss these treasons to thy head,
139 With the hell-hated lie o'erwhelm thy heart,
140 Which, for they yet glance by and scarcely bruise,
141 This sword of mine shall give them instant way
    Where they shall rest forever. Trumpets, speak!
        Alarums. [They] fight. [Edmund falls.]
    ALBANY
143 Save him, save him!
    GONERIL   This is practice, Gloucester.
    By th' law of war thou wast not bound to answer
145 An unknown opposite. Thou art not vanquished,
146 But cozened and beguiled.
    ALBANY   Shut your mouth, dame,
    Or with this paper shall I stop it. *[To Edmund]* Hold, sir,
    Thou worse than any name, read thine own evil.
        [To Goneril]
    No tearing, lady; I perceive you know it.
    GONERIL
150 Say if I do, the laws are mine, not thine.
151 Who can arraign me for't?   *Exit.*
    ALBANY
    Most monstrous! *[To Edmund]* O, know'st thou this
    paper?

---

133 *In . . . name* (because one was not obliged to fight with an inferior, nor
with an unknown adversary)   135 *say* touch, sign   136 *safe and nicely* cau-
tiously and correctly   139 *hell-hated* hateful as hell   140 *Which, for they*
since those treasons   141 *way* access   143 *Save him* i.e., don't kill him; *This
is practice* i.e., you've been tricked   145 *opposite* opponent   146 *cozened*
cheated   150 *the . . . mine* (Goneril is queen; Albany is her consort)   151
arraign try (the monarch, having no peers, could not be prosecuted)

EDMUND
  Ask me not what I know.
ALBANY
  Go after her. She's desperate; govern her.   154
                              [Exit Attendant.]
EDMUND
  What you have charged me with, that have I done,
  And more, much more. The time will bring it out.
  'Tis past, and so am I. *[To Edgar]* But what art thou
  That hast this fortune on me? If thou'rt noble,   158
  I do forgive thee.   159
EDGAR   Let's exchange charity.
  I am no less in blood than thou art, Edmund;   160
  If more, the more thou'st wronged me.
      [Removing his helmet]
  My name is Edgar, and thy father's son.
  The gods are just, and of our pleasant vices
  Make instruments to plague us.
  The dark and vicious place where thee he got   165
  Cost him his eyes.
EDMUND   Thou'st spoken right; 'tis true.
  The wheel is come full circle; I am here.   167
ALBANY   *[To Edgar]*
  Methought thy very gait did prophesy
  A royal nobleness. I must embrace thee.
  Let sorrow split my heart if ever I did hate   170
  Thee or thy father.
EDGAR   Worthy prince, I know't.
ALBANY
  Where have you hid yourself?
  How have you known the miseries of your father?
EDGAR
  By nursing them, my lord. List a brief tale,   174

---

154 *govern* take care of   158 *fortune on* victory over   159 *charity* forgiveness
165 *dark . . . place* adulterous bed, illicit genitals; *got* begot   167 *I . . . here*
i.e., at the bottom of Fortune's wheel again   174 *List* hear

And when 'tis told, O that my heart would burst!
176 The bloody proclamation to escape
177 That followed me so near – O our lives' sweetness,
That we the pain of death would hourly die
Rather than die at once! – taught me to shift
180 Into a madman's rags, t' assume a semblance
That very dogs disdained; and in this habit
182 Met I my father with his bleeding rings,
Their precious stones new lost; became his guide,
Led him, begged for him, saved him from despair;
Never – O fault! – revealed myself unto him
Until some half hour past, when I was armed.
Not sure, though hoping, of this good success,
I asked his blessing, and from first to last
Told him our pilgrimage; but his flawed heart,
190 Alack, too weak the conflict to support,
'Twixt two extremes of passion, joy and grief,
Burst smilingly.
EDMUND   This speech of yours hath moved me,
And shall perchance do good. But speak you on;
You look as you had something more to say.
ALBANY
If there be more, more woeful, hold it in,
196 For I am almost ready to dissolve
Hearing of this.
          Enter a Gentleman [with a bloody knife].
GENTLEMAN
Help, help, O help!
EDGAR   What kind of help?
ALBANY   Speak, man!
EDGAR
What means this bloody knife?
GENTLEMAN   'Tis hot, it smokes.
200 It came even from the heart of – O, she's dead!

---

176 *bloody proclamation* (declaring him an outlaw) 177 *our . . . sweetness*
how sweet life is to us 182 *rings* sockets 196 *dissolve* (in tears)

ALBANY
  Who dead? Speak, man!
GENTLEMAN
  Your lady, sir, your lady; and her sister
  By her is poisoned. She confesses it.
EDMUND
  I was contracted to them both; all three
  Now marry in an instant.   205
EDGAR   Here comes Kent.
      Enter Kent [as himself].
ALBANY
  Produce the bodies, be they alive or dead.
      [Exit Attendant.]
  This judgment of the heavens that makes us tremble
  Touches us not with pity. – O, is this he?
      [To Kent]
  The time will not allow the compliment
  Which very manners urges.   *210*
KENT   I am come
  To bid my king and master aye good night.   211
  Is he not here?
ALBANY   Great thing of us forgot!
  Speak, Edmund, where's the king, and where's Cordelia?
      Goneril's and Regan's bodies brought out.
  Seest thou this object, Kent?   214
KENT
  Alack, why thus?
EDMUND   Yet Edmund was beloved.
  The one the other poisoned for my sake,
  And after slew herself.
ALBANY
  Even so. Cover their faces.
EDMUND
  I pant for life. Some good I mean to do,
  Despite of mine own nature. Quickly send,   *220*

---

205 *marry* unite   **211** *aye* forever   **214** *object* sight, spectacle

221   Be brief in it, to th' castle, for my writ
       Is on the life of Lear and on Cordelia.
       Nay, send in time.
       ALBANY   Run, run. O run!
       EDGAR
224   To who, my lord? Who has the office? Send
       Thy token of reprieve.
       EDMUND
       Well thought on. Take my sword.
       Give it the captain.
       EDGAR   Haste thee for thy life.
                                   [Exit Gentleman.]
       EDMUND   *[To Albany]*
       He hath commission from thy wife and me
       To hang Cordelia in the prison, and
230   To lay the blame upon her own despair,
231   That she fordid herself.
       ALBANY
       The gods defend her. Bear him hence awhile.
                         [Edmund is borne off.]
       Enter Lear with Cordelia in his arms [, followed by the
       Gentleman].
       LEAR
       Howl, howl, howl! O you are men of stones.
       Had I your tongues and eyes, I'd use them so
       That heaven's vault should crack. She's gone forever.
       I know when one is dead and when one lives.
       She's dead as earth. Lend me a looking glass;
238   If that her breath will mist or stain the stone,
239   Why, then she lives.
       KENT   Is this the promised end?
       EDGAR
240   Or image of that horror?

---

221 *brief* quick; *writ* order of execution   **224** *office* commission   **231** *fordid*
destroyed   **238** *stone* mirror of polished stone   **239** *promised end* Judgment
Day   **240** *Fall . . . cease* let the world end

ALBANY   Fall and cease.

LEAR
  This feather stirs. She lives. If it be so,
  It is a chance which does redeem all sorrows
  That ever I have felt.

KENT   O my good master –

LEAR
  Prithee, away.

EDGAR   'Tis noble Kent, your friend.

LEAR
  A plague upon you, murderers, traitors all.
  I might have saved her; now she's gone forever!
  Cordelia, Cordelia, stay a little. Ha?
  What is't thou say'st? – Her voice was ever soft,
  Gentle and low, an excellent thing in woman.
  I killed the slave that was a-hanging thee.   250

GENTLEMAN
  'Tis true, my lords, he did.

LEAR   Did I not, fellow?
  I have seen the day, with my good biting falchion   252
  I would have made him skip. I am old now,
  And these same crosses spoil me. *[To Kent]* Who are you? 254
  Mine eyes are not o' th' best, I'll tell you straight.

KENT
  If fortune brag of two she loved and hated,   256
  One of them we behold.

LEAR
  This is a dull sight. Are you not Kent?   258

KENT
  The same, your servant Kent. Where is your servant 259
    Caius?

---

252 *falchion* small sword   **254** *crosses spoil* vexations weaken   **256** *loved and
hated* first loved, then hated (Lear and a hypothetical other? Lear and
Cordelia? Lear and Kent, who are looking at each other?)   **258** *dull sight* dis-
mal spectacle   **259** *Caius* (obviously Kent's alias; but the name appears
nowhere else in the play)

LEAR

260   He's a good fellow, I can tell you that.
    He'll strike, and quickly too. He's dead and rotten.

KENT

    No, my good lord, I am the very man –

LEAR

263   I'll see that straight.

KENT

264   That from your first of difference and decay
265   Have followed your sad steps.

LEAR   You are welcome hither.

KENT

266   Nor no man else. All's cheerless, dark, and deadly.
267   Your eldest daughters have fordone themselves,
268   And desperately are dead.

LEAR   Ay, so I think.

ALBANY

    He knows not what he says, and vain is it
270   That we present us to him.

EDGAR   Very bootless.

      Enter a Messenger.

MESSENGER

    Edmund is dead, my lord.

ALBANY

    That's but a trifle here.
    You lords and noble friends, know our intent.
274   What comfort to this great decay may come
    Shall be applied; for us, we will resign
    During the life of this old majesty
    To him our absolute power. *[To Edgar and Kent]* You
      to your rights,

---

263 *I'll . . . straight* I'll attend to it shortly   **264** *difference and decay* quarrel and decline   **265** *You . . . hither* (Lear fails to make the connection)   **266** *Nor . . . else* i.e., no one is welcome here   **267** *fordone* killed   **268** *desperately* in despair   **270** *bootless* pointless   **274** *decay* ruin, Lear

With boot and such addition as your honors   278
Have more than merited. All friends shall taste
The wages of their virtue, and all foes   280
The cup of their deservings. – O see, see!

LEAR

And my poor fool is hanged. No, no, no life.   282
Why should a dog, a horse, a rat have life,
And thou no breath at all? Thou'lt come no more.
Never, never, never, never, never.
Pray you, undo this button. Thank you, sir.
Do you see this? Look on her! look, her lips,
Look there, look there –

> *He dies.*

EDGAR   He faints. My lord, my lord!

KENT

Break, heart, I prithee break.

EDGAR   Look up, my lord.

KENT

Vex not his ghost. O, let him pass. He hates him   290
That would upon the rack of this tough world   291
Stretch him out longer.

EDGAR   He is gone indeed.

KENT

The wonder is he hath endured so long.
He but usurped his life.

ALBANY

Bear them from hence. Our present business
Is general woe.
        [To Edgar and Kent]
                    Friends of my soul, you twain
Rule in this realm, and the gored state sustain.   297

---

278 *boot* reward   **282** *fool* (A term of endearment; here, Cordelia. The fool disappears after III.6.)   **290** *ghost* spirit   **291** *rack* a torture instrument **297** *gored* wounded

KENT
    I have a journey, sir, shortly to go;
    My master calls me, I must not say no.

EDGAR
300   The weight of this sad time we must obey,
    Speak what we feel, not what we ought to say.
    The oldest hath borne most; we that are young
    Shall never see so much, nor live so long.

                    Exeunt with a dead march.

---

300 (Edgar speaks the final lines as the inheritor of Lear's kingdom. In the quarto, Albany speaks them, as the highest-ranking person left alive.)